In Him

Experiencing the Riches of Christ in Ephesians

DONNA GAINES

JEAN STOCKDALE

DAYNA STREET

ANGIE WILSON

ABBEY DANE

In Him: Experiencing the Riches of Christ in Ephesians

Cover and book design: Amanda Weaver

Handwriting: Melissa Bobo Hardee

Map design: Paige Warren

Editing: Dayna Street, Donita Barnwell, Melissa Bobo Hardee, Lauren Gooden, Paige Warren, Vera Sidhom

CONTENTS

HOW TO USE THIS STUDY

Welcome to *In Him: Experiencing the Riches of Christ in Ephesians!*

Long before the foundations of the world were laid, God had a plan to redeem, restore, and reconcile all things in Christ. And now, through the life, death, and resurrection of Jesus, that plan has been set in motion. In his first-century letter to the Ephesians, Paul lifts our eyes to see the breathtaking beauty of God's eternal purposes. And he not only reveals what God has done, he calls us to live in light of who we are *In Him.*

Paul's Ephesian letter is more than a theological masterpiece; it's a spiritual treasure map, guiding us through the vast riches of our inheritance in Christ. In just six short chapters, Paul unveils the magnitude of our position: We've been chosen, adopted, redeemed, sealed, raised, and seated with Christ. But he doesn't stop with who we are, he goes on to tell us how we are to live. Our new identity should reshape everything: how we think, how we love, how we walk in unity, how we live on mission, and how we stand firm in a world at war.

In our study of Ephesians, we'll discover that the first half of the letter celebrates all that God has done for us in Christ. The second half shows us how to live it out and resist when the enemy attacks. This study is designed to provide an opportunity for personal study throughout the week, leading up to small group discussion and large group teaching time once a week. Before you begin, you will want to make sure to have a purple pen to mark the phrases "In Him," "In Christ," or the equivalent in your Bible or the reference text beginning on page 7. Each of the ten weekly lessons is divided into five daily homework assignments centered on comprehending the text as well as personal application. We cannot do what we do not know. Throughout our study, we will keep four goals in mind:

> Observation: What does the text say? (Who? What? Where? When? Why? How?)
> Interpretation: What does the text mean?
> Application: What difference should this make in my life?
> Transformation: The goal! Am I becoming more like Jesus?

For the first eight weeks in our Day Five study, we'll take a closer look at the methods the enemy uses and learn how to stand firm against the subtle, and not-so-subtle, ways he schemes against us. During the final two weeks, we will focus on strategies to equip ourselves to move forward in the victory that is already ours in Christ.

Friend, everything God has promised is already yours. As you walk through this study, may your eyes be opened to the vastness of His grace, and may you experience the riches of Christ in a deeper, more personal way. You have been chosen by the Father, dearly loved by the Son, and empowered by the Spirit. You are equipped for the battle and invited to live in the fullness of all that is yours *In Him*. Let the journey begin!

The Letter of Paul to the Ephesians

EPHESIANS 1

The Blessings of Redemption

1 Paul, an apostle of Christ Jesus by the will of God,

To the saints who are at Ephesus and who are faithful in Christ Jesus: 2 Grace to you and peace
from God our Father and the Lord Jesus Christ.

3 Blessed be the God and Father of our Lord Jesus Christ, who has blessed us with every spiritual
blessing in the heavenly places in Christ, 4 just as He chose us in Him before the foundation
of the world, that we would be holy and blameless before Him. In love 5 He predestined us
to adoption as sons through Jesus Christ to Himself, according to the kind intention of His
will, 6 to the praise of the glory of His grace, which He freely bestowed on us in the Beloved.
7 In Him we have redemption through His blood, the forgiveness of our trespasses, according
to the riches of His grace 8 which He lavished on us. In all wisdom and insight 9 He made known
to us the mystery of His will, according to His kind intention which He purposed in Him 10 with
a view to an administration suitable to the fullness of the times, that is, the summing up of all
things in Christ, things in the heavens and things on the earth. In Him 11 also we have obtained
an inheritance, having been predestined according to His purpose who works all things after
the counsel of His will, 12 to the end that we who were the first to hope in Christ would be to the
praise of His glory. 13 In Him, you also, after listening to the message of truth, the gospel of your
salvation – having also believed, you were sealed in Him with the Holy Spirit of promise, 14 who
is given as a pledge of our inheritance, with a view to the redemption of God's own possession,
to the praise of His glory.

15 For this reason I too, having heard of the faith in the Lord Jesus which exists among you
and your love for all the saints, 16 do not cease giving thanks for you, while making mention of
you in my prayers; 17 that the God of our Lord Jesus Christ, the Father of glory, may give to you
a spirit of wisdom and of revelation in the knowledge of Him. 18 I pray that the eyes of your
heart may be enlightened, so that you will know what is the hope of His calling, what are the
riches of the glory of His inheritance in the saints, 19 and what is the surpassing greatness of
His power toward us who believe. These are in accordance with the working of the strength of
His might 20 which He brought about in Christ, when He raised Him from the dead and seated
Him at His right hand in the heavenly places, 21 far above all rule and authority and power and
dominion, and every name that is named, not only in this age but also in the one to come.
22 And He put all things in subjection under His feet, and gave Him as head over all things to the
church, 23 which is His body, the fullness of Him who fills all in all.

EPHESIANS 2

Made Alive in Christ

[1] And you were dead in your trespasses and sins, [2] in which you formerly walked according to the course of this world, according to the prince of the power of the air, of the spirit that is now working in the sons of disobedience. [3] Among them we too all formerly lived in the lusts of our flesh, indulging the desires of the flesh and of the mind, and were by nature children of wrath, even as the rest. [4] But God, being rich in mercy, because of His great love with which He loved us, [5] even when we were dead in our transgressions, made us alive together with Christ (by grace you have been saved), [6] and raised us up with Him, and seated us with Him in the heavenly places in Christ Jesus, [7] so that in the ages to come He might show the surpassing riches of His grace in kindness toward us in Christ Jesus. [8] For by grace you have been saved through faith; and that not of yourselves, it is the gift of God; [9] not as a result of works, so that no one may boast. [10] For we are His workmanship, created in Christ Jesus for good works, which God prepared beforehand so that we would walk in them.

[11] Therefore remember that formerly you, the Gentiles in the flesh, who are called "Uncircumcision" by the so-called "Circumcision," which is performed in the flesh by human hands – [12] remember that you were at that time separate from Christ, excluded from the commonwealth of Israel, and strangers to the covenants of promise, having no hope and without God in the world. [13] But now in Christ Jesus you who formerly were far off have been brought near by the blood of Christ. [14] For He Himself is our peace, who made both groups into one and broke down the barrier of the dividing wall, [15] by abolishing in His flesh the enmity, which is the Law of commandments contained in ordinances, so that in Himself He might make the two into one new man, thus establishing peace, [16] and might reconcile them both in one body to God through the cross, by it having put to death the enmity. [17] And He came and preached peace to you who were far away, and peace to those who were near; [18] for through Him we both have our access in one Spirit to the Father. [19] So then you are no longer strangers and aliens, but you are fellow citizens with the saints, and are of God's household, [20] having been built on the foundation of the apostles and prophets, Christ Jesus Himself being the corner stone, [21] in whom the whole building, being fitted together, is growing into a holy temple in the Lord, [22] in whom you also are being built together into a dwelling of God in the Spirit.

EPHESIANS 3

Paul's Stewardship

[1] For this reason I, Paul, the prisoner of Christ Jesus for the sake of you Gentiles – [2] if indeed you have heard of the stewardship of God's grace which was given to me for you; [3] that by revelation there was made known to me the mystery, as I wrote before in brief. [4] By referring to this, when you read you can understand my insight into the mystery of Christ, [5] which in other generations

was not made known to the sons of men, as it has now been revealed to His holy apostles and
prophets in the Spirit; 6 to be specific, that the Gentiles are fellow heirs and fellow members of
the body, and fellow partakers of the promise in Christ Jesus through the gospel, 7 of which I
was made a minister, according to the gift of God's grace which was given to me according to
the working of His power. 8 To me, the very least of all saints, this grace was given, to preach to
the Gentiles the unfathomable riches of Christ, 9 and to bring to light what is the administration
of the mystery which for ages has been hidden in God who created all things; 10 so that the
manifold wisdom of God might now be made known through the church to the rulers and the
authorities in the heavenly places. 11 This was in accordance with the eternal purpose which He
carried out in Christ Jesus our Lord, 12 in whom we have boldness and confident access through
faith in Him. 13 Therefore I ask you not to lose heart at my tribulations on your behalf, for they
are your glory.

14 For this reason I bow my knees before the Father, 15 from whom every family in heaven and
on earth derives its name, 16 that He would grant you, according to the riches of His glory, to
be strengthened with power through His Spirit in the inner man, 17 so that Christ may dwell in
your hearts through faith; and that you, being rooted and grounded in love, 18 may be able to
comprehend with all the saints what is the breadth and length and height and depth, 19 and to
know the love of Christ which surpasses knowledge, that you may be filled up to all the fullness
of God.

20 Now to Him who is able to do far more abundantly beyond all that we ask or think, according
to the power that works within us, 21 to Him be the glory in the church and in Christ Jesus to all
generations forever and ever. Amen.

EPHESIANS 4

Unity of the Spirit

1 Therefore I, the prisoner of the Lord, implore you to walk in a manner worthy of the calling
with which you have been called, 2 with all humility and gentleness, with patience, showing
tolerance for one another in love, 3 being diligent to preserve the unity of the Spirit in the
bond of peace. 4 There is one body and one Spirit, just as also you were called in one hope of
your calling; 5 one Lord, one faith, one baptism, 6 one God and Father of all who is over all and
through all and in all.

7 But to each one of us grace was given according to the measure of Christ's gift. 8 Therefore it
says,

> "When He ascended on high,
> He led captive a host of captives,
> And He gave gifts to men."

9 (Now this expression, "He ascended," what does it mean except that He also had descended
into the lower parts of the earth? 10 He who descended is Himself also He who ascended far
above all the heavens, so that He might fill all things.) 11 And He gave some as apostles, and
some as prophets, and some as evangelists, and some as pastors and teachers, 12 for the
equipping of the saints for the work of service, to the building up of the body of Christ; 13 until
we all attain to the unity of the faith, and of the knowledge of the Son of God, to a mature man,
to the measure of the stature which belongs to the fullness of Christ. 14 As a result, we are
no longer to be children, tossed here and there by waves and carried about by every wind of
doctrine, by the trickery of men, by craftiness in deceitful scheming; 15 but speaking the truth
in love, we are to grow up in all aspects into Him who is the head, even Christ, 16 from whom
the whole body, being fitted and held together by what every joint supplies, according to the
proper working of each individual part, causes the growth of the body for the building up of
itself in love.

The Christian's Walk

17 So this I say, and affirm together with the Lord, that you walk no longer just as the Gentiles
also walk, in the futility of their mind, 18 being darkened in their understanding, excluded
from the life of God because of the ignorance that is in them, because of the hardness of their
heart; 19 and they, having become callous, have given themselves over to sensuality for the
practice of every kind of impurity with greediness. 20 But you did not learn Christ in this way,
21 if indeed you have heard Him and have been taught in Him, just as truth is in Jesus, 22 that,
in reference to your former manner of life, you lay aside the old self, which is being corrupted
in accordance with the lusts of deceit, 23 and that you be renewed in the spirit of your mind,
24 and put on the new self, which in the likeness of God has been created in righteousness and
holiness of the truth.

25 Therefore, laying aside falsehood, speak truth each one of you with his neighbor, for we are
members of one another. 26 Be angry, and yet do not sin; do not let the sun go down on your
anger, 27 and do not give the devil an opportunity. 28 He who steals must steal no longer; but rather
he must labor, performing with his own hands what is good, so that he will have something to
share with one who has need. 29 Let no unwholesome word proceed from your mouth, but only
such a word as is good for edification according to the need of the moment, so that it will give
grace to those who hear. 30 Do not grieve the Holy Spirit of God, by whom you were sealed for
the day of redemption. 31 Let all bitterness and wrath and anger and clamor and slander be put
away from you, along with all malice. 32 Be kind to one another, tender-hearted, forgiving each
other, just as God in Christ also has forgiven you.

EPHESIANS 5

Be Imitators of God

1 Therefore be imitators of God, as beloved children; 2 and walk in love, just as Christ also
loved you and gave Himself up for us, an offering and a sacrifice to God as a fragrant aroma.

3 But immorality or any impurity or greed must not even be named among you, as is proper
among saints; 4 and there must be no filthiness and silly talk, or coarse jesting, which are not
fitting, but rather giving of thanks. 5 For this you know with certainty, that no immoral or impure
person or covetous man, who is an idolater, has an inheritance in the kingdom of Christ and
God.

6 Let no one deceive you with empty words, for because of these things the wrath of
God comes upon the sons of disobedience. 7 Therefore do not be partakers with them;
8 for you were formerly darkness, but now you are Light in the Lord; walk as children of
Light 9 (for the fruit of the Light consists in all goodness and righteousness and truth),
10 trying to learn what is pleasing to the Lord. 11 Do not participate in the unfruitful deeds of
darkness, but instead even expose them; 12 for it is disgraceful even to speak of the things which
are done by them in secret. 13 But all things become visible when they are exposed by the light,
for everything that becomes visible is light. 14 For this reason it says,

> "Awake, sleeper,
> And arise from the dead,
> And Christ will shine on you."

15 Therefore be careful how you walk, not as unwise men but as wise, 16 making the most of your
time, because the days are evil. 17 So then do not be foolish, but understand what the will of the
Lord is. 18 And do not get drunk with wine, for that is dissipation, but be filled with the Spirit,
19 speaking to one another in psalms and hymns and spiritual songs, singing and making melody
with your heart to the Lord; 20 always giving thanks for all things in the name of our Lord Jesus
Christ to God, even the Father; 21 and be subject to one another in the fear of Christ.

Marriage Like Christ and the Church

22 Wives, be subject to your own husbands, as to the Lord. 23 For the husband is the head of the
wife, as Christ also is the head of the church, He Himself being the Savior of the body. 24 But as
the church is subject to Christ, so also the wives ought to be to their husbands in everything.

25 Husbands, love your wives, just as Christ also loved the church and gave Himself up for her,
26 so that He might sanctify her, having cleansed her by the washing of water with the word,
27 that He might present to Himself the church in all her glory, having no spot or wrinkle or any
such thing; but that she would be holy and blameless. 28 So husbands ought also to love their
own wives as their own bodies. He who loves his own wife loves himself; 29 for no one ever hated
his own flesh, but nourishes and cherishes it, just as Christ also does the church, 30 because we

are members of His body. 31 For this reason a man shall leave his father and mother and shall be joined to his wife, and the two shall become one flesh. 32 This mystery is great; but I am speaking with reference to Christ and the church. 33 Nevertheless, each individual among you also is to love his own wife even as himself, and the wife must see to it that she respects her husband.

EPHESIANS 6

Family Relationships

1 Children, obey your parents in the Lord, for this is right. 2 Honor your father and mother (which is the first commandment with a promise), 3 so that it may be well with you, and that you may live long on the earth.

4 Fathers, do not provoke your children to anger, but bring them up in the discipline and instruction of the Lord.

5 Slaves, be obedient to those who are your masters according to the flesh, with fear and trembling, in the sincerity of your heart, as to Christ; 6 not by way of eyeservice, as men-pleasers, but as slaves of Christ, doing the will of God from the heart. 7 With good will render service, as to the Lord, and not to men, 8 knowing that whatever good thing each one does, this he will receive back from the Lord, whether slave or free.

9 And masters, do the same things to them, and give up threatening, knowing that both their Master and yours is in heaven, and there is no partiality with Him.

The Armor of God

10 Finally, be strong in the Lord and in the strength of His might. 11 Put on the full armor of God, so that you will be able to stand firm against the schemes of the devil. 12 For our struggle is not against flesh and blood, but against the rulers, against the powers, against the world forces of this darkness, against the spiritual forces of wickedness in the heavenly places. 13 Therefore, take up the full armor of God, so that you will be able to resist in the evil day, and having done everything, to stand firm. 14 Stand firm therefore, having girded your loins with truth, and having put on the breastplate of righteousness, 15 and having shod your feet with the preparation of the gospel of peace; 16 in addition to all, taking up the shield of faith with which you will be able to extinguish all the flaming arrows of the evil one. 17 And take the helmet of salvation, and the sword of the Spirit, which is the word of God.

18 With all prayer and petition pray at all times in the Spirit, and with this in view, be on the alert with all perseverance and petition for all the saints, 19 and pray on my behalf, that utterance may be given to me in the opening of my mouth, to make known with boldness the mystery of the gospel, 20 for which I am an ambassador in chains; that in proclaiming it I may speak boldly, as I ought to speak.

21 But that you also may know about my circumstances, how I am doing, Tychicus, the beloved
brother and faithful minister in the Lord, will make everything known to you. 22 I have sent him
to you for this very purpose, so that you may know about us, and that he may comfort your
hearts.

23 Peace be to the brethren, and love with faith, from God the Father and the Lord Jesus Christ.
24 Grace be with all those who love our Lord Jesus Christ with incorruptible love.

Experiencing the Riches of Christ in Ephesians

Introduction

In Him

You are in Christ. It is this connection between what Christ has been made of God to us, and how we have it only as also being in Him, that we must learn to understand better. [1]
~ Andrew Murray

There's a phrase found repeatedly on the pages of the New Testament, so often, in fact, that we are likely to skim over it without stopping to take it in. It's a simple term, just two words: "In Christ." Not beside Him. Not behind Him. Not just near Him. In Him.

Don't let the simplicity of the phrase mislead you. Those two words are the very heartbeat of the Christian life. They hold the weight of eternity. They speak of union, identity, security, and belonging. They remind us not just where we are spiritually, but who we now are because of Christ. *In Him*, we find forgiveness (Ephesians 1:7). *In Him*, we are made new (2 Corinthians 5:17). *In Him*, we live and move and have our being (Acts 17:28).

Dear believer, His life is your life. His strength is your hope. You aren't just loosely connected to Jesus; you are situated *In Him*. This is no distant relationship, no mere association. As John Stott describes it, "The relationship…is something much more than a formal attachment or nodding acquaintance, something more even than a personal friendship; it is nothing less than a vital, organic, intimate union with Jesus Christ, involving a shared life and love." [2]

That "shared life and love," that abiding union, is the very essence of Christianity. And on the night before His crucifixion, that was the message Jesus wanted most to leave with His disciples. He didn't give them a pep talk or five-year strategic plan to follow. Instead, He gave them a truth that would anchor them for the rest of their lives: Life, real life, is found in union with Him.

To drive the point home, Jesus used a picture His friends would have immediately understood: a vine and its branches. These were men acquainted with the soil. They had walked past vineyards all their lives. They had seen vines flourish under careful hands, and they had watched them wither when neglected. So, in John 15:1-8, Jesus took what they knew and used it to build a bridge between their world and the Kingdom He was ushering in.

Interestingly, the metaphor Jesus used wasn't new. His reference to the vine and the branches echoed back through centuries of Jewish history. It was a familiar picture, woven into the fabric of Israel's national identity. Long before, God had used the vine to describe His covenant people. So, to truly grasp what Jesus was saying, we need to step back into the world where that image first took root.

The Vine that Withered

The custom of most nations is to adopt a national symbol drawn from the natural world, something that reflects their values, story, or spirit. England has the lion, a majestic, but somewhat unlikely symbol, given that you won't find one roaming the English countryside. More authentically, Ireland has the shamrock. Less authentically, Scotland has the unicorn. The United States claims the bald eagle, a creature as striking as it is indigenous.

In the Old Testament, the symbol for Israel was the vine. That might not be the kind of image you would expect for a nation. Vines don't intimidate. They don't conquer. But they do grow. They flourish. They produce. And that's what God intended for His people. They existed not for their own glory, but for His, to bear fruit for Him. In their national character, they were to reflect who He was and what He was about. The psalmist gives voice to Israel's experience:

> You brought us from Egypt like a grapevine; You drove away the pagan nations and transplanted us into Your land. You cleared the ground for us, and we took root and filled the land (Psalm 80:8-9, NLT).

For 400 years, Israel lived as refugees within the civilization of Egypt, first welcomed, then later enslaved. Over time, they absorbed much of the Egyptian culture, its language, and customs. But God, the Master Gardener, sovereignly pulled them out of that soil and "transplanted" them in a new land of promise: Canaan. There, they became the focus of His special care and attention. And in that new place, they began to prosper:

> Our shade covered the mountains; our branches covered the mighty cedars. We spread our branches west to the Mediterranean Sea; our shoots spread east to the Euphrates River (Psalm 80:10-11, NLT).

Then, something went wrong. Pride crept in. Sin set in. The vine that God intended to be fruitful, grew wild. Israel turned away from the One Who had planted them and nourished their growth. And He was grieved:

> What more could I have done for My vineyard that I have not already done? When I expected sweet grapes, why did My vineyard give me bitter grapes? (Isaiah 5:4, NLT).

The vine God had intended to flourish and grow, began to wither. So, God withdrew His protection and allowed the vine to be ravaged by other nations. In the wake of the resulting devastation, the psalmist laments:

> But now, why have You broken down our walls so that all who pass by may steal our fruit? The wild boar from the forest devours it, and the wild animals feed on it (Psalm 80:12-13, NLT).

Yet, God wasn't finished. Judgment would not be His last word. Grace was still coming. He had a plan, not to abandon the vineyard, but to replant it. He would start over with a "shoot from the stem of Jesse" (Isaiah 11:1). That single shoot would be the true Vine.

You can almost hear the anguish in the psalmist's voice as he pleads with God for restoration:

> Come back, we beg You, O God of Heaven's Armies. Look down from Heaven and see our plight. Take care of this grapevine that You Yourself have planted, this son You have raised for Yourself…Strengthen the man You love, the son of Your choice. Then we will never abandon You again. Revive us so we can call on Your name once more. Turn us again to Yourself, O Lord God of Heaven's Armies. Make Your face shine down upon us. Only then will we be saved (Psalm 80:14-15; 17-19, NLT).

The people had failed, the vine had withered, but hope was not lost. Centuries later, the psalmist's prayer was answered.

The True Vine

It was the night before the cross. Judas had already slipped away. The upper room had grown quiet. The eleven remaining disciples sat with troubled hearts, trying to make sense of Jesus' words about leaving, betrayal, denial, and glory. Into the silence, Jesus spoke, "Get up, let us go from here" (John 14:31).

The men followed Jesus down the stairs and out into the narrow, winding streets of Jerusalem. Avoiding the Temple Mount with its noise and Passover crowds, Jesus turned and led them outside the city through the Kidron Valley to their destination. As they made their way toward the Mount of Olives, where Gethsemane and betrayal awaited, Jesus stopped. Perhaps they had come to a vineyard with rows of neatly tended grapes stretched across the hillside. Picture Jesus reaching for a grape branch, with its woody stem and new spring growth, as He then said something no one expected: "I am the true Vine and My Father is the Vinedresser" (John 15:1).

It was a powerful claim. Israel had always been the vine: God's chosen people, planted to bear fruit for His glory. But where the nation had failed, Jesus succeeded. He was the faithful Son, the fruitful Vine, the fulfillment of Israel's story. He was rooted in the Father's will and yielded the fruit of righteousness, obedience, and love.

And then came the beautiful summons: "Abide in Me" (John 15:4). Stay attached. This was more than just theology. It was an invitation into intimacy, into relationship, into Life. The kind of "life" Jesus came to give was not just a pulse - it was vibrant, soul-deep overflowing life (John 10:10).

This was a seismic shift. No longer was identity rooted in a nation or a system, but in a Person. And *In Him*, everything changed. Jesus continued:

> Live in Me. Make your home in Me just as I do in you. In the same way that a branch can't bear grapes by itself but only by being joined to the vine, you can't bear fruit unless you are joined with Me. I am the Vine, you are the branches. When you're joined with Me and I with you, the relation intimate and organic, the harvest is sure to be abundant. Separated, you can't produce a thing. Anyone who separates from Me is deadwood, gathered up and thrown on the bonfire. But if you make yourselves at home with Me and My words are at home in you, you can be sure that whatever you ask will be listened to and acted upon. This is how my Father shows Who He is – when you produce grapes, when you mature as My disciples (John 15:4-8, MSG).

Andrew Murray captures the substance of this turning point:

> During the life of Jesus on earth, the word He chiefly used when speaking of the relationship of the disciples to Himself was: "Follow Me." When about to leave for Heaven, He gave them a new word, to express their more intimate and spiritual union. That chosen word was "Abide in Me." [3]

In Greek, the word for "abide" is *meno* and it means "to remain, to dwell, to stay." [4] But it means more than just staying in one place. It means staying in one Presence.

In His final hours, Jesus was giving His disciples something far deeper than a new rule to follow; He was revealing a new reality to live in. A relationship so close, so intertwined, that His very life would flow into theirs. Spoken in the shadow of the cross, His words would shape the understanding of those who heard them and all who came after.

Come. Abide. And live - truly, abundantly, eternally.

Paul's Favorite Phrase

No one grasped the wonder of that invitation more than Paul. From his own encounter with the risen Christ on the road to Damascus, he understood what it meant to be united to the Vine, rooted and alive, no longer bound by the old, but living in the new. That union, that connection, became the foundation for the phrase Paul used to describe the reality of the Christian life. You can't read his letters without hearing it: *In Christ... In Christ Jesus...In Him.* It's like the truth was too amazing to say just once, so he returned to this phrase over 160 times as the default term for those who follow Christ. [5]

To Paul, those two words - "in Christ" - carried the essence of everything salvation means. This wasn't a figure of speech. It was a spiritual reality. The very moment we come to Christ, something extraordinary happens: His death becomes our death. His resurrection becomes our resurrection. His righteousness becomes our covering. And from that point on, we are no longer who we once were. We are completely transformed.

Throughout Paul's letters, he invites us into a new way of being - *In Him*:

- "There is now no condemnation for those who are in Christ Jesus" (Romans 8:1). Those twelve words dissolve the hardest places in our hearts. In Christ, shame has lost its voice. Not because of our goodness, but because the perfect love of Jesus has drawn the lines of grace so wide, even our worst mistakes collapse into His forgiveness.
- "For as in Adam all die, so also in Christ all will be made alive" (1 Corinthians 15:22). In Christ, we no longer live in the shadow of death, but in the dawn of resurrection. The story is rewritten, not with ink, but in His precious blood. Where death once ruled with finality, life now rises, with the promise of eternity. The grave is no longer the end, it's only the beginning.
- "If anyone is in Christ, he is a new creature; the old things passed away; behold, new things have come" (2 Corinthians 5:17). In Christ, the soul's geography is changed. What was once barren ground, now springs forth with fresh hope. The past isn't erased; it's redeemed, folded in a greater story, a story of how grace makes all things new.
- "He made Him who knew no sin to be sin on our behalf, so that we might become the righteousness of God in Him" (2 Corinthians 5:21). This is the great exchange. He took our place so we could take His. Our sin, every stain, is laid upon the sinless Savior. And in return, His perfect righteousness is placed over us, covering us completely. In Christ, we are no longer defined by what we've done, but by what He has done for us.
- "Blessed be the God and Father of our Lord Jesus Christ, Who has blessed us with every spiritual blessing in the heavenly places in Christ" (Ephesians 1:3). Every blessing is already given. Nothing has been withheld. Nothing more can be earned. Every blessing has been poured out lavishly, waiting only for open hands to receive. In Christ, we lack nothing - not now, not ever.

Paul's words resonate deep within us. We nod in agreement. We sing the songs. We say we believe all that Christ has done for us. And yet, if we're honest, when we look at our lives, something feels off. There's a tension, a dissonance between the riches Scripture promises and the reality we are living. We read about freedom, but still feel bound to old ways. We read about peace, but wrestle with anxiety. We read about joy, but find ourselves tired, restless, and running on empty.

What is the missing piece? Why do the truths we believe feel so distant from the lives we're living? Could it be that we've embraced only part of the gospel - Christ in us - while overlooking the invitation to live fully *In Him*?

Life In Him

Most believers understand, at least in part, what it means for Christ to live in us. We remember the day grace found us, when we opened the door and Christ, through His Spirit, came in and made His home in our hearts. It was a holy beginning, a sacred first breath.

But to stop there is to live on the front porch of the gospel, never stepping fully inside.

In his letter to the Ephesians, Paul's words swing the door wide open: "In Christ" - not merely Christ in us, but we *In Him.* A life that is hidden in His righteousness, anchored in His love, and seated with Him in the heavenly places. Paul isn't inviting us to a moment. He's inviting us to step inside - into a dwelling, a way of life, a place to abide, a Presence.

Jesus didn't go to the cross just to forgive our sins. He gave His life for us to form His life in us. He didn't come only to claim us as His own, but to transform us into His likeness.

As Ann Voskamp simply and beautifully writes, "You belong to Jesus to become like Jesus." [6] What your soul truly longs for is found not in striving, but in staying. It's not in effort, but in abiding - in Christ, always, only.

The gospel isn't just a message to believe, it's an invitation to live a new kind of life: a life *In Him.*

The disciples said yes to that invitation and turned the world upside down. Paul said yes and the gospel spread across nations and generations. What will happen if you say yes?

Come. Abide. And live - truly, abundantly, eternally. *In Him.*

Introduction to Ephesians

Ephesians – carefully, reverently, prayerfully considered – will change our lives.
It is not so much a question of what we will do with the epistle, but what it will do with us. [1]
~ Ken Hughes

Imagine checking your mailbox today and finding – not junk mail, not a bill – but a handwritten letter, addressed to you. As you open it, the words inside reach beyond ink and paper. They remind you of who you are, why you're here, and how your life fits into a story far grander than you ever dreamed. That's what the letter to the Ephesians is. Paul pulls back the curtain on a cosmic drama – a story that began before time with a God Who chose you, adopted you, and redeemed you. A loving Father Who is now weaving all things – even the broken pieces of your life – into His grand design under Christ. This is no ordinary letter. It's a mirror that shows you who you really are. It's a map that charts a new way to live. It's a call to live not just better, but altogether differently. Because in Christ, you are no longer who you once were. You are who you were always meant to be.

To grasp the message of Ephesians, we must first trace the journey of the messenger, a journey, like the letter he wrote, that reminds us no one is beyond the reach of God's transforming hand.

Paul

From the very beginning, the writer of Ephesians identifies himself as Paul (1:1), but that wasn't always his name. Once he was Saul, a Roman citizen from Tarsus, a trade city close to the Mediterranean coast in what is now modern-day Turkey. Raised in a devout Jewish family, Saul was immersed in both the cultural and religious traditions of Judaism from an early age.

At some point, his family either moved to Jerusalem or made lengthy visits there. In Jerusalem, Saul became a student of Gamaliel, one of the most respected rabbis of the time (Acts 22:3). Brilliant and disciplined, Saul quickly rose in the ranks of the Pharisees and became one of first-century Judaism's most promising young leaders. Saul was in such a high position that when the first Christians were put on trial, he had a vote in deciding their punishment (Acts 26:10). The first time we see him in Scripture, he's standing by as Stephen is stoned to death – watching with approval and holding the coats of those throwing the stones (Acts 7:58–8:1).

Saul's loyalty to the Law of Moses was unwavering, and he viewed the growing movement of Jesus-followers as a threat to everything he believed. The Messiah crucified? Heresy! And then risen from the dead? No way! Determined to preserve the purity of Judaism, Saul became a fierce opponent of the early church and set out to destroy it. House by house. City by city.

But God had other plans.

On his way to persecute believers in Damascus, Saul's life took an amazing turn: A blinding light. A voice from Heaven. And a question from the risen Christ that pierced his soul, "Saul, Saul, why are you persecuting me?" (Acts 9:4). In that sacred moment, everything changed. Saul found out that Jesus was alive. He went from denying the Messiah to living for Him. Paul never got over that encounter. How could he? One minute, he was Saul, resolved to erase the name of Jesus from the pages of history. The next, he was Paul, apprehended by the Savior's love and captured by His grace.

Grace has a way of rewriting our stories. And God rewrote Paul's: He became the apostle chosen by God to carry the name of Jesus beyond the borders of tradition, beyond the walls of Jerusalem, right into the heart of the Gentile world (Acts 9:15). While serving faithfully in the church at Antioch, the Holy Spirit called Paul to take the message of Jesus to the Gentiles (Acts 13:1-3). What followed was nothing short of remarkable. The book of Acts traces three powerful journeys as Paul carried the name of Jesus across the Roman Empire. It was one of the most far-reaching evangelistic missions the world has ever seen. And interestingly, the place he stayed longer than anywhere else was Ephesus.

Ephesus

Take a moment to picture the most influential cities of our day: New York, London, Tokyo. Now rewind the clock two thousand years and step into Ephesus. Strategically situated about two-and-a-half miles inland from the Aegean Sea, along the western coast of what is now Turkey, Ephesus was a political, cultural, and commercial powerhouse in the ancient world. With a population nearing 250,000, it wasn't just large, it was the crown jewel of Asia Minor. In the Roman Empire, it ranked just behind Rome and Athens in prestige and was famously known as the "Supreme Metropolis of Asia." [2]

Ephesus in the Time of Paul c. AD 60

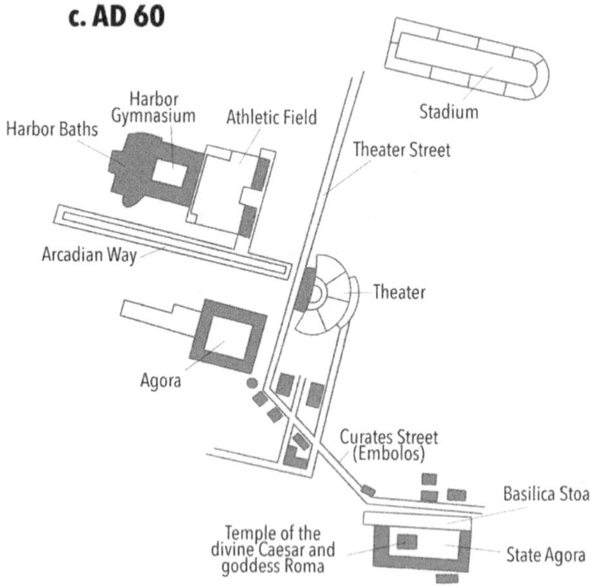

Ephesus was the capital of the wealthy Roman province of Asia, making it a central administrative center. It housed the governor's residence and was home to a major Roman court, drawing people from across the province to settle legal matters. As a free city, Ephesus enjoyed a degree of self-governance, a privilege that contributed to its considerable wealth and influence. [3]

Situated along key land and sea routes from Rome, Ephesus served as a vital gateway to the East and was the largest trading center in Asia Minor. The city had a magnificent theater, with a seating capacity of 24,000. Ingeniously designed, the theater's acoustics allowed a speaker standing at a specific spot on the stage to whisper and still be heard throughout the entire audience. [4] The city's famous agora (marketplace) and complex network of streets and colonnades bore witness to its commercial vitality. Wealthy citizens often financed public buildings, baths, fountains, and statues, contributing to the city's grandeur. [5]

Towering over Ephesus, about a mile outside of town, was a temple built for the worship of the goddess Artemis, as the Greeks called her, or Diana, as she was known by the Romans. They believed Artemis to be the goddess of fertility, and her temple was so stunning, it was considered one of the Seven Wonders of the Ancient World. Larger than a modern-day football field, and four times the size of the Parthenon in Athens, the temple had more than a hundred columns set in double rows around the shrine. Many of the columns were sculpted with mythological scenes and overlaid with gold. [6] In Paul's day, the temple wasn't just a tourist attraction, it was the heart of Ephesian life. Howard Vos explains the stronghold Artemis had in Ephesus:

> Artemis represented a form of the Asian mother goddess...the goddess of fertility in man, beast, and vegetation. As the mother-goddess figure, she represented more than fertility – also resurrection, the eternal return of life to earth. She had become the patroness of maidens of marriageable age, the helper of women in childbirth. She was also the moon goddess, the goddess of wild nature, and of the hunter and fisherman. In the peasant's mind, such a divinity would ensure that his beasts and land were fruitful. To the intellectual, she presented the idea of an all-creating mother who sustained the universe. [7]

The cult of Artemis drew thousands of pilgrims, creating a thriving business in religious artifacts and souvenirs, such as silver shrines (Acts 19:24). The temple complex also functioned as a bank, adding to the city's economic standing.

In the first century, Ephesus' political importance was boosted when Domitian awarded the city an imperial temple dedicated to the Flavian Dynasty. As a "temple warden" of the imperial cult in Asia Minor, Ephesus benefited from political and commercial benefits. Prominent Ephesians were appointed to the Provincial Assembly, whose mission was to promote and enforce emperor worship throughout the province. [8]

In addition to cult worship, Ephesus was an epicenter for sorcery and the occult. The people were "obsessed with demons and magic," [9] as attested by the stories of the seven sons of Sceva and the burning of magic books in Acts 19:13-20.

It's into this city that Paul arrives. A city that will never be the same again.

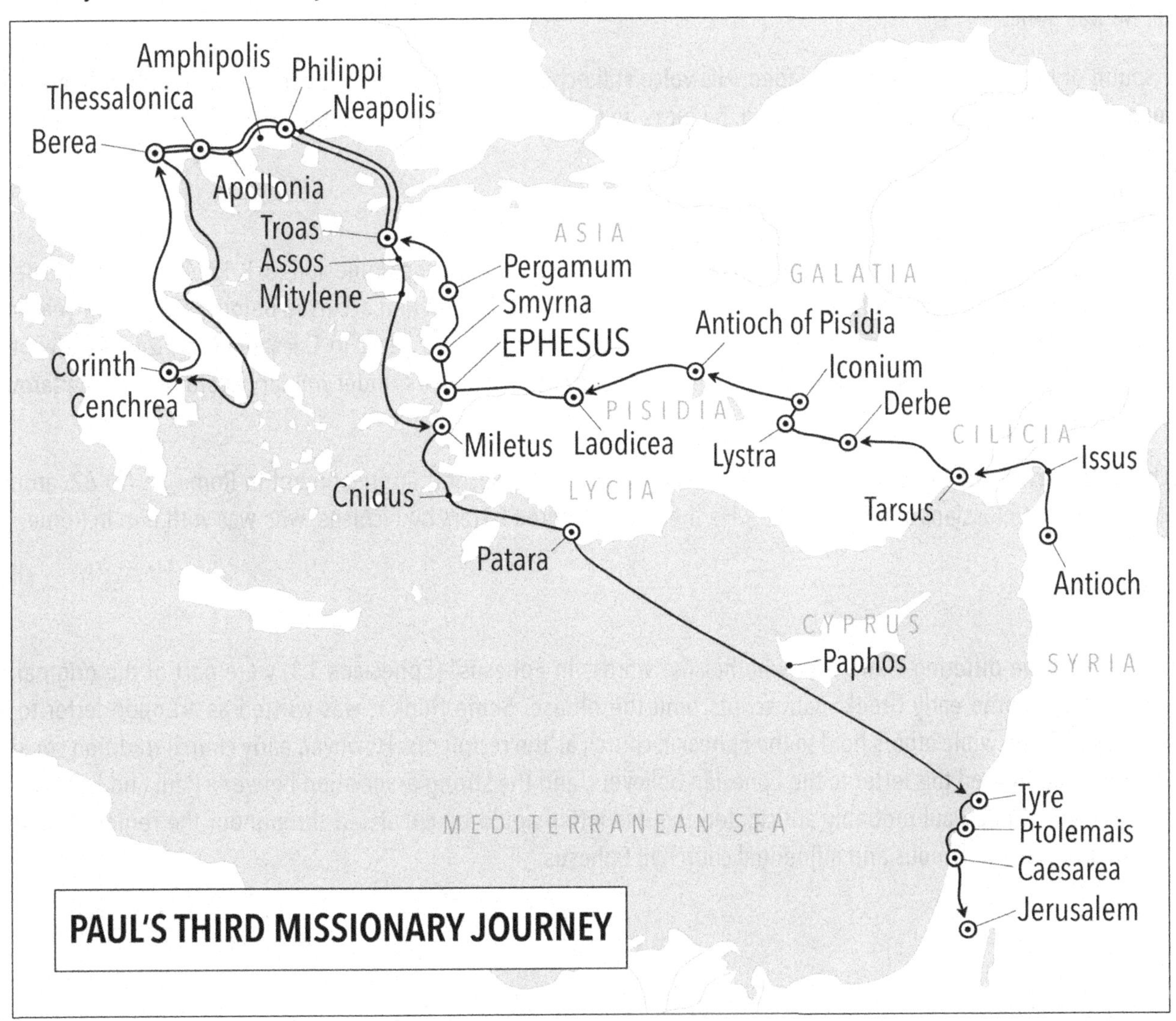

Paul in Ephesus

During Paul's second missionary trip, he made a brief stop in Ephesus (Acts 18:19-21). But it was during his third missionary journey that he returned and stayed. For nearly three years, Paul poured his heart into the city (Acts 19:10; 20:31). He reasoned in the synagogue, taught daily in the lecture hall of Tyrannus, and shared the message of Jesus as he walked the crowded streets.

And God moved.

Right there, in the shadow of the Temple of Artemis, the gospel took hold and spread like wildfire, reaching not just the city but the entire region. Many people believed in Christ. Those who had practiced sorcery brought their books and burned them in the streets. Others walked away from idols and turned to Christ. The sick were healed. Demons fled at the name of Jesus. The oppressed were set free.

But not everyone was happy. Silversmiths feared their profits; the gospel was bad for the idol-making business. One of them, Demetrius, stirred up a riot. The whole city was thrown into chaos, shouting, surging through the streets, dragging believers into the theater. But in the end, the name of Jesus still stood, unshaken (Acts 19:23-41).

When the time came for Paul to leave, he called the elders to meet him on the shore at Miletus. There, he gave them a heartfelt charge to remain faithful shepherds, warning them of coming dangers, and urging them to guard the flock with vigilance, humility, and unwavering devotion to Christ.

And then he was gone.

But the sound of his sandals never really faded. His voice still echoed in the hearts of those whose lives had been changed. Then, years later, from Rome, chained to a guard, he picks up his pen to write them a letter.

Time Stamp

Paul's letter gives us an important clue about when it was written: He was in prison (Ephesians 3:1, 13; 4:1; 6:20). Acts describes two imprisonments of Paul. His first incarceration in Philippi was relatively brief and occurred before Paul's three-year ministry in Ephesus (Acts 16:23-34). His second and longer confinement included two years in Caesarea (Acts 24:27), a winter as a prisoner at sea and on the Island of Malta (Acts 27:9-28:14), and then two years under military custody in Rome (around AD 60-62). [10]

Most scholars believe Paul wrote to the Ephesians near the end of his second imprisonment in Rome, in AD 62, around the same time he wrote Colossians and Philemon. [11] He then sent all three letters by Tychicus, who was with him in Rome.

A Side Note

Modern scholars have differing views over whether the words "in Ephesus" (Ephesians 1:1) were part of the original text of Ephesians, because some early Greek manuscripts omit the phrase. Some think it was written as an open letter to all the churches in Asia Minor, while others hold to the Ephesian church as the recipients. However, early church tradition consistently affirms that Paul addressed this letter to the Ephesian believers, and the strong association between Paul and Ephesus in Acts supports this view. While Paul probably anticipated that his letter would be circulated throughout the region, "his first and primary audience was the famous and influential church in Ephesus." [12]

The Message

Paul writes to the first-century believers in Ephesus with a central message: Because they've been made new in Christ, they should live in an entirely new way.

New life = New lives

The phrase "in Christ" reverberates throughout the entire letter. Ephesians unveils what it means to live in light of God's redemptive work through Christ. Far more than a set of moral instructions, Paul's letter offers a vision of transformed humanity – rooted in grace, shaped by love, and empowered by the Spirit. And it is all because of Jesus: His life, death, resurrection, and ascension.

Paul's message can be divided into three main sections. The first section, chapters 1-3, lays a theological foundation: who believers are in Christ. The second two sections, chapters 4-5 and chapter 6 are practical, demonstrating how this new way of being human shapes daily life. Throughout the letter, life "in Christ" not only defines the believer's position, but also fuels the transformation of their practice.

Part One

- ***In Him*: We are.** Paul begins by revealing a new identity for believers: We are chosen, adopted, redeemed, and sealed by God, not because of anything we've done, but because of His eternal purpose and grace. From this identity flows a new kind of community, where old divisions – ethnic, social, religious – are erased. In Christ, Jew and Gentile become one new humanity, reconciled not only to God but also to one another.

Part Two

- ***In Him*: We mature.** As members of this new humanity, we are beckoned to a radically different walk – one that leads us toward spiritual maturity. Paul urges us to put off the old self, shaped by corruption and deceit, and to put on the new self, created to be like God in righteousness and holiness. Life in Christ is a journey of transformation, where character is shaped by grace and relationships reflect His love.
- ***In Him*: We win.** To live this new way requires an awareness of the spiritual battle around us. Strengthened by the armor of God, we learn to stand firm against the unseen forces of darkness and live in victory.

Ephesians is not just a letter to the early church, it's a call for us to live fully alive, fully free, and fully known – being formed by the image of Christ and joining Him in the grand adventure of redeeming the world.

Key Words

Paul had a remarkable gift with words – his writing is theologically profound, yet personal and passionate. He didn't write merely to convey information but to ignite transformation. With rich, multi-layered language, he invited his readers to grasp the mystery of Christ and see the big picture of God's redemptive plan. In Ephesians, several key words emerge that shape the letter's message:

Adoption
Armor of God
Be subject
Chose
Dead
Faith
Filled with the Spirit
Fullness of God
Gift
Gifts
Grace
Holy Spirit
Imitators
In Christ
In Christ Jesus
In Him
Inheritance
Inner man
Lay aside
Light
Love of Christ
Made alive
Manifold wisdom
Mature
Mystery
One body
One new man
Peace
Power
Predestined
Put on
Reconciliation
Redemption
Renewed
Revelation
Saints
Sealed
Spirit-filled
Stand
Truth in love
Unity
Walk in love
Wisdom
Workmanship

Ephesians Today

Ephesians remains profoundly relevant today because it speaks to the deepest needs of our hearts and the challenges of our culture. In a world that's lost its moral compass, and where people are struggling to figure out who they are, Paul's letter is like a breath of fresh air. It reminds us that our identity isn't something we achieve – it's something we receive – in Christ. And with that new identity comes a new way of being human, an entirely different way to live: *In Him.*

Because Christ stepped into death to bring us life,
we no longer walk in the graveclothes of our former selves.
The old has passed. The new has come.

And with every breath the Spirit gives,
we rise, again and again,
into the kind of life Jesus died to give us.
A life not just changed, but exchanged:
our sin for His righteousness,
our striving for His strength,
our emptiness for His fullness.

This is not just a better life.
It is a brand-new life.
A Spirit-led life.
A life that looks like Him.

And Can It Be That I Should Gain? 107

CHARLES WESLEY THOMAS CAMPBELL

1. And can it be that I should gain An in - terest in the
2. He left His Fa - ther's throne a - bove, So free, so in - fi -
3. Long my im-pris - oned spir - it lay Fast bound in sin and

Sav-iour's blood? Died He for me, who caused His pain? For me, who
nite His grace; Emp-tied Him - self of all but love, And bled for
na-ture's night; Thine eye dif - fused a quick-'ning ray, I woke, the

Him to death pur-sued? A - maz - ing love! how can it be That
A - dam's help-less race; 'Tis mer-cy all, im - mense and free; For,
dun - geon flamed with light; My chains fell off, my heart was free; I

Thou, my God, shouldst die for me?
O my God, it found out me.
rose, went forth, and fol-lowed Thee.

REFRAIN

A - maz-ing love! how
A - maz-ing love!

can it be That Thou, my God, shouldst die for me.
How can it be That Thou, my God,

Blessed ... with every spiritual blessing
Ephesians 1:1-14

one

"Blessed...with every spiritual blessing"

Ephesians 1:1-14

Union with Christ is the fountainhead from which flows
the Christian's every spiritual blessing. [1]
~ Robert Reymond

If you found out you had inherited six million dollars, would you claim it? If an attorney told you, "This money belongs to you. Rightfully. Legally. No strings attached. No fine print. Just sign here." Would you take it?

I imagine most of us would rush to that attorney's office, sign the papers, and walk away wealthy. But there was one man who did not. His name was Tomas Martinez.

Tomas, originally from Chile, spent years wandering the streets of Bolivia, panhandling and sleeping wherever he could find a spot. And yet, he was a millionaire. He just didn't know it. Let me explain.

Tomas Martinez had once been a respectable, middle-class man. Married. Stable. But after a few bad decisions, and writing some checks he couldn't cover, he panicked. He fled to Bolivia to escape prosecution. And there, his life unraveled: Alcohol. Addiction. Despair.

Meanwhile, back in Chile, his wife, Ines, the woman he had left behind, lived a quiet life. The couple never officially divorced. And when she died, she left behind a fortune. A fortune with no one to claim it but her one legal heir: sixty-seven-year-old Tomas Martinez.

Detectives were hired. They followed the trail, and eventually tracked him down. As they approached to give him the good news, Tomas saw them coming. Believing the men had come to arrest him for crimes committed decades before, he ran. In that moment, before they could make him a millionaire, he was gone. Vanished. Never to be seen again. His disappearance led to one newspaper calling Tomas a "new millionaire paradoxically not knowing his fortune." [2]

While you are undoubtedly shaking your head over Tomas' failure to claim his inheritance, I have to ask: Have you claimed yours? You see, as a child of God and a co-heir with Christ, you, too, have been given an inheritance, one that far exceeds any monetary value.

Yet, like Tomas, far too many live as though they are spiritual beggars, unaware that Heaven's riches are theirs to claim. Fear keeps them running, shame keeps them hiding, and unbelief blinds them to the truth that they have been chosen, redeemed, and sealed with the promise of eternal life. Paul begins his letter to the Ephesians with a profound message. Everything your heart desires, every longing, every blessing, flows from one awe-inspiring truth: You are united with Jesus. He is the Source of your life, the deep, unshakable well from which every spiritual blessing comes. *In Him*, untold wealth is yours.

Day One

Ephesians 1:1-2

At the time Paul writes his Ephesian letter, he has been a Christ-follower for about thirty years. He has been on three missionary journeys and has established churches all around the Mediterranean Sea. At the end of his third mission trip, he is arrested in Jerusalem on the trumped up charges that he brought a Gentile, Trophimus the Ephesian, into the temple, and incited a riot (Acts 21:27-36). Since he desires to go to Rome to preach the gospel (Acts 19:21), Paul claims his right as a Roman citizen to have his case tried before Caesar and is eventually sent to the capital city of the Empire.

In Rome, Paul is placed under house arrest while awaiting his trial, but that doesn't stop him from preaching the gospel. Although confined to his rented house, he is still allowed to have visitors. For the next two years, Paul's incarceration becomes his platform for "boldly proclaiming the Kingdom of God and teaching about the Lord Jesus Christ" (Acts 28:31, NLT).

During this time, he writes Ephesians and gives it to Tychicus to deliver to the believers in Asia Minor.

When Paul's dispatch arrives in Ephesus, the news will spread fast, and the entire congregation of Jewish and Gentile believers will gather to hear his words read aloud in one sitting.

Reading through the entire letter at one time is valuable, not only because it gives us a feel for the way Paul's letter was experienced in the first century, but it also gives us an overview of the epistle. Let's begin our journey through Ephesians by reading through all six chapters in Paul's letter. (It will take you about twenty minutes.) Before you begin, pray and ask the Lord to reveal His truth to you, to give you spiritual wisdom and insight so that you might grow in your knowledge of Him.

1. What is Paul's general tone in the letter?

2. After reading Paul's entire letter, what one verse stands out to you the most? Why?

Now that you have a general understanding of the content of Paul's message to the Ephesians, let's take a deeper look at our passage for this lesson.

Read Ephesians 1:1-14.

3. In Scripture, a key word or phrase is fundamental to the text and is usually repeated by the writer to emphasize his message. As you read Ephesians 1:1-14, underline the key words (including synonyms) or phrases that you see. List them in the box below.

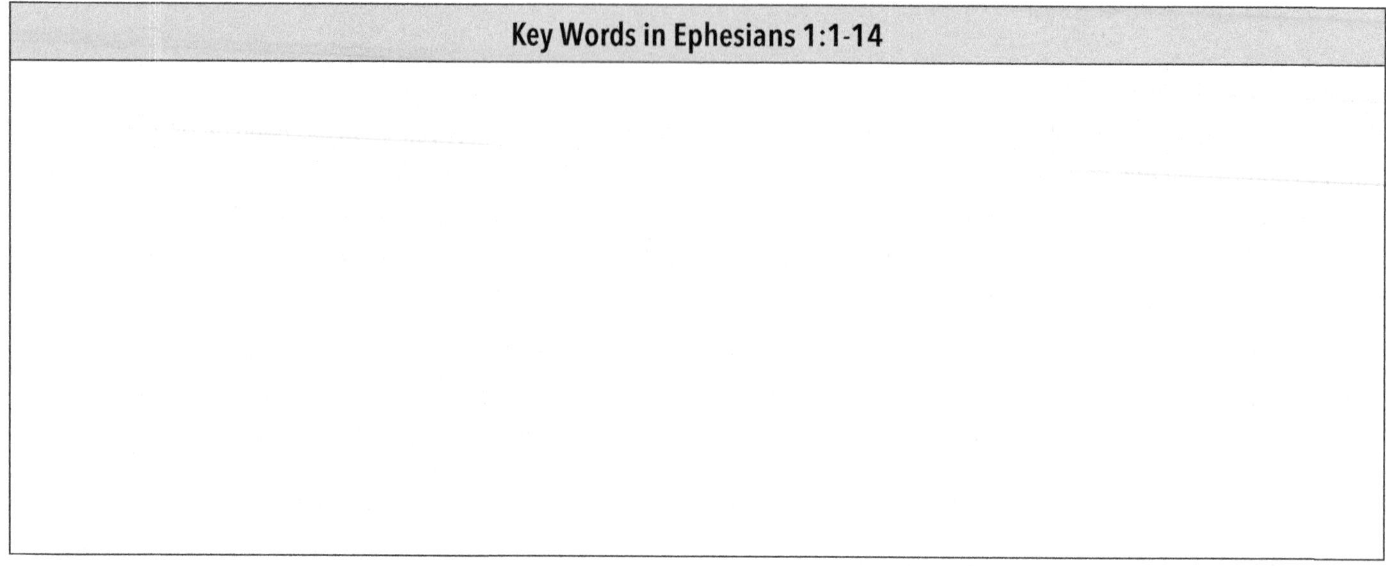

Key Words in Ephesians 1:1-14

4. How many times does Paul use the phrase "in Him" or an equivalent ("in Christ," "in Christ Jesus," "in the Beloved") in these fourteen verses? Mark those with a purple pen.

5. Write a one-sentence summary of Ephesians 1:1-14.

First-century Hellenistic letters typically began with a salutation, which identified the writer and the recipients, and then offered greetings. The opening words of Ephesians follow this standard.

Read Ephesians 1:1-2.

Paul begins Ephesians by identifying himself as the author. The mention of Paul's name would have immediately grabbed the attention of his recipients. At the close of his second missionary journey (around AD 52), Paul left Achaia (Greece) and took Aquila and Priscilla with him. They made a brief stop in Ephesus, where Paul visited the synagogue to talk with the Jews about Jesus. Although the Ephesians urged Paul to stay in the city longer, he declined, but left Aquila and Priscilla behind to spread the gospel throughout the city. His parting words, "I will return to you again if God wills" (Acts 18:21), came to fruition a year later. During his third missionary journey, he spent close to three years in Ephesus (Acts 20:31) and won large numbers of people to Christ. His ministry in Ephesus was a time of spiritual awakening that spread throughout the city and nearby region.

6. Read Luke's account of Paul's time with the Ephesians in Acts 19:1-20:2 and complete the following chart to gain an understanding of what took place during Paul's extended visit to Ephesus around AD 53-56.

Scripture	What Happened
Acts 19:1-7	
Acts 19:8	
Acts 19:9-10	
Acts 19:11-12	
Acts 19:13-17	
Acts 19:18-20	
Acts 19:23-27	
Acts 19:28-20:2	

Charles Swindoll reflects on Paul's experience in Ephesus, "Time, tears, trials, teaching, and testifying – these things summed up Paul's ministry in Ephesus. They were the essential ingredients for his fruitful ministry in that great city." [3]

After the tear-filled farewell between Paul and the Ephesian elders on the shores of Miletus in Acts 20:36-38, there is no record that Paul ever returns to Ephesus in person. So, imagine how excited they are, several years later, to receive a letter from their spiritual father!

7. What phrase does Paul use to describe himself? (v. 1)

The word "apostle" is the Greek word *apostolos*, "one who is sent." [4] Paul's use of the word is an acknowledgement that he has been selected as God's emissary to fulfill a specific mission. Not one of Jesus' twelve original disciples (later called apostles), Paul makes it clear in Ephesians 1:1, that it is only "by the will of God" that he is an apostle. And it is upon that ground that he will address the Ephesians.

8. What noun does Paul use to describe the recipients of his letter? (v. 1)

When you hear the word "saint," what comes to mind? Do you think of a dead person who has been given the title of "saint" due to some kind of extraordinary spiritual achievement? Warren Wiersbe provides helpful commentary:

> No word in the New Testament has suffered more than this word saint. Even the dictionary defines a saint as a "person officially recognized for holiness of life." Who makes this official recognition? Usually some religious body, and the process by which a person becomes a saint is technically known as canonization. The deceased person's life is examined carefully to see whether he qualifies for sainthood. If the candidate's character and conduct are found to be above reproach, if he has been responsible for working at least two miracles, then he is qualified to be made a saint. As interesting as this procedure is, we do not find it authorized in the Bible. [5]

Paul will use the word "saint" nine times in Ephesians to address his readers. [6] So, what does Paul mean by "saint"? He is talking about people just like us, people who struggle and stumble. People who have problems at work, issues in their families, and difficulties in relationships. But through it all, they remain remarkably different. The Greek word for "saint," *hagios,* is derived from the word for holy. Holy means distinct, different, and set apart to God. [7]

To be clear, it's not that saints don't have problems, but they handle them differently. They live differently. James Boice gives a rich summary of what it means to be a saint:

> Every Christian is a saint, and every saint is a Christian. Moreover, every true Christian is in some sense separated from the world. It does not mean that we are taken out of the world. That is not the way God operates. But it does mean that we are removed from it in the sense of not really belonging to the world any longer. If we are truly Christ's, we have a new nature, a new set of loyalties, and a new agenda. [8]

Not only are Paul's recipients separated from the world and set apart to God, but he also uses a second phrase to describe them: "faithful in Christ Jesus" (Ephesians 1:16). Since their initial profession of faith in Christ Jesus, the Ephesian saints have faithfully continued to grow *In Him.* Right in the middle of a city that is a seedbed for paganism, materialism, idolatry, and the occult, these believers are flourishing, and the gospel is spreading. Amid all the darkness surrounding them, they are a shining light.

Notice the words Paul uses to designate the realm of their faithfulness: "in Christ Jesus." Paul will use this phrase and its equivalents over thirty times in this one letter, so it will help us to have a clear understanding of the term. John Stott explains that everyone who gives their heart and life to Jesus is "joined to Christ in one spiritual body so that what is true of Him is also true of us." [9]

Stott then goes on to explore what this profound truth means:

> To be "in Christ" is to be personally and vitally united to Christ, as branches are to the vine and members to the body, and thereby also to Christ's people. For it is impossible to be part of the Body without being related to both the Head and the members.... According to the New Testament – and especially Paul – to be a Christian is in essence to be "in Christ," one with Him and with His people. [10]

Take a moment and marinate on that phrase "in Christ." In those two small words, Paul defines the spiritual position of the believer: Christ is in us, and we are *In Him.* His identity is our identity. And that changes everything. *In Him,* we can live from the abundance of God's Kingdom, allowing His actions to be what naturally flow out of us in our daily living.

After Paul identifies himself and his audience, he then gives his customary greeting, "Grace to you and peace from God our Father and the Lord Jesus Christ" (v. 2). Paul's greeting celebrates the way the gospel works. Grace comes first, and as it fills our lives through the Holy Spirit, it brings us peace.

Grace and peace are not contingent upon our circumstances. When the world is falling in, God's grace and peace hold us up:

> Grace and peace flooded H.P. Spafford when he sailed over the watery graves of his daughters and strengthened him to write a hymn of praise to a God Who knows how it feels to lose a child, "When peace like a river attendeth my way, When sorrows like sea billows roll; Whatever my lot. Thou hast taught me to say, 'It is well, it is well with my soul.'" [11]
>
> Grace and peace became the companions of Joseph Scriven after his first fiancé drowned the night before their wedding, and his second fiancée died of pneumonia before they could marry. In the midst of his grief, he penned the hymn, "What a Friend We Have in Jesus." [12]
>
> Grace and peace surrounded Elisabeth Elliot after her husband Jim was martyred by the Auca Indians and enabled her to continue ministering to the very people who had killed her husband. She would later write, "I really believe that God can give His peace no matter what the situation…Peace does not dwell in outward things, but in the heart prepared to wait trustfully and quietly on Him who has all things safely in His hands." [13]

DID YOU KNOW?

By using the words "grace" and "peace," Paul is combining expressions from both Jewish and Gentile traditions. Jews would greet each other with "peace" (*shalom*); Gentiles wished each other grace (*charis*). [14] Paul is basically saying, "What you have been hoping for through your own greetings is now offered to you in Christ." *In Him*, the future hope of grace and peace become a present reality.

Grace and peace are the heritage available to every child of God, and that includes you.

9. In what situation do you long for grace and peace today?

Thank you, Father, for including me in Christ, calling me to be Yours, and setting me apart.
Your grace sought me and saved me; Your grace is sufficient to hold me fast in what I am facing right now.
May Your peace rule in my heart, permeating my soul and calming every storm.
I receive Your grace and peace today. Fill me with the fullness of Your Spirit, and lead me
deeper into Jesus today. Help me to live each day in the power of Your presence
and reflect Your goodness in all that I do.
In Jesus' name, Amen.

Day Two

Ephesians 1:3-6

As Paul transitions from the introduction to the heart of his letter, he unleashes an avalanche of praise to God. Ephesians 1:3-14 is one long, beautiful sentence that focuses on the Triune God who has lavished His blessings upon us. While Paul is writing, he is imprisoned in Rome, chained to a Roman soldier, and yet, he is so overwhelmed with the goodness of God that he cannot help but burst out in praise.

As we begin our study of one of the richest passages in Scripture, let's think of it as a hymn composed of three stanzas. The first, verses 3-6, centers on the gracious plan of the Father. The second, verses 7-12, exalts the redemptive work of Jesus, the Son. The third, verses 13-14, magnifies the ministry of the Holy Spirit. Each stanza will close with a refrain of praise that invites us to rejoice in all the Godhead has done for us.

In the first stanza, verses 3-6, Paul directs his praise to God, the Father. He begins with a general topic phrase in verse 3 before widening out with expression after expression of God-centered worship and praise. In these verses, Paul summons the praise of our hearts and draws our focus upward to God, Who is infinitely worthy of all our worship.

Read Ephesians 1:3.

1. Who is Paul blessing and why?

Paul begins with an ascription of praise to our Creator that will echo throughout his entire hymn: "Blessed be God...Who has blessed us with every spiritual blessing." Paul uses three closely related words, *eulogetos, eulogeo,* and *eulogia,* right here in this one verse.

- *Eulogetos* is an adjective used exclusively in the New Testament to describe God and means "worthy of praise," "to speak well of," "blessed." We have an English word that is derived from this word, "eulogy," which basically means "a commendation or good word." Paul begins with the joyful declaration that God is supremely worthy of our worship.
- The second word, *eulogeo,* is the verb translated "bless" and means "to benefit, to prosper, to give contentment," which describes what God has done for us. Paul uses the past tense "has blessed" as an indication that this blessing of believers had already occurred in eternity past.
- And with what has God blessed us that should motivate us to bless him? Paul pronounces God has blessed us with "every spiritual blessing." The noun "blessing" is *eulogia* and here denotes the benefits the Father has bestowed upon us. [15]

So, with an adjective, a verb, and a noun that are all related, Paul opens his praise hymn with a call for us to worship God as a response to the blessings we have received from Him.

2. In Whom are we blessed? (v. 3)

All our blessings are in Christ. Everything we are and everything we have is ours only *In Him.*

The blessings Paul is talking about here are not material, but spiritual. Swindoll explains they are "benefits already bestowed upon believers because of their intimate association with the Savior, Jesus Christ (Ephesians 1:3). Such blessings, sealed by Christ and reserved in Heaven, can never be taken away." [16]

Because God has already generously poured out these eternal blessings upon His people through Christ, we don't have to ask for them. We simply accept them and apply them to our lives. In Christ, we can enjoy these blessings now, and will enjoy them for all eternity.

Did you notice the word right before "spiritual blessings?" "Every." No blessing is withheld. Each believer has received "in Christ" every possible spiritual blessing from God.

3. Where does Paul say these blessings are found? (v. 3)

"In the heavenly places" is a phrase Paul will repeat five times in Ephesians. Richard Coekin helps us understand the meaning of the term:

> The heavenly places are the spiritual dimension in which God and all spiritual powers are dwelling. They are not just for Heaven (for evil powers exist in the heavenly places but not in Heaven), and not earth (for this is not a matter of flesh and blood) and not the future (for we wrestle with our spiritual enemies in the heavenly places now). [17]

Simply stated, "the heavenly places" refer to the spiritual dimension, the sphere beyond the material world. This is the place where:

- We have already been blessed (Ephesians 1:3).
- Christ is seated right now (1:20).
- We have already been raised and are seated with Him (2:6).
- The victory of Christ over evil powers at the cross is spiritually manifested in the gathering of the church under His authority and revealed in the unity of our earthly church gatherings under His Word (3:10).
- We stand firm against the attacks of the enemy (6:10-12).

Wiersbe explains that the believer actually "operates in two spheres: the human and the divine, the visible and the invisible." [18] He then elaborates:

> Physically, he is on the earth in a human body, but spiritually he is seated with Christ in the heavenly sphere – and it is this heavenly sphere that provides the power and direction for the earthly walk. The president of the United States is not always seated at his desk in the White House, but that executive chair represents the sphere of his life and power. No matter where he is, he is the president, because only he has the privilege of sitting at that desk. Likewise with the Christian: No matter where he may be on this earth, he is seated in the heavenlies with Jesus Christ, and this is the basis of his life and power. [19]

No wonder Paul is expressing such heartfelt praise and thanksgiving to the Father!

Read Ephesians 1:4-6.

4. As we work through our passage for this lesson, Paul will elaborate on the spiritual blessings that are ours because we are "in Christ." Throughout the lesson, use the following chart to compile a list of the specific blessings Paul attaches to the term "in" or "through" Christ. Beginning with verses 4-6, list the spiritual blessings Paul writes about.

Scripture	Spiritual Blessing Received
v. 4	
v. 5	
v. 6	
v. 7	
v. 7	
vv. 7-8	
vv. 9-10	
vv. 11-12	
vv. 13-14	

The other day, while I was paused at a stop sign, I noticed surveyors marking property lines where a new subdivision was being built. The three men were standing at one corner of the property. One of them was holding what appeared to be a plat map, the other two were focused on the piece of surveying equipment (which I have since then discovered is called a total station) in front of them. A little while later, I drove back by and the trio were still in that same spot, no property lines yet marked.

As I watched, the men adjusted the total station two or three times, apparently trying to get it in an exact spot. The men were looking for what surveyors call the "point of beginning," the place that needed to be marked exactly before any boundary lines could be marked. If a surveyor gets the initial spot wrong, even if just by a few feet, all the property lines will be off, and houses will be misplaced. No builder begins their work until the survey is complete and the legal property lines have been marked.

In Ephesians 1:4-6, Paul elaborates on the benefits of knowing Christ and addresses the "point of beginning" in our relationship with Christ, tracing it back to eternity past.

5. What did God do before He created the world? (v. 4)

Entire books have been written on these verses because they form the basis for the doctrine of election, God's sovereign will as it relates to our salvation. And still, no one has been able to adequately unravel the mysteries of election and predestination because it is beyond the realm of our finite understanding. Swindoll relieves us of the pressure of trying to fully comprehend these mysteries:

> We aren't asked to understand the ins and outs of election, how it fits with free will, or why God chose that person rather than this person. We'll go mad if we try to get our minds around the infinite mind of God, to grapple with His wisdom, to understand His greatness, or to question His goodness. Instead, we're expected to accept the doctrine of election by faith and praise God for it. [20]

The fact remains: God saved us according to His eternal plan. We cannot take any credit for our salvation or boast regarding our own choice.

When was the last time you took a moment to say "Thank you Lord for choosing me"? Why don't you stop and do that right now?

And now for the "flip side" of this doctrine, which is equally true: Anyone who desires to choose Jesus, to be saved, can! As Paul makes clear in Romans 10:9, "If you confess with your mouth Jesus as Lord, and believe in your heart that God raised Him from the dead, you will be saved." We are never commanded to choose to be the elect. We are commanded to choose Jesus as our Savior and Lord!

DID YOU KNOW?

The structure of the 202 words in Ephesians 1:3-14 is called a *berakhah* or "praise cry." [21] In the Jewish tradition, a *berakhah* usually begins with "Blessed are You, Lord our God" and is followed by praising Him for a specific reason. These blessings are central to Jewish daily life, intentionally fostering a mindset of gratitude and praise to God.

6. What is God's purpose for redeeming us? (v. 4)

The Greek word for "holy" is *hagios* (the same word we saw translated "saint" in verse 1) and means to be set apart for God to reflect His nature. [22] God chose us not just to be saved, but to live changed lives here on earth. "Blameless" (*amomos*) means without fault or free from accusation. [23] Living "blameless" does not imply that we do the impossible – live perfect lives. In fact, it has nothing to do with us and everything to do with Christ. God sees us as blameless because we are *In Him.* Because we belong to God through Jesus Christ, He looks upon us as if we had never sinned.

Yet, our status in Christ is not a free pass to sin, but rather a motivation to live our lives like Him. That is Kingdom living. In the words of Dallas Willard, "To live in the kingdom means to live within the range of God's effective will with His life flowing through mine. Another good way of putting this is to say that as a disciple I am learning from Jesus to live my life as He would live my life if He were I." [24]

7. In God's love, what has He predestined? (v. 5)

"Predestined" comes from the Greek word, *proorizo*, which means to "determine in advance." [25] God did not have to call an emergency meeting after the fall of man in Genesis 3; He knew from the beginning what would happen and had already set into motion our adoption plan. Under Roman law, the backdrop for Paul's epistle, adopted children had the same rights and privileges as biological children. Even those who had once been slaves, became full heirs when they were adopted into their new family.

In the same way, the "Abba" relationship that Christ has with the Father is extended by grace to everyone who believes in Christ. And not only was our adoption part of God's plan from the very beginning, He did so "according to the kind intention of His will" (Ephesians 1:5). The word for "will" in the Greek language is *thelematos* and "conveys more emotion than volition; God's will, therefore, means God's heart desire. Predestination, election, and adoption are all part of God's purpose and God's will, a magnificent expression of God's character." [26]

Not only are we chosen (v. 4) and adopted (v. 5), but we are also accepted (v. 6). The NKJV makes our eternal position clear: "He made us accepted in the Beloved." Because of the grace of God in Christ, we stand secure *In Him*.

However, God's overarching purpose in saving us goes beyond the blessings that we receive.

8. What is God ultimate goal in our salvation? (v. 6)

We have been saved to bring glory to Him and to praise His holy name! It was His eternal plan to save us and make us His very own. As John Phillips exclaims, "The endless ages of eternity will prove to be all too short a time to sing His praise for such matchless love and grace." [27]

As I have been writing today's study, I have found myself repeatedly humming the "Doxology." Close out your time in God's Word by lifting your heart in praise to Him:

Praise God, from Whom all blessings flow;
Praise Him, all creatures here below;
Praise Him above, ye heav'nly host;
Praise Father, Son, and Holy Ghost.
Amen. [28]

Day Three
Ephesians 1:7-12

John Newton was born in 1725 in London, England. The son of a shipmaster, Newton went to sea at an early age, and ended up becoming a slave trader, capturing and transporting enslaved Africans under brutal conditions. As a young man, his hardened heart was ambivalent to the suffering his actions caused. His recklessness led to many hardships, including his own forced servitude and near-death experiences at sea.

But then, in 1748, his ship was caught in a violent storm at sea, and Newton feared for his life. As his ship was battered by waves, he cried out to God for mercy. Miraculously, the storm subsided, and the ship was saved. This experience marked the beginning of his spiritual transformation. Newton later gave his life fully to Christ and repented of his role in the slave trade. Over time, he became a pastor and an advocate for the abolition of slavery. He worked closely with William Wilberforce, a leader in the movement to end slavery in Britain. [29]

One of Newton's greatest legacies is the hymn "Amazing Grace," which he wrote as a testimony of his journey from sin to redemption. The lyrics of this great hymn of the faith reflect the foundation of the passage we are studying today:

In Him we have redemption through His blood, the forgiveness of sins, according to the riches of His grace.
Ephesians 1:7

As we saw in our examination of Ephesians 1:3-6, the first stanza of Paul's anthem of praise found its bearings in the past and lauded the work of God: blessed, chosen, predestined, bestowed. Now, as Paul begins the second stanza, he shifts to the present and pours out a litany of praise for the second person of the Trinity, Jesus, the Son. In verses 7-12, Paul's words build with intensity as he gives us five reasons to lift our praise to God.

Read Ephesians 1:7-8.

The opening words of verse 7, "In Him," point back to the last words in verse 6, "in the Beloved," a reference to Jesus Christ the Son.

1. According to verse 7, what do we have through Christ's blood?

Here, we see the first reason Paul gives us in this passage for praising God: **He redeemed us.**

Redeemed is one of the most beautiful words in the English language. In the original Greek, the word for redemption is *apolutrosin,* which means "release effected by payment of ransom." [30] At the time Paul is writing, slavery was a deeply entrenched institution in the social and economic fabric of the Roman Empire, a society that literally had millions of slaves. For a slave to be set free from servitude, a price, a ransom, would have to be paid. Paul uses the term, redemption, in verse 7, to "point to the fact that God has redeemed believers, setting them free from the bondage of sin." [31]

Paul's use of the present tense "we have" indicates that our redemption is a present reality. It is not past tense – you were redeemed at one point but have to keep being redeemed over and over. It is not future tense – one day you will be redeemed. Redemption is our present standing in Christ. *In Him*, in every moment of our present, we are free!

2. What was the ransom price for our sin? (v. 7)

All of humanity was in the slave market of sin, but Christ willingly purchased our freedom with an infinite price! And as wonderful as that is, His death is about even more. The Lamb of God gave His life so that we could be in union with Him, so that we could live *In Him*. Ann Voskamp writes, "The atonement was always about 'at-one-ment.' God has always wanted more than to forgive us of our sins – He has always wanted to give us Himself." [32]

3. Read Mark 10:45; Hebrews 9:12; and 1 Peter 1:18-19. What do these verses tell us about the price paid for our sin?

What reason to sing His praise! In fact, our redemption will be the theme of one of the songs we will join with the angels and sing in eternity:

> And they sang a new song, saying, "Worthy are You to take the book and to break its seals; for You were slain, and purchased for God with Your blood men from every tribe and tongue and people and nation. You have made them to be a kingdom and priests to our God; and they will reign upon the earth…Worthy is the Lamb that was slain to receive power and riches and wisdom and might and honor and glory and blessing" (Revelation 5:9-10, 12).

To the idea of redemption, Paul adds a second reason to praise God: **He forgave us.**

The word "forgive" means "to carry away." [33] As David writes, "As far as the east is from the west, so far has He removed our transgressions from us" (Psalm 103:12). In the Old Testament, on the Day of Atonement (Yom Kippur), the high priest would select two goats. The first goat would be sacrificed for the sins of the people, and its blood sprinkled before God on the Mercy Seat. Then, the high priest would place his hands on the second goat, known as a "scapegoat," confess the sins of Israel over it, and the goat would be sent out into the wilderness to "carry away" the sins of the people, never to return (Leviticus 16). At Calvary, Christ fulfilled the role of the both goats: His sacrificial death covered our sins, and then as our "scapegoat," He carried our sins away!

4. Read John 1:29. How did John the Baptist describe Jesus?

Because our sins have been taken away, no accusation remains against us! Coeklin beautifully frames our redemption through the blood of Christ:

> For God to allow such a sacrifice for our sins is grace. For God to provide such a sacrifice for our sins is amazing grace. For God to become such a sacrifice for our sins is grace beyond our comprehension! [34]

5. What does Paul say about the riches of God's grace? (vv. 7-8)

Here we see the third reason Paul gives us to praise God: **He lavished His grace upon us.**

The verb "lavish" means to heap, to give readily, and in large quantities. [35] God is not a miser who dribbles out His blessings to us a little at a time. God has generously and abundantly showered us with the abundance of His grace that "is greater than all our sin!" [36]

Read Ephesians 1:9-10.

6. What has God made known to us? (v. 9)

The Greek word *mysterion* is a reference to a truth formerly hidden, but now made known. Grant Osborne writes:

> From eternity past God had decided how He would bring humanity back to Himself through the death of His Son (see 1:5) and how He would bring history to an end, but He kept many of the details hidden until He determined the time was right. Paul's point was that the time of fulfillment had arrived (see Mark 1:15), and the mysteries have now been made known. [37]

Paul's excitement is mounting as he gives us this fourth reason to praise God: **He has made known the mystery of His will to us.**

David Shepherd notes that Paul uses two terms – wisdom and understanding – to describe the believer's comprehension of the mystery of God's will and distinguishes the difference between them:

> Wisdom is the ability to see into the heart of things and understand them. It is the knowledge that satisfies the intellect.
>
> Understanding is insight that leads to wise action. It enables a person to handle the day-to-day problems of practical life and living. [38]

7. What is the purpose of God's will? (vv. 9-10)

Here in this broken world, we see the devastating accumulation of the effect of sin. But one day, in Christ, God will restore everything back to the way it was supposed to be before sin entered the world. As Paul anticipates God's eternal plan to bring everything together in Christ, who is already raised in triumph to rule over every evil power, he can hardly contain himself. But then, it gets even better!

Read Ephesians 1:11-12.

8. What does Paul say that believers have obtained? (v. 11)

Paul's explosion of worship in verses 7-12 gives us a fifth reason to join in praise to God: **He has given us an inheritance.**

We are redeemed! We are forgiven! But, too often, we forget that we are heirs! God hasn't just given us knowledge of His redemptive purpose; He has made us heirs of its blessing. Just as ancient Israel obtained an inheritance in the Promised Land, as children of God, we have an inheritance: the Promised Life as co-heirs with Christ. As Paul explains in Romans 8:17, "And since we are His children, we are his heirs. In fact, together with Christ we are heirs of God's glory" (NLT). The word "heirs" means "those who receive their allotted possession by right of sonship." [39] Because God has adopted us as His children, we have full rights to share in the inheritance of Jesus, the Son: His power, His authority. All that is His, is ours!

9. Who is to bring praise of God's glory? (v. 12)

That's right, we are! God's ultimate plan in creating us and saving us, is that we might bring glory to Him.

10. Turn to the "Spiritual Blessings Received" chart on page 38 and fill in the five blessings we have studied in the passage today. Which of these five blessings (reasons to praise God) stood out the most to you and why?

Day Four
Ephesians 1:13-14

In Acts 19:1-7, Luke recounts an experience Paul had soon after his arrival in Ephesus during his third missionary trip. As he was settling in for his extended stay in the city, he met a group of men who were known as believers. These men knew about Jesus, but Paul sensed that something was missing. So, he asked them a simple question: "Did you receive the Holy Spirit when you believed?"

They replied, "No, we haven't even heard that there is a Holy Spirit."

At this point, I imagine Paul was nodding his head as he realized what the issue was: These men were sincere, but had not yet given their lives to Jesus. Paul then probed, "What baptism did you experience?" Their answer, "The baptism of John," told Paul exactly what he needed to know to help them understand the shortfall of their faith.

Then Paul explained, "John's baptism called for repentance from sin. But John himself told the people to believe in the One who would come later, meaning Jesus."

These men had repented, but they had not yet believed in Christ. They believed the Messiah was coming, but they were still living in the economy of the Old Testament. As soon as the twelve men heard Paul's words, they realized their error and asked Paul to baptize them "in the name of the Lord Jesus." Right then and there, Paul baptized them, and as he placed his hands on the men, they were filled with the Holy Spirit. [40]

Twelve men. Ordinary men. But now, filled with extraordinary power.

As we come to the final stanza in Paul's Ephesians anthem, he celebrates the astounding work of the Holy Spirit and celebrates the spiritual blessings that are ours through the third Person of the Trinity.

Read Ephesians 1:13-14.

1. Turn back to the chart on page 38 and fill in the spiritual blessing Paul praises God for in Ephesians 1:13-14.

During Paul's time in Ephesus, the Holy Spirit moved, and revival broke out. Multitudes were radically saved. Now, he takes them back to their salvation experience.

2. What two things happened after these believers listened to the message of truth? (v. 13)

-

-

DID YOU KNOW?

In the ancient world, a seal was used in legal documents as a mark of identification. The seal was usually made from hot wax, which was dropped on the document and then imprinted with a signet ring. The wax seal identified the document with the name and authority to which the signet belonged. Likewise, the Holy Spirit shows that we belong to God, identifying us as God's treasured possession.

The entire process of salvation is covered in just this one verse. First, the Ephesian believers heard the "gospel of salvation." Then, they "believed" and were saved by their faith. As the Apostle explains in his letter to the Romans, "So faith comes from hearing, and hearing by the word of Christ" (Romans 10:17). Once they heard "the message of truth" and believed, they were immediately "sealed" by the Holy Spirit.

The word "seal," *sphragizo*, means to make something secure and permanent. [41]

Why is the sealing of the Holy Spirit significant?

- First, it refers to a completed transaction. Today, when legal documents are signed, a notary stamps them to signify the agreement is finalized.
- Second, it indicates ownership. God has placed His seal on us because He has purchased us with the precious blood of His Son to be His very own.
- Third, it also implies security and protection. As God's own possession, the believer is safe and protected because he or she is part of the finished work of Christ at Calvary.

All who believe in Jesus are irreversibly sealed and eternally secure.

3. How does knowing that you are sealed with the Holy Spirit impact your daily life?

4. Read John 14:16-17. How long will the Holy Spirit be with those who are in Christ?

While it is possible for us to grieve the Holy Spirit and forfeit the blessings of His ministry in our lives (Ephesians 4:30), He will never leave us.

5. In addition to being our seal, what other role does the Holy Spirit play in the believer's life? (vv. 13-14)

The word "pledge" is rendered in some translations as "earnest," "down payment," or "guarantee." [42] This metaphor is similar to the earnest money put down on a house today, a down payment guaranteeing the future full payment of the amount promised. God has promised an inheritance to everyone who is "in Christ" and the Holy Spirit is the first installment to guarantee that what He has begun, He will bring to completion.

Interestingly, the word "pledge" can also mean an engagement ring. Wiersbe explains that the word is used that way in Greece today:

> After all, isn't an engagement ring an assurance – a guarantee – that the promises made will be kept? Our relationship to God through Christ is not simply a commercial one, but also a personal experience of love. He is the Bridegroom and His church is the bride. We know that He will come and claim His bride because He has given us His promise and His Spirit as the "engagement ring." What greater assurance could we want? [43]

The "pledge" is a reference to the indwelling presence of the Holy Spirit in the lives of believers.

6. Look up the verses in the chart that follows and make a list what the Holy Spirit does in our lives.

Scripture	Ministry of the Holy Spirit
1 Corinthians 3:16	
Ephesians 1:13	
John 14:26	
Acts 1:8	
John 16:8	
Romans 8:26	
Ephesians 3:16	
2 Corinthians 3:17	
2 Corinthians 3:18	
Romans 8:16	

The Holy Spirit is active in the life of every believer, working to guide, empower, convict, teach, and transform us into the image of Christ! But even so, our present experience of the Holy Spirit is just a sneak preview of what is yet to come!

"The redemption of God's own possession" (Ephesians 1:14) points to the time to come when we will receive our full inheritance as a child of God: the resurrection and glorification of our bodies (1 Corinthians 15:51-54; 1 Thessalonians 4:15-17). What a day of celebration that will be!

Stanza by stanza, the volume of Paul's hymn has gradually increased. Now, with the final refrain, it reaches *fortississimo*, as he exclaims, "to the praise of His glory." What about you? Is your heart overflowing with gratitude and praise in response to the spiritual blessings that are ours *In Him*? As Kent Hughes contends, "Our theology must become doxology." [44] In other words, what we believe about God must lead us to praise God. We have been chosen by God the Father, redeemed by Jesus, the Son, and sealed by the Holy Spirit. All to the praise of His glory!

7. Look back over the list of spiritual blessings you have compiled from Ephesians 1:3-14. What are some ways you can live in gratitude for the spiritual blessings Paul has described?

Our highest response to the spiritual blessings that have been bestowed upon us by the Triune God is to join Paul in his boundless praise of the One who reigns above! Will you do that now? As you consider all that He has done for you, respond to Him in prayer and praise.

Let everything that breathes sing praises to the Lord!
Psalm 150:6

Day Five

Satan's strategy: Distraction

As we begin today's study, let's consider a question that naturally arises from exploring Ephesians 1:1-14:

> If God has chosen me, Christ has redeemed me, and the Holy Spirit has sealed me, why do I still find it so difficult to live out the Christian life?

God's intention for you is to live from the fullness of life in Christ. But you have an opponent who has a different agenda. Satan knows who you are in Christ, he knows the wealth of spiritual blessings that are yours, but he hopes you will forget. And he will use everything at his disposal to accomplish his goal.

Right now, in the heavenlies, a war is being waged to control the story of your life. In Ephesians 6:11, Paul urges us to "stand firm against the schemes of the devil." The Greek word he uses for "schemes" is *methodia*, from which we get our English word method. [45] Make no mistake, Satan is not passive in his ways. He is active, deceptive, and wickedly skilled. His strategies are ruthless. So, we need a strategy as well. And Paul gives it to us in 2 Corinthians 10:3-5:

> For though we walk in the flesh, we do not war according to the flesh. For the weapons of our warfare are not carnal but mighty in God for pulling down strongholds, casting down arguments and every high thing that exalts itself against the knowledge of God, bringing every thought into captivity to the obedience of Christ (NKJV).

Paul makes it clear that we have an arsenal of weapons at our disposal to conquer every ploy of Satan. But in order to defeat the enemy, we must first recognize his tactics and schemes. Satan will do his best to pull us toward him and away from Jesus. If we fail to understand Satan's methods, we risk succumbing to them.

In our Day Five study, during each of the first eight weeks, we will examine one of the methods the enemy uses against us and learn how to stand firm against that scheme. During the final two weeks, we will focus on strategies to equip ourselves for victory in our spiritual battle.

The first of Satan's tactics we will consider is **distraction**. One of Satan's favorite strategies is to subtly draw our attention away from the spiritual blessings we have in Christ by filling our minds with other things that keep us from focusing on God's truth and purpose for our lives.

1. What are some of the common distractions Satan uses to keep us from recognizing and embracing the spiritual blessings we have in Christ?

In an essay for the *New York Times Magazine*, Andrew Sullivan, a secular writer, makes this glaring indictment, "This new epidemic of distraction is our civilization's specific weakness. And its threat is not so much to our minds, even as they shape-shift under pressure. The threat is to our souls. At this rate, if the noise does not relent, we might even forget we have any." [46]

Reading Sullivan's article, I recalled a quote from C.S. Lewis' classic work, *The Screwtape Letters.* In this fictional correspondence between a senior demon and his inexperienced nephew, Screwtape writes to his apprentice Wormwood: "We will make the whole universe a noise in the end. We have already made great progress in this direction as regards the Earth. The melodies and silences of Heaven will be shouted down in the end." [47]

Interestingly, Lewis' book was published in 1941 when the background noise in the world was a physical war. Now, decades later, the noise has reached deafening levels. Yet, it is not a physical war we are engaged in, but a spiritual war. And it is even more deadly. For while military engagement threatens our earthly lives, spiritual battles have eternal consequences. Never before has mankind had to contend with the level of clamor vying for our attention that we have today. Facebook, X, the 24-hour news cycle, and an overwhelming flood of information and misinformation have drawn us into a digital wind tunnel with unprecedented outcomes:

- The World Health Organization reported that problematic social media use among adolescents rose sharply from 7% in 2018 to 11% in 2022. Additionally, the study found that 12% of adolescents are at risk of addictive gaming. [48]
- A study published in the *Monitor on Psychology* found that U.S. teens spend an average of 4.8 hours daily on social media platforms. Among those with the highest social media use, 41% rated their mental health as poor or very poor, compared to 23% among those with the lowest use. [49]
- The American Psychiatric Association's 2024 poll revealed that 43% of U.S. adults feel more anxious than the previous year, with significant concerns about current events. Factors raising anxiety include notification overload, social comparison, and "fear of missing out" (FOMO), all of which are fueled by social media. [50]

2. How much time do you estimate that you spend on social media every day?

If you have a smart phone, look under your settings for Screen Time (iPhone) or Digital Wellbeing (Android) for your daily average this past week. How close was your estimate to the actual amount of time you spent on your device every day? And that doesn't even account for the time on your other devices or watching television.

This incessant noise diverts our attention from the goodness of God's blessings and drowns out the stillness needed to hear God's voice. Tyler Staton explains that "God's native language is a whisper, and a whisper is hard to hear and easy to ignore." [51] He goes on to say, "One of the reasons it's difficult to hear God's voice is because He's got a lot of competition. It's hard to hear a whisper amid all that noise." [52] It is possible (and entirely likely) that God is speaking to you more than you realize, but you fail to hear Him because of all the counterfeit noise coming at you from the deceiver.

And if all the noise around us isn't distracting enough, Satan will keep us so busy with our responsibilities, obligations, and schedules that we find ourselves merely giving God our leftovers of time (if we have any), rather than making Him priority one. Richard Foster explains that the if enemy "can keep us engaged in 'muchness' and 'manyness,' he will rest satisfied." [53]

To keep us from embracing the blessings and engaging in the purposes of God, Satan strategically distracts us by dangling all the world has to offer in effort appeal to our natural worldly desires. And he has a pretty high success rate. As Jesus said in the Parable of the Sower, "All too quickly the message is crowded out by the worries of this life, the lure of wealth, and the desire for other things, so no fruit is produced" (Mark 4:19, NLT).

3. Read Matthew 28:19-20. Before Jesus ascended back to Heaven, what was His final "message," the last instructions He gave to His followers?

We call these verses The Great Commission. Jesus was giving His followers their marching orders: Take everything you have learned from Me and share it with others. More than 2000 years later, His instructions for us are the same. We are to believe in Jesus, live like Jesus lived, and teach others to do the same. Sounds pretty simple and straightforward, doesn't it? So, why is it so hard to stay the course? Because we get distracted.

In 1 Peter 5:8, Peter tells us how to stand firm against Satan's distracting schemes: "Be of sober spirit, be on the alert. Your adversary, the devil, prowls around like a roaring lion, seeking someone to devour" (1 Peter 5:8). The opposite of being distracted is being "alert." Jonathan Pokluda shares this insight:

> When I think about that command, I think of all the professions where we need people to be alert and of sober mind. The pilot of every airplane should be alert and sober-minded. The surgeon in every hospital should be alert and sober-minded. Why? Because if they are distracted by anything, the consequences are grave. That's what Peter was trying to get across to his audience. If the Christian is distracted by other things, the consequences are dire. [54]

Dire indeed! If we allow the enemy to distract us, we will show up as the "Daily Special" on Satan's lunch menu! How can we avoid the cycle of distraction so that we can finish well the work Christ has for us? First, **stay alert**.

And then, **be obedient**. In Acts 20, when it was time for Paul to leave his friends in Ephesus to sail to Jerusalem, he knew it was likely that he would be imprisoned when he arrived. As he bid farewell to the community of believers he had grown to love, he spoke these stirring words:

> My life is worth nothing to me unless I use it for finishing the work assigned me by the Lord Jesus the work of telling others the Good News about the wonderful grace of God (Acts 20:24, NLT).

While life would certainly have been easier for Paul had he remained in Ephesus, to be obedient, he had to get on the ship. He would not be deterred or distracted. His sole focus was to complete the task Jesus had given him. How focused are you on "finishing the work" Jesus has given to you?

4. What specific changes do you sense the Lord leading you to make to lessen the pull of distractions in your life?

5. In what other ways has God spoken to you through His Word in Ephesians 1:1-14?

Father, thank You for loving me, choosing me, and redeeming me. Thank You for forgiving my sins, granting me the righteousness of Christ, and making me complete in Him. Thank You for giving me every spiritual blessing in Christ Jesus. I claim His immeasurable riches over my life today. Keep me alert to the schemes of the enemy and his distracting ways. I stand firm in Your truth. Give me the strength to resist every attempt of the enemy to pull me away from Your will. Keep my focus on You and You alone.
In Jesus' name, Amen.

314 Amazing Grace! How Sweet the Sound

st. 1–5 John Newton, 1779
st. 6 anon.

NEW BRITAIN
CM

Columbian Harmony, 1829

That the eyes of your heart may be enlightened

Ephesians 1:15-23

"That the eyes of your heart may be enlightened"

Ephesians 1:15-23

The utmost need in every ministry group, every missionary outreach, every denomination, is to rediscover the Lord Jesus Christ and the indispensability of His indwelling presence within the believer. [1]
~ Ian Thomas

As we move into the second half of Ephesians 1, Paul's focus shifts from praise for all we have received "in Christ" to prayer for our hearts to be "enlightened" to comprehend the riches of the inheritance that we have been given. Paul's prayer is that the readers of his letter (which includes us) will be able to grasp the magnitude of spiritual blessings that we have inherited in Christ.

In Ephesians 1:1-14, we learned that *In Him* we are:

- Chosen
- Holy
- Blameless
- Adopted as sons
- Graced
- Redeemed
- Forgiven
- Recipients of an inheritance
- Sealed by the Holy Spirit

Read over that list once again. These are astonishing truths! Yet, there is truly no way to fully comprehend all that we have received "in Christ" apart from the Holy Spirit's revelation. Only He can help us not merely <u>know</u> these realities intellectually but <u>live</u> them experientially.

In a sense, being *In Him* means that Christ <u>represents</u> us before the Father. All that Christ is and has belongs to us.

Many analogies have been used to help us understand what it means to be "in Christ." One that especially resonates with me is the battle between David and Goliath. You may recall that Goliath, the nine-foot, nine-inch-tall champion fighter represented the Philistines. For forty days and nights, Goliath stood and taunted the army of Israel, challenging them to a "winner takes all" duel. But not one soldier in Israel's ranks dared to face the giant.

Finally, David, a young shepherd from the tribe of Judah, courageously stepped forward to represent the Israelites. His boldness didn't come from his stature, his military training, or his battle armor. It was rooted in a deep experiential knowledge of the living God. With unshakeable confidence, David confronted Goliath, not in the name of Israel, but in the name of their God – *Yahweh*:

> "You come to me with a sword, a spear, and a javelin, but I come to you in the name of the Lord of hosts, the God of the armies of Israel, whom you have taunted. This day the Lord will deliver you up into my hands, and I will strike you down and remove your head from you. And I will give the dead bodies of the army of the Philistines this day to the birds of the sky and the wild beasts of the earth, that all the earth may know that there is a God in Israel, and that all this assembly may know that the Lord does not deliver by sword or by spear; for the battle is the Lord's and He will give you into our hands" (1 Samuel 17:45b-47).

How was David able to stand strong while the rest of Israel's army cowered in fear? Because David knew God – not just information about Him, but firsthand experience of His faithfulness and power. The rest of the army only knew of Him. That made all the difference.

Author Rankin Wilbourne makes this correlation:

> In the same way, Christ represents those who place their faith in Him. If we are united to Christ, then we are united to Him in all that He has done for us. Christ represents those who come to be His so thoroughly that we are said to have been "crucified with Christ" (Galatians 2:20), "buried…with Him" (Romans 6:4), and "raised with Christ" (Colossians 3:1). We are even "seated…with Him in the heavenly places" (Ephesians 2:6) now as we walk about with both feet on the ground. [2]

For many believers, there exists a profound disconnect between what we know to be true in Christ and the way we live on a daily basis. As we continue through Ephesians, we will be challenged to bridge that gap – not merely to understand truth, but to walk in it. We have been "blessed with every spiritual blessing in the heavenly places in Christ" (Ephesians 1:3). May the Holy Spirit awaken our hearts to live from that abundance!

Day One

Ephesians 1:15-17

What if the greatest need in your life isn't for God to give you something new, but to open your eyes to what He's already given you in Christ? That's the heart of Paul's rich, one-sentence prayer in Ephesians 1:15-23. He's not asking for new blessings, but for new sight: A spiritual awakening to the hope, riches, and power already present in every believer.

Read Paul's prayer in Ephesians 1:15-23.

1. As you read, mark the key words in the passage and then write them down. Mark any occurrence of "In Him," "In Christ," or the equivalent in purple.

Key Words in Ephesians 1:15-23

2. What does Paul's prayer for the Ephesians reveal about his priorities for their spiritual growth?

3. Paul's prayer is full of rich phrases. Choose one of them that especially stood out to you and commit to meditate on it for five minutes a day over the next week. Mull it over in your mind. Allow its truth to sink in deeply. Which phrase did you choose?

In our study today, we will focus on Ephesians 1:15-17, a passage that beautifully captures Paul's deep gratitude and his earnest prayer for the spiritual growth of the Ephesian believers.

Read Ephesians 1:15-16.

The "for this reason" that begins verse 15 points back to the beautiful doxology that we studied last week. Paul pivots from the blessings we all receive because we are *In Him,* to praying for the Ephesians to fully grasp what they now possess.

4. What has Paul heard about the Ephesians? (v. 15)

The faith Paul is talking about in verse 15 is not a reference to their original conversion. Charles Swindoll elaborates:

> Paul himself had spent enough time with the Ephesians to already know the genuineness of their original faith in Christ. Rather, he's referring to the condition of their faith as they grew in Christ. Over the years, the Ephesians' faith had grown steadily stronger. They had built well on the foundation laid by Paul and other ministers (1 Corinthians 3:10). [3]

Their reputation has reached Paul. Jesus said, people will know we are His disciples by our love for one another (John 13:35). The Ephesian Christians are known for their faith in Christ and their love for the saints.

5. What does Paul say he does (and does not do) in verse 16?

As Paul begins his prayer, he immediately breaks out in thanksgiving for the believers' faithfulness. Having invested more time in the church in Ephesus than any other, Paul is like a proud spiritual father who is overwhelmed with gratitude that they are living out their faith in such a public and Christ-honoring way.

Thanksgiving is the natural overflow of a life centered on Christ. It also reflects our trust *In Him*, even in the midst of difficult circumstances. In fact, thanksgiving is one of the common elements in Paul's letters.

Read 1 Thessalonians 5:16-19.

6. Is it possible that ingratitude quenches the Holy Spirit?

Ask the Lord if a spirit of murmuring and complaining (like the Israelites in the desert) has taken the place of thanksgiving in your heart.

Read Philippians 4:4-7.

Notice that the peace of God only guards our heart and mind after we have prayed and given thanks. We can choose to be anxious for nothing because "the Lord is near" (Philippians 4:5b). Yes, He is near. He is with us and within us!

7. Do you include thanksgiving in your prayers?

As we were preparing for this study, I read Kyle Worley's book, *Home with God: Our Union with Christ.* Kyle devotes an entire book to describing our union with Christ and all that we have received because we are *In Him.* He summarizes, "So when we say that our union with Christ is the believer's incorporation in and with the life, death, resurrection, ascension, and heavenly session of the Son of God Jesus the Christ, we are saying that the believer now belongs to all that is in Christ Jesus." [4]

Not only is Christ in us, but we are also *In Him.* He is "with us" and will never leave us or forsake us.

8. Write your own doxology of thanksgiving for all that you have received "in Christ."

The promise is His Presence! We need Him! We are all born looking for acceptance. Babies come into this world searching for their mother's face. They are born knowing her voice and have an insatiable desire to be seen by her.

Recently, I attended a seminary graduation ceremony. When I looked at the program, I was surprised to discover that one of the young women I had discipled when she was in high school was graduating with a Master of Theological Studies degree. I was so excited that I jumped up as she came off the stage and hugged her! As we embraced, one of the things she said to me was, "You saw me." She went on, "Not many people 'saw' me as God created me. But, you did, and I cannot believe He allowed you to be here for this day!" Truly, His tender mercies never cease to amaze me!

We all long to be seen, to be known fully and delighted in. That is one of the reasons I love the Tabernacle and all of the symbolism in it that points to Jesus. God has desired from the beginning to dwell with us. As I have studied the articles of the Tabernacle, I have learned that the "Table of Showbread" could more accurately be translated "The Bread of the Presence" or "The Bread of the Face." Jesus is the Bread of Life. We are invited to partake of Him – to be *In Him.* To see and be seen.

Worley points out:

> The tabernacle was purposefully designed to mirror aspects of the garden of Eden. It was the place where God's priests would meet with God and the people would worship God. The tabernacle is a picture of living *coram deo*, the old Latin phrase meaning "before the face of God." Even as Moses spoke with God as one would speak with a friend, "face to face," all of Israel had now been invited to live their lives oriented around the presence of God. [5]

To be "in Christ" is to be enveloped by His righteousness and filled with His Spirit. To be intimately acquainted with Him. To <u>know</u> Him experientially. To be "before the face of God."

When we pray, we are entering into the very throne room of God. We are invited to come "boldly" before His throne (Hebrews 4:16, NLT). We come before the Father in the name of the Son and in the power of His Spirit. We come boldly because we are *In Him*, and He is interceding for us, as is the Holy Spirit. Reminding ourselves of these truths enables us to view prayer as the gift of God that allows us to get in on what He is doing on earth: To see "His Kingdom come, and His will be done on earth as it is in Heaven" (Matthew 6). When you pray and intercede for others, you are lifting them before God's throne and asking for His will to be done in their lives.

Do you have a list of people that you mention to the Lord in prayer?

One of the most beneficial things I have done throughout the years is to have a prayer notebook. I am not saying that is the only way to pray or record your prayer requests. Some people use a journal. My husband uses blank business cards that he carries around in his pocket. The method is not important. What is important is that you have one.

My three-ring binder is tabbed and filled with prayer requests. I have my notebook divided into the following sections:

- Praise/Thanksgiving
- Family
- Church
- Friends in Ministry/SBC Entities
- Intercession
- Government
- Missions/World Atlas

I use notebook paper in each section to record my requests. When God answers a prayer, I record the answer and date it. This practice has been a beautiful way to remember the faithfulness of God. I once heard someone say, "The palest ink is better than the best memory." What a treasure my notebook contains of all the answered prayers through the years!

Read Ephesians 1:17.

As Paul keeps on praying, he moves from thanksgiving to petition.

9. How does Paul describe God? (v. 17a)

10. What does Paul ask God to give to the Ephesian believers? (v. 17b)

11. What does it mean for God to give a spirit of wisdom and revelation?

12. Write your own paraphrase of verse 17.

Close your time with the Lord today by asking Him for wisdom and revelation as you proceed in your study.

DID YOU KNOW?

The literal meaning of wisdom, the Greek word *sophia,* is "skill in matters of common life, sound judgment, intelligence, practical wisdom." [6] The further away we get from God, the less true wisdom we possess. That is why what was once considered "common sense" is no longer common. As our culture moves away from a foundational Judeo/Christian understanding of life, we are losing our moral bearings. The Greek word *apokalupsis* means revelation: "uncovering, disclosing, revelation, especially of divine mysteries." [7] *Apokalupsis* conveys the idea of making something fully known or visible, especially truths that come directly from God and can not be discovered by human reason alone.

Day Two

Ephesians 1:18-19

In addition to Paul's prayer for a deeper knowledge of God through wisdom and revelation (v. 17), Paul then asks the Father to give the Ephesians the ultimate outcome of that knowledge: an enlightened heart (v. 18). The "knowledge" Paul is talking about is more than just knowing facts about God; it is a deep, personal knowledge by acquaintance. Harold Hoehner explains the difference:

> One can know many facts about the leader of a nation through the news media, but that is quite different from personally knowing that leader as his or her family does. Thus, one acquires this knowledge of God not only by facts from the Bible but by the Holy Spirit's giving insight and disclosure in the knowledge of God Himself. [8]

The knowledge of God Paul desires for believers is not a microwave process. It requires time, time spent with Him, getting to know Him intimately. J.I. Packer insightfully writes, "If ever man is to come to a knowledge of God…two veils must be taken away: that which hides God's mind and that which clouds our heart. God in His mercy removes both. Thus, our knowledge of God, first to last, is His gracious gift." [9]

Did you notice the photo at the beginning of our lesson? The streetlight is on, but it is dimmed by fog that has crept in. Before you go further in this lesson today, please stop and spend some time in prayer with God. Ask Him to remove anything that is dimming your vision and to open your heart to see Him more clearly, to know His truth more deeply, and to understand His love more fully. As you prepare your heart to pray, reflect on these lyrics:

> *O soul, are you weary and troubled?*
> *No light in the darkness you see?*
> *There's light for a look at the Savior,*
> *And life more abundant and free.*
>
> *Turn your eyes upon Jesus,*
> *Look full in His wonderful face,*
> *And the things of earth will grow strangely dim,*
> *In the light of His glory and grace.* [10]

Read Ephesians 1:18-19.

Using a color other than purple, underline the phrase "eyes of your heart" in verse 18. That is not a phrase we use often, but perhaps it should be added to our vocabulary. What does Paul mean by "eyes of your heart"? The *Life Application Bible Commentary* gives us helpful context, "For the Jew, the heart was the core of the personality, the total inner person, the center of thought and moral judgment. The imagery of the *eyes of your heart* pictures an ability to see the reality…." [11] This spiritual insight given by the Holy Spirit leads us as believers to comprehend all that God has made available to us through Christ.

Wilbourne invites us to consider how deeply Paul's prayer speaks to the inner life of the believer – not just to our intellect, but to the imagination of the heart formed by faith.

> The apostle Paul prays that "the eyes of your heart [would be] enlightened, that you may know what is the hope to which he has called you, what are the riches of his glorious inheritance" (Ephesians 1:18). Paul prays for the eyes of your heart – what are they if not your imagination? My hope, then, is that with them you would see what is true, so that you may know God, and enjoy him, and be filled with hope. This glorious adventure begins in union with Christ. [12]

Did you notice what Wilbourne calls the Christian life a "glorious adventure"? Is that how you describe your life with Christ? If not, why? Could it be that you have settled for works of the flesh, which cause our relationship with Him to degenerate into duty?

In verses 18-19, Paul specifies three things that he desires the Ephesians to know, to really know, in their innermost being. Let's look at them in the order Paul does.

First, Paul wants them to know **the hope of God's calling**.

1. Look up the following verses and record what you learn about hope.

- 1 John 3:2-3 –

- Romans 15:4;13 –

When we hear the word, "calling," we tend to think of it in terms of an individual's calling to ministry, but that is not the meaning here. Paul's use of "calling" in verse 18 has a broader application; it applies to all believers. John Stott elaborates:

> [God] has called us to Christ and to holiness, to freedom and peace, to suffering and glory. More simply, it was a call to an altogether new life in which we know, love, obey, and serve Christ, enjoy fellowship with Him and each other, and look beyond our present suffering to the glory which will one day be revealed. [13]

And the hope he is talking about? It applies to every believer as well. Our hope is not in some vague feeling that everything will eventually be okay. It is a complete and total confidence that what God has promised, He will do.

Second, Paul wants the Ephesians to know the **riches of the glory of His inheritance**. Our inheritance includes everything God has given to us in salvation through the person and work of Christ.

2. Read the following verses and note what you learn about our riches in Christ.

- Colossians 1:12 –

- 1 Peter 1:3-5 –

Don't you just love Peter's reminder in 1 Peter 1:4 that our inheritance is "imperishable and undefiled and will not fade away, reserved in Heaven for you"? Swindoll encourages us, "At that time, when we stand in glory, basking in our eternal inheritance, all of our human limitations, physical diseases and disabilities, emotional baggage, hardships, and handicaps will be put away forever." [14] What a glorious day that will be!

Third, Paul wants the believers in Ephesus to know **the boundless greatness of His power toward us who believe**.

3. Read the following verses and write down what you learn about the greatness of the power of God.

- Hebrews 1:3 –

- 1 Corinthians 4:20 –

Could it be that verses 18-19 build upon one another? It takes confident hope to be able to appropriate the very riches that we have in Christ. Then, as we begin to live what we possess, we encounter the surpassing great power that can only be attributed to His Presence. Consider Stott's words:

> It is because of Christ's resurrection from the dead and enthronement over the powers of evil that he has been given headship over the church. The resurrection and ascension were a decisive demonstration of divine power. For if there are two powers which man cannot control, but which hold him in bondage, they are death and evil. Man is mortal; he cannot avoid death. Man is fallen; he cannot overcome evil. But God in Christ has conquered both, and therefore can rescue us from both. [15]

DID YOU KNOW?

In verse 19, Paul uses four almost synonymous words to express the power of God. Alone, each word has a slightly different meaning. (1) "power" (*dunamis*) means ability or potential; (2) "working" (*energeian*) means active energy/power; (3) "strength" (*ischuos*) in humans refers to bodily strength, in God, it is His inherent strength; (4) "might" (*kratous*) means dominion, a force that overcomes resistance (this word is only used to describe God). When combined, these words exhibit the "boundless greatness" and completeness of the power of God. [16]

4. How would you summarize what we have received through our hope, His riches, and His power?

5. Let's pause in our journey through Paul's prayer in Ephesians 1:15-23 and take a few moments to look at Paul's prayer life. Read the following verses and note what Paul says in the chart below.

Scripture	Paul's Admonition
Romans 12:12	
Ephesians 6:18	
Colossians 4:2	
1 Thessalonians 5:17	

Paul's prayers always include thanksgiving. Yesterday, you were asked if you included thanksgiving in your prayers. I believe you will experience a decisive shift in your perspective and attitude if you will focus on thanking God for all the ways He has provided for you and blessed you with His Presence.

6. Close out your time in God's Word today by writing a prayer of thanksgiving to the Lord for all that you have received *In Him.*

Day Three

Ephesians 1:19b-21

As we begin today, read Paul's entire prayer in Ephesians 1:15-23 once again.

Now, read our verses for today, 19b-21, aloud. In these verses, Paul is proclaiming the magnificence of our King Jesus! He has conquered sin, death, hell, and the grave for us by taking our place on the cross and paying our sin debt (Colossians 2:9-15).

1. What did the "working of the strength of God's might" do in Christ? (Ephesians 1:19b-20)

Paul is emphasizing the operative side of God's power, first in Christ's resurrection and then in our lives. Grant Osborne explains Paul's perspective:

> To Paul everything in Christianity is derived from the implications of the resurrection. If there is no resurrection, "our preaching is useless and so is your faith...your faith is futile; you are still in your sins... [and] we are of all people most to be pitied" (1 Corinthians 15:14, 17, 19). But Paul knows that Christ was indeed raised, so the Christian claims are the central truths that bring meaning to life in this world. The incomparable divine power was unleashed at Jesus' resurrection and continues today for all the saints. [17]

Let that sink in for a moment. God's power at work in the lives of believers is resurrection power! The resurrection wasn't just a historical miracle; it was a demonstration of divine energy beyond compare. It shattered the grip of death and defeated the forces of darkness. As we tap into that "same power that rose Jesus from the dead" [18] (as the song says), it has the potential to profoundly transform our lives. God freely makes His power available, and He exerts it for us, but it is faith that sets it in motion in our lives. We must trust *In Him*, not our own strength, to live the Christian life. Are you living like you have resurrection power available to you?

2. In what areas of your life are you relying on your own strength instead of the power of God?

3. Read the following verses and take notes on what you learn about God's power through Christ that is accessible to you.

- Romans 8:11 –

- 2 Corinthians 4:5-7; 12:9-10 –

- John 14:12-14 –

God's power was not only revealed in raising Jesus from the dead, but also in exalting Him to the highest place of honor.

4. Where is Jesus now seated? (v. 20)

Forty days after rising victoriously from the grave, the resurrected Messiah completed preparing His disciples to carry the gospel to the ends of the earth. Then, before their very eyes, God exalted Him to the highest place of honor – the right hand of the Father, enthroned above all (Acts 1:1-10; 2:33). What a demonstration of God's amazing power!

5. Over what does Christ have authority? (v. 21)

Jesus' name is far above all others. Enthroned at the right hand of God, Christ now reigns far above every ruler, every authority, every name, spiritual or earthly, now or in eternity. There is no throne, no title, no power that outranks Him. His name eclipses them all. "So that at the name of Jesus every knee will bow, of those who are in Heaven and on earth and under the earth, and that every tongue will confess that Jesus Christ is Lord, to the glory of God the Father" (Philippians 2:10-11).

6. What does it look like to live fully surrendered to the One who reigns above all?

As we come to the end of today's study, pause and let the truth of Ephesians 1:19-21 settle deeply in your heart. Meditate on Christ's life, death, burial, resurrection, ascension, and glorification. How is it even possible to grasp the truths of all He has purchased for those who are *In Him*?

DID YOU KNOW?

Paul's statement in Ephesians 1:20, "seated Him at His right hand in the heavenly places," comes from Psalm 110:1, "The Lord says to my Lord: 'Sit at My right hand until I make Your enemies a footstool for Your feet.'" It is the most often quoted Old Testament verse in the New Testament (more than 30 times) because it gives the basis for the exaltation of Christ. Psalm 110 is a coronation psalm that the Jews believed referred to the coming Messiah. However, "the early church understood the psalm to have been fulfilled in Jesus, anchoring His authority, power, and glory. For us this means that Christ is now in the place of power, and the entire Godhead is at work in this world on behalf of God's people. The heavenly realms, as we saw in 1:3, refer to the arena in which believers now dwell spiritually. Here this includes Heaven itself, as Christ dwells alongside His Father in glory." [19]

7. What are some of the truths that came to mind as you were thinking though all that you have *In Him*?

Jesus is alive. Jesus is exalted. Jesus is reigning.

He is not a distant King, but a risen Savior whose power is at work in us today, empowering us to overcome sin, endure trials, and walk in victory.

Stand in awe of His majesty. Rest in His authority. Walk in His power. And let your life proclaim: Jesus is Lord – now and forever.

Day Four

Ephesians 1:21-23

Today, we pick back up with Paul's beautiful portrait of Christ's exalted position – seated at the right hand of the Father – a place of honor and absolute authority.

Jesus isn't just alive, He is enthroned. He has been given all authority over every power, every name, and every realm. God's sovereignty isn't just a theological truth; it's an anchor for our souls. Whatever you are going through today, allow yourself to take great comfort in this reality.

As my husband and I have walked through the valley of cancer over the past year-and-a-half, God's sovereignty has granted us supernatural peace. Our all-knowing, all-powerful, and compassionate Father has carried us through each and every day, giving us His calm, His peace, in the midst of every circumstance we've faced.

That peace hasn't always come easily – or automatically. In fact, some days it feels like a full-on wrestling match just to shake off anxiety and refuse to give it a place in my heart. But I have learned to treasure those hard-fought days, those days when victory finally comes, as faith rises above fear, and peace floods my heart. As Jesus says in John 10:10, the evil one has come to "steal, kill and destroy." He hates the presence of Christ "in you" and will use any means to distort and pervert our perception of God and drain us of our peace. But Jesus came that we might have "life and have it abundantly" (John 10:10b).

Some days just feel like a battle ground, don't they? We often encounter military language in Scripture to describe the spiritual battle we face each day. Yet many of us would rather imagine ourselves in a garden retreat or floating around on a peaceful cruise ship. The reality is far more urgent: we are in hostile territory, stationed on a battleship, not a pleasure boat. Our weapons are not of this world. They are rooted in the very character of Christ and the power of His Word. And though the conflict is real, we are not powerless.

We have a choice:

> Be anxious for nothing, but in everything by prayer and supplication with thanksgiving let your requests be made known to God. And the peace of God, which surpasses all comprehension, will guard your hearts and your minds in Christ Jesus (Philippians 4:6-7).

In the midst of the battle, peace is possible, but it all comes down to choice. We must choose to believe God's Word and then act on it. So, let me ask: How are you doing today? In today's culture, anxiety seems to be in the very air we breathe. Are you weighed down with fear or unrest? Having an accurate view of God enables us to believe and cast out fear.

Close your eyes. Ask the Lord to allow you to see what Isaiah saw, "the Lord sitting on a throne, lofty and exalted, with the train of His robe filling the temple" (Isaiah 6:1).

Let that vision fill your soul. He is glorious, exalted, and reigning as King of Kings and Lord of Lords.

1. Read Isaiah 6:1-7. What was Isaiah's response to seeing the Lord?

Isaiah was undone. He was changed. Once he saw the holiness and majesty of God, once he experienced His Presence, he could never be the same again.

As we saw in the introduction to this week's lesson, David knew the Lord. He had experienced His Presence. That is the reason he was able to confront Goliath without fear. He knew Who was with him. He went forward in the name of the Lord and defeated Israel's taunting enemy.

Today, the enemy still taunts, intimidates, and instills fear. But we can stand firm against his "schemes" (Ephesians 6:11) and trust our resurrected, ascended, and reigning King.

Read Ephesians 1:21-23.

2. Make a list of what Christ is seated above. (v. 21)

3. Now, read Ephesians 6:12. Make a list of what we struggle against.

Compare the list from Ephesians 1:21 with the list from Ephesians 6:12. These two passages reflect a similar structure – a hierarchy of spiritual forces. Paul wants us to see that Christ reigns "far above" every demonic power, every spiritual threat, every foul spirit that attempts to intimate or accuse. He is enthroned over them all!

4. What is the significance of Christ's position? (vv. 21-23)

Did you notice that Jesus is not only seated in authority, He is "head over all things to the church which is His Body"? If you are a part of the Church universal, Christ's Body, the enemy is under your feet as well. We have positional authority because we are *In Him.* We have no fear because we know our God and He is with us. The promise is His Presence and His Presence is all we need.

As we saw in Lesson One, right before He ascended, Jesus told His disciples:

> "All authority has been given to Me in Heaven and on earth. Go therefore and make disciples of all the nations, baptizing them in the name of the Father and the Son and the Holy Spirit, teaching them to observe all that I commanded you; and lo, I am with you always, even to the end of the age" (Matthew 28:18b-20).

At His ascension, Jesus was given all authority in "Heaven and earth." And because He is "with us," we stand in that authority with Him. John Eldredge writes, "By the grace of God, we share in that authority with Jesus…Satan and his emissaries bank an awful lot of their work on the fact that Christians don't know the power and authority we now have in Christ. When we begin to exercise that fierce mastery, everything begins to change." [20]

5. Let's look at some other verses in the New Testament that teach us about the authority of Christ. Summarize what you learn.

    - Matthew 10:1 –
    - Mark 6:7 –
    - Luke 10:19-20 –
    - Luke 12:4-7 –
    - Colossians 2:9-12 –
    - Revelation 12:10 –

Francis Foulkes writes:

> The sequence of thought here seems to be: by His resurrection and ascension Christ is exalted to be Lord of all, He is head of all things for the church; the church is His body intended to express Him in the world; more than that, the church is intended to be a full expression of Him by being filled by Him whose purpose it is to fill everything there is. [21]

6. How can you, as part of the church, better reflect Christ and thus fill the earth with His glory?

Close your time today by thanking the Lord for giving you authority "in Christ Jesus" as well as "every spiritual blessing in heavenly places in Christ" (Ephesians 1:3).

Day Five

Satan's strategy:
Deception

When Satan slithered into the Garden of Eden, his intent was to drive a wedge between God and Adam and Eve. He correctly assumed that the man and woman were unlikely to go along with anything that looked like a direct attack on God. So, he came up with a strategy that was cunning and calculated: **deception**.

The enemy didn't approach Eve with obvious evil or outright rebellion. Instead, he slid in with subtle suggestions and questions designed to undermine her trust in God. "Did God really say...?" (Genesis 3:1, NLT), was more than a question – it was a seed of doubt. In that moment, Satan twisted God's Word, reframing His command not to eat "from the tree of the knowledge of good and evil" (Genesis 2:17) as restrictive. In doing so, he painted the Creator not as generous but as withholding. He appealed to Eve's desires, convincing her that she could be "like God," without God.

That's how deception works – it always carries a fragment of truth wrapped in a deadly lie. The tragedy is that Eve, and Adam with her, chose to listen to the deceiver instead of remembering the faithfulness and goodness of the God who had provided everything they needed. And because they believed the lie, they were separated from the Presence of God.

So, it's no surprise that deception is still one of the enemy's favorite tactics. He causes us to question God's heart, by whispering lies that sound like truth: "God's holding out on you," "You know better than He does," "This one compromise won't matter." And if we're not deeply rooted in the Word of God, we will find ourselves easily swayed. That's why it's essential to fill our minds daily with truth, to walk in humility and obedience, and to remain watchful. We are in a battle, not against flesh and blood, but against spiritual forces of evil (Ephesians 6:12). And the only way to stand firm is to cling to what is true, trust the character of God, and reject the seductive voice of the serpent that still speaks today.

Right now, if we could peel back the heavens, we would see a spiritual war raging all around us. As Jesus tells us in John 8:44, Satan is the father of lies. His favorite lies fall into two categories. First, he lies about God. Those lies come in the form of "God is not." He sends messages like:

- God is not good, or that wouldn't have happened.
- God is not listening to your prayers; He doesn't really care about you.
- God is not able; He is not going to come through for you.

Second, he lies to you about you about your identity in Christ. He deludes us with lies that begin with "You are not":

- You are not forgiven.
- You are not wanted.
- You are not loved.

Attacking our identity in Christ is a favorite ploy of the enemy. *In Him*, you have a new life and are a new creation. Wilbourne explores what your new life means, "Union with Christ tells you a new story about who you are. If you are 'in Christ,' you too have been given a new identity. God has called you into a new life, rooted in a history that predates you, anchored in the life, death, and resurrection of Jesus." [22]

The evil one does not want you to know or live from your identity "in Christ." That is why you must be discerning and aware of your thoughts. Not every thought originates with you. You must run every thought through the grid of God's Word.

1. Define deception.

The next time you experience a negative, critical, or anxious thought, stop and ask, "Is it true"?

The enemy is crafty. He rarely attacks head-on, but often twists the truth or plants subtle doubts about God's Word. First, he whispers his cunning lies into our ear. If we listen instead of refusing the lie, our emotions begin to engage. Once our feelings get involved, the lies gain momentum and volume. Often, it seems like our emotions sit on the front row of our lives, screaming for our attention. But we are not called to live controlled by our emotions, we are called to live by the truth.

When you sense your chest tightening and anxiety trying to force its way into your mind and emotions, remember, "God has not given us a spirit of fear, but of power and of love and of a sound mind" (2 Timothy 1:7, NKJV). Refuse fear and anxiety. Turn those thoughts into prayer requests. Look to Jesus, the Author and Perfector of our faith. Trust Him. Believe Him. No excuses!

Let truth take charge. For every lie the enemy throws at you, there is a corresponding truth for you to stand upon. Take up your Sword of the Spirit (the Word of God) and stand firm against the fiery darts of the enemy (Ephesians 6:16).

2. What is the primary emotion you're feeling right now?

If your answer lists fear, anxiety, discouragement, depression, or anything else not from the Lord, ask Him for a Word from His Word to combat the lies of the enemy. His voice brings life and peace. "The mind governed by the flesh is death, but the mind governed by the Spirit is life and peace" (Romans 8:6, NIV).

3. Write out the truth from God's Word that He revealed to you. (You might also want to begin building a list that you can keep in your Bible or on your phone that you can refer back to when needed, of the common lies or accusations you receive from the enemy and the truths of God's Word to combat them.)

God builds up and encourages. Refuse condemnation and accusation. The enemy is called "the accuser of the brethren," but God declares something different over you: "There is now no condemnation for those who are in Christ Jesus" (Romans 8:1). You are no longer under condemnation. You are forgiven and have been given the very righteousness of God in Christ (2 Corinthians 5:21). Jesus Christ is the Truth! Stand in truth and you will be able to detect and defeat the enemy's lie.

Allow the words of Watchman Nee to encourage and embolden you:

> God makes it quite clear in His Word that He has only one answer to every human need – His Son, Jesus Christ. In all His dealings with us, He works by taking us out of the way and substituting Christ in our place. The Son of God died instead of us for our forgiveness: He lives instead of us for our deliverance. [23]

Hallelujah! What a Savior!

379 Turn Your Eyes upon Jesus

H. H. L. HELEN HOWARTH LEMMEL

A dwelling of God in the Spirit

Ephesians 2

"A dwelling of God in the Spirit"

Ephesians 2

We are taken out of the great graveyard of sin and placed into the throne room of glory. [1]
~ Warren Wiersbe

When I prepare to write, I always begin by reading the text in multiple translations. As I opened Ephesians 2 in *The Message,* the chapter heading stopped me in my tracks:

He Tore Down the Wall

These five little words encompass a heart-penetrating truth that serves as a beautiful summation of Ephesians 2. I pray as you walk through this chapter, you will be reminded: It is finished. The work of Christ on the cross is complete. And the only aspect for which you are responsible is accepting this indescribable gift by grace through faith.

Sin had created a wall between us and God – a wall of sin, shame, and separation. Jesus Christ, the sinless Son of God, tore down that wall, by humbling Himself "by becoming obedient to the point of death, even death on a cross" (Philippians 2:8).

Paul begins Ephesians 2 by taking us back to the darkness in which we lived prior to encountering the marvelous light of the truth of the gospel. And then he masterfully guides us through streams of mercy into the miracle of God's grace. Much like a powerful "before and after" transformation, Paul describes how believers were once spiritually dead, trapped by the darkness of sin. But now, made alive in Christ, we walk in the radiance of His light.

Invite the Holy Spirit into your space right now as you open the pages of Scripture. Be reminded that, as a child of God, you have been rescued from the kingdom of darkness and transported into the Kingdom of Light…forevermore.

The veil was torn, the wall demolished, the separation forever dissolved so that *In Him*, we could "become a dwelling in which God lives by His Spirit" (Ephesians 2:22b, NIV).

Day One

Ephesians 2:1-7

Begin today by reading Ephesians 2 in its entirety. As you read, underline the key words in the chapter.

1. Grab a purple pen and mark every instance of "In Him," "In Christ," or the equivalent. Make a list of the key words from Ephesians 2.

Key Words in Ephesians 2

2. What do Paul's words "you were dead" (v. 1) mean to you?

3. How do we move from death to life?

4. As a child of God, what do we experience as a result of being made alive in Christ?

Now let's look at today's passage in more depth.

Reread Ephesians 2:1-3.

Paul begins Ephesians 2 by describing the bad news of what life apart from Christ is like. His opening words may serve as a painful reminder of our past as we consider our lives prior to coming to Christ. But this is not his intention. Remember Paul's words from Romans 8:1: "There is now <u>no</u> condemnation for those who are in Christ Jesus" (emphasis mine). God does not condemn us for our sin; therefore, we should not walk in condemnation. To drag us into the quicksand of guilt and shame is a tactic of the enemy. Again, this is <u>not</u> what Paul is doing here. His desire is for us to ponder the depth of our own sin, so that our hearts are awakened to the magnitude and wonder of His salvation gift.

5. What word does Paul use to describe us prior to our conversion? (v. 1a)

Dead means dead. As you consider Paul's words here, take a moment to notice how *Merriam-Webster* defines dead: "Deprived of life, no longer alive; lacking power to move, feel, or respond; incapable of being stirred emotionally or intellectually; grown cold." [2]

Wiersbe captures the reality of our spiritual state apart from Christ: "The unbeliever is not sick; he is dead! He does not need resuscitation; he needs resurrection." [3] Before we come to Christ, we are dead in the only sphere of life that really matters: a relationship with God, the very Source of Life.

6. What was your life like prior to coming to a saving knowledge of Jesus Christ? Do you remember the "deadness" of living in sin?

Paul is obviously talking to a group of living, breathing people, so they are not dead physically. He is speaking to their spiritual state. Just as a corpse cannot resuscitate itself, neither can an unbeliever revive his or her own spirit. Try as we might, nothing gives us the life we were originally created to have. We can chase after success, relationships, and all kinds of experiences, hoping they'll make us feel alive. But apart from God, "you were dead." All of us were dead.

Paul then goes on to explain what our "dead" life was like in verses 2-3. Because to grasp the greatness of our salvation, we must understand our condition prior to receiving it.

7. How does a person live prior to conversion and who are they obeying? (v. 2a)

We were walking in a God-less way, "according to the course of this world" (v. 2). As Eugene Peterson paraphrases it in *The Message*: We "let the world, which doesn't know the first thing about living, tell us how to live." But, it's even worse: In our sin, we were unknowingly cooperating with the enemy who despises Jesus.

8. How is Satan described? (v. 2b)

Different translations offer varying descriptions of Satan here, but the general idea is that he and his demons have some measure of authority in the world system in which we live. N.T. Wright describes it this way, "His deadly ideas, his schemes for defacing God's beautiful creation and particularly His image-bearing human creatures, are, as we say, 'in the air.' You can sense their power 'in the atmosphere' of a place." [4]

John Piper expounds on Satan's authority with a reminder of his limitations: "He's not God. He does not share God's omniscience and omnipresence, but we do know that he has many unclean spirits, demons, at his disposal, and they are deployed all over the world in the air. The air is where his flaming arrows fly." [5]

We also read in verse 2 that the devil is the spirit at work in the hearts of those who refuse to obey God. Have you heard the phrase, "Lost people act like lost people"? Those who refuse to obey God and surrender their lives to Him by following His Word do so because the spirit of the evil one is at work in their lives. This may pack more of a punch than we would like, but it does not negate the truth of it. Charles Swindoll elaborates:

> So potent is the power of Satan that he can get people to believe that truth is a lie and that a lie is the truth. He fills the world with temptations and traps, and he reigns over his kingdom of darkness like a malevolent dictator oppressing his powerless victims. Paul includes even himself in the category: "Among [the sons of disobedience] we too all formerly lived" (2:3). [6]

9. Why do we live disobediently prior to salvation? (v. 3)

Self. We cannot point a finger at anything or anyone else because of our sin. Wright says, "We live in a world where human beings, left to themselves, not only choose the wrong direction, but remain cheerfully confident that it is in fact the right one." [7]

DID YOU KNOW?

In our English translations of Ephesians 2:1-3, we have two sentences. There is a period at the end of verse 2 and a period at the end of verse 3. But in the original Greek, those periods are actually commas. That is because verses 1-3 are part of one sentence, with 124 words, that goes all the way through verse 7. Paul liked long sentences! He began the letter reminding us of our spiritual blessings in Christ with a 202-word sentence (Ephesians 1:3-14). Then he shared his prayer for the Ephesians and us in a 164-word sentence (Ephesians 1:15-23).

Sadly, we see this rampant in today's culture, do we not? The depravity of human nature is so evident in our world today, in ways we would never have imagined just a decade ago. And those who walk in outright defiance to the ways of God are convinced they are right – with a culture cheering them on unashamedly. Left to ourselves, we will follow our own desires and the inclinations of our sinful flesh, and because of that, we subject ourselves to the wrath of God (v. 3b).

Read Ephesians 2:4-7.

And now…the good news!

"<u>But God</u>." We need to put these two words on a notecard and post them on our mirrors, car dashes, refrigerators, and closet doors. Just whispering them now brings tears to my eyes as I think back on my life prior to making the choice to surrender my life to Jesus, to follow Him purposefully and intentionally with my whole heart. "<u>But God</u>." Behind those simple words stands a divine plan so vast in love and eternal in scope that the human mind can't fully grasp it – we can only receive it with open hearts. Rather than abandoning a sinful humanity to hopelessness and death, God acted.

This is where the tide turns. As Paul continues, he begins to knit together the great redemption thread.

10. What adjectives does Paul use to describe God's mercy and love? (v. 4)

11. What are the three ways God's mercy and grace are revealed to us? (vv. 5-6)

-
-
-

In Christ, we are made "alive," raised," and "seated." All three verbs are past tense actions that describe our present state. We are "alive," "raised," and "seated" now. Paul is referring back to his earlier prayer for us, that we might know "the surpassing greatness of [God's] power toward us…which He brought about in Christ, when He raised Him from the dead and seated Him at His right hand in the heavenly places, far above all rule and authority and power and dominion…" (Ephesians 1:19-21).

Rankin Wilbourne provides us with fascinating commentary regarding the verbs Paul uses to depict our union with Christ:

> Paul actually invented new words to describe this new reality. The phrases "crucified with," "raised with," "buried with," and "seated with" are each a single word in Greek beginning with the prefix syn, meaning "with." Those words didn't exist before Paul coined them. But something so unique had happened that there were no words for it! A new vocabulary was necessary. It was the only way he could describe who he had become because of Jesus. [8]

If we can only grasp what Paul is saying here! Jesus was crucified, but God made Him "alive" again. When He was lying in the tomb, God "raised" Him from the dead. And then the Father "seated" the Son on the throne of the universe. What God did for Jesus, He does for all who believe *In Him!* As Wilbourne explains, "When we are in Christ, every part of Christ's life, not only His death, has significance for us. We share in His life and obedience, His death and His resurrection, even His ascension! We participate in another's victory. All that is His becomes ours." [9]

And what does God achieve through His costly plan? It is all "so that in the ages to come He might show the surpassing riches of His grace in kindness toward us in Christ Jesus" (v. 7). God's plan is to spend all of eternity showering us with His blessings!

Consider Wright's reflection, "Whenever anyone says, or implies, that God is after all a bit stingy, or mean, or small-minded, look at these verses and think again." [10]

As you close today, take a few minutes to slowly reread and meditate on verses 4-7.

12. How do these truths impact you?

In Him, you are alive. *In Him*, you are raised from spiritual death to new life. Right now, you are seated with Him in the heavens. This is who you are as a child of God…linked with Him, united with Him. For all of eternity, *In Him*.

Without God's mercy and grace, we're stuck in imperfect. We're stuck without hope. We're just plain stuck.
But God's mercy comes and gets us unstuck. His mercy saves us through Jesus Christ. [11]
~ Max Lucado

Day Two
Ephesians 2:8-10

Take a moment to reflect on the time when you said "yes" to Jesus, that day when your heart was awakened to grace and you accepted Christ into your heart.

For me, that happened when I was a six-year-old child. I remember it well. Through tears, I recognized my need for a Savior, and I made the choice to repent, believe, and receive Him. And then, I think back to my young adulthood when God so clearly called me to abandon my own way of doing things. I was broken over my sin and all the years wasted in disobedience and rebellion. At that point, God called me deeper. A few years later as a young mother, I had an encounter during an early morning quiet time when God called me to get serious about following Him, to dig deep into His Word and to make prayer a way of life. God took me deeper still. I was transformed.

As Paul teaches in Ephesians 2:8-10, I cannot take any credit for my salvation or transformation. They were accomplished entirely by God. He alone is the One who opens our blind eyes to the truth of the gospel, giving us the ability to grasp its message and receive the promise of forgiveness offered to all who believe.

In these verses, Paul gives us a concise outline for Biblical salvation – the "gospel in a nutshell," if you will. We can often gloss over these verses, especially if we were raised in church or saved as a young child. Many of us can quote them with ease from memory. But oh, the richness and the depth, the truth and the power of these words from the Apostle Paul.

This is the good news of the gospel, the foundation of our faith. I urge you to sit down with your Bible, a pen, and an open heart. Allow the Lord to take you back to the basics, the most elementary principles of our faith. May the Holy Spirit make the wonder of God's grace fall fresh on you again.

Read Ephesians 2:8.

1. How are we saved? (v. 8)

By grace. Through faith. That's it. No other way. No other explanation. Yesterday, we saw that before we came to Christ, we were spiritually dead (Ephesians 2:1, 5). Steven Cole adds, "Dead men can do absolutely nothing to remedy their condition. They can't work toward being raised from the dead. They can't pray for it. They can't even muster up the faith to get raised from the dead. It takes an act of God to impart life to a dead man. Even so, it takes an act of God to save those who are dead in their sins." [12]

Grace (undeserved kindness) is the basis for everything God has done for us, and faith is the means by which we receive and embrace that grace.

2. What word does Paul use to describe our salvation? (v. 8b)

Imagine opening a beautifully wrapped package on Christmas morning and turning to the giver and saying, "Oh, what a nice gift! How much do I owe you?" That sounds ridiculous, doesn't it? The only appropriate response is, "Thank you." The same is true for the gift of salvation. We do not owe God anything other than the "thank you" of a grateful and surrendered heart. Wiersbe reiterates, "Salvation is a gift, not a reward." [13]

In our "give to get" society, we may struggle to grasp that salvation is absolutely free and only requires that we believe it and receive it. Most, if not all, other religions require that we must do something to earn our way to Heaven. Christianity is the only religion where Jesus comes to us, a sinful people, and offers a way to forgiveness, freedom, and life forever with God.

DID YOU KNOW?

Soli Deo gloria is a phrase that came out of the Protestant Reformation. Johann Sebastian Bach affixed the initials *SDG* at the bottom of every composition that he wrote "to communicate the idea that it is God and God alone who is to receive the glory for the wonders of His work of creation and of redemption." [14]

Read Ephesians 2:9.

3. What is salvation not and why? (v. 9)

As human beings, we naturally crave recognition for our accomplishments and achievements – promotions, awards, trophies, medals, raises, accolades. These things aren't inherently wrong. But our human nature, often riddled with pride, longs to be acknowledged (and if we are honest, sometimes praised) for our efforts. When we succeed, we like people to take notice. It's simply part of who we are.

God's primary reason for redeeming mankind was His love for the world (John 3:16). However, He created us and knows us. I am convinced that His redemption plan was a gift, in part, because He knew we might find some way to take credit for it or feel as though it depended upon us. God does not leave any room for boasting when it comes to salvation. We aren't saved as a reward for good deeds or religious performance. Even as God planned to rescue us, He did it with our frailty and flesh in mind. He wants us to fully acknowledge that all glory and honor are His alone for the great gift of salvation and eternal life.

Soli Deo gloria. Glory to God alone.

4. What areas in your life do you find yourself still trying to "earn" God's love instead of resting in His grace?

These verses offer another foundational truth on which we can stand. Since there is nothing we can do to earn salvation, why would we ever believe there is anything we can do to lose it? It is a gift. No one takes a gift back after freely giving it. And our Heavenly Father, the perfect Giver, surely does not.

5. How does John 10:28 speak to the permanence of our salvation?

Paul has reminded us how we are saved. Now, he goes on to tell us why we are saved.

Read Ephesians 2:10.

6. What word does Paul use to describe us? (v. 10a)

This is one of my favorite verses in all of Scripture. It was a truth I discovered at a pivotal time in my life when it seemed my world was falling apart. I felt alone, rejected, and (honestly) worthless, especially to the Kingdom of God. In the NLT, this verse reads, "For we are God's masterpiece." This truth stood against every lie with which the enemy taunted me, and it began to reveal to my heart that God had transformed me, changed me, and reworked me like an artist or a potter tends to a creative piece. I repeated this verse to my boys daily as they would get out in the school car line (they will still say it today). I wanted them to know, to be convinced, that they are an exquisite and perfect masterpiece in the hands of Almighty God, made to do everything He planned for them to do.

The Greek word for "workmanship" is *poiema* from which we get our word *poem*. The church is His poem and His new creation. [15] Wilbourne beautifully expounds on the meaning of *poeima*:

> You are God's poem, His work of art. There's no one else He made quite like you. So when He becomes one with you, He still preserves and delights in your unique particularity. As he restores His image in you, as you become more like His Son, you are becoming more and more yourself – more and more the you God dreamed up when He first dreamed you up." [16]

This is life-changing truth. This is life-giving truth. This is your identity *In Him*.

7. What are some things that can speak into your heart and mind causing you to doubt that you are a masterpiece, His workmanship?

Poeima is only used twice in the New Testament, in Romans 1:20 and Ephesians 2:10. [17] In Romans, it refers to God's first work of creation and is translated "what has been made." In the beginning God wrote a beautiful poem, the world and all who lived in it. But His first poem was ruined when it was marred by sin. So, He wrote a new poem; He made a new creation, His "workmanship." God made us, His people alive in Christ.

8. For what purpose has God made us a new creation? (v. 10b)

The "good works" mentioned in verse 10 have nothing to do with earning salvation. Swindoll explains, "Ephesians 2:10…refers to the good works of those who are already born-again believers in Christ and who are now empowered by the Holy Spirit to determine and then do things that please God (Philippians 2:13)." [18]

God didn't just save us from something; He saved us for something. As His workmanship, we've been created in Christ Jesus for a life that reflects His character and purposes. These "good works" aren't about earning favor; they're about living out the new identity we've been given. God has already prepared opportunities for us to walk in that and display His glory through our lives.

As we reflect on our salvation by grace through faith, let's also embrace the calling that comes with it: to live as His masterpiece, shaped by His hands, sent into the world to reflect His goodness.

What "good works" might God be calling you to walk in today, not to earn His favor, but as a response to His grace?

Our conversion is not the end; it is the beginning. God continues to work in us to make us what He wants us to be. His purpose is to make us more like Christ. [19]
~ Warren Wiersbe

Day Three

Ephesians 2:11-18

Therefore...remember...
Ephesians 2:11a

As Paul continues, he entreats his readers once again to remember. At the beginning of Ephesians 2, he reminds believers in general of their spiritual state prior to salvation. Now, he once again tells his audience to remember their pre-Christian past and what they have been saved from, this time focusing in specifically on the Gentiles. Paul begins verse 11 with "Therefore, remember." The "remember" command opens verse 12 as well.

Paul's reminder isn't just about looking back for the sake of it. It's about grounding believers in the bigger story God is telling, where the past helps us understand who we are and where we're going:

> In an age of information and trending topics, the present can seem more relevant than the past. With all the advancing technologies, it can be easy to think that the past represents a step backward. From a biblical perspective, however, the future informs the past and the past informs the future and everything in between. The early chapters of Genesis, for example, are not fully comprehended without the final chapters of Revelation, forming one comprehensive goal for creation from a sovereign God. Our confidence in the Word and the reasons to remember Him are deeply rooted in God's unchanging character. [20]

Read Ephesians 2:11-12.

Most of the converts in the church at Ephesus were Gentiles who were aware that the Old Testament was largely about God's covenant relationship with the Jews. For centuries, the Jews (the "Circumcision") had looked down on the Gentiles (the "Uncircumcision") as outsiders. William Barclay offers insight into the visceral hatred that existed between the Jews and Gentiles:

> The Jews had an immense contempt for the Gentiles. They said that the Gentiles were created by God to be fuel for the fires of hell, and that God loved only Israel of all the nations that He had made. "The best of the serpents crush," they said, "the best of the Gentiles kill." It was not even lawful to give help to a Gentile woman in childbirth, for that would be to bring another Gentile into the world. [21]

The *Life Application Study Bible* adds, "Jews and Gentiles alike could be guilty of spiritual pride – Jews for thinking their faith and traditions elevated them above everyone else, Gentiles for trusting in their achievements, power, or position." [22]

Wiersbe notes that the word that "best describes Gentiles is <u>without</u>. They were outside in several respects." [23]

1. In verse 12, what does Paul remind the Gentiles of specifically? (Hint: They are without five things.)

-
-

-
-
-

Of all the things Paul lists, the last two sting a little deeper than the others. "You lived in this world without God and without hope" (Ephesians 2:12b, NLT).

2. Has there been a time when you lived without God and without hope? What was that like?

Memories can sometimes be painful, and the devil can use those to discourage us and keep us away from the abundant life Christ offers. On the other hand, remembering can be beneficial as it sets the stage for awe-filled worship because of what God has done for us. I can think back on two specific periods in my life that I was without hope. I was a Christian, so intellectually I knew I belonged to Christ and that nothing would change my eternity. However, the enemy used my circumstances to paralyze me with fear, worry, loneliness, sadness, and hopelessness. As I remember those days, my heart grows warm, and my eyes often brim with tears as I recount God's faithfulness, love, and presence. I have often said I would not go back and undo those painful moments (although a part of me wishes I had not endured them), because what I learned of God forever changed my view of Him. It sealed upon my heart what I knew to be true in my head. I experienced Him like never before, and I never want to forget it.

I imagine Paul is painting a similar scenario for the Gentiles as he pens these words. And then once again comes one of the most beautiful conjunctions in all the Bible. But. The "But now" in Ephesians 2:13 correlates with the "But God" in Ephesians 2:4. Both passages reveal God's gracious action on behalf of sinful mankind.

Read Ephesians 2:13.

3. What contrast does Paul offer to a life without Christ, without citizenship, without covenant, without hope, and without God? (v. 13)

4. What is the only thing that brings us near to God? (v. 13b)

Only the blood of Christ unites us with Him and brings us near to Him. This points us back to the truth and foundation of our salvation as we saw yesterday: Only God's rich and merciful love displayed through the bloodshed of Jesus Christ can raise us from death to life and provide a life full of hope. This had to be such a powerful reminder for the Gentiles who once lived as outsiders apart from Christ!

Pause for a moment and turn these verses into a prayer of praise and thanksgiving.

Oh Father, I was an outsider, living apart from You, excluded from the citizenship of Heaven,
unaware of Your covenant and promises, living without You and without hope.
Thank You, that because of the blood of Jesus, I am united with Christ
and have been brought near to You.

I deeply love this passage of Scripture because it encompasses so much of Who God is and what He does for us.

Paul has pointed us to the hope we have *In Him* and the nearness we have to Him because of the blood of Jesus. Now, he turns our attention to another stunning characteristic of our Savior.

Read Ephesians 2:14-16.

5. What did Christ bring us? (v. 14)

6. Have you ever been without peace? How does a life without peace compare to a life filled with peace because of Jesus?

7. How did Jesus bring peace to the Jews and Gentiles? (vv. 14b-15)

8. How did Christ reconcile the two groups and what was the result? (v. 16)

Wright elaborates on this oneness in Christ of which Paul speaks:

> The point of it all was to create a single new humanity in place of the two. Today's church may no longer face the question of the integration of Jew and Gentile into a single family, though there are places where that is still a major issue. But we face, quite urgently, the question which Paul would insist on as a major priority. If our churches are still divided in any way along racial or cultural lines, he would say that our gospel, our very grasp of the meaning of Jesus' death, is called into question. [24]

Read Ephesians 2:17-18.

9. How are the Gentiles described? How are the Jews described? (v. 17)

The *Life Application Study Bible* makes this distinction: Jews – near to God because they already knew of Him through the Scriptures and worshiped Him in their religious ceremonies. Gentiles – far away because they knew little or nothing about God. [25] The Jews and Gentiles had a shared problem: They both needed to be reconciled to God. As Paul writes in Romans 3:22b-23: "There is no distinction; for all have sinned and fall short of the glory of God." Wiersbe explains how God settled the sin problem man, both Jews and Gentiles, had:

> A God of love wants to reconcile the sinner to Himself, but a God of holiness must see to it that sin is judged. God solved the problem by sending His Son to be the sacrifice for our sins, thereby revealing His love and meeting the demands of His righteousness. [26]

Because of Christ's sacrificial death at Calvary, we now "come through Christ directly into the presence of God the Father. Those who come to Him are removed from their little departments and are placed in Christ, the new Temple where there are no departments. The Cross dissolves the fences, and the gospel is preached to the Gentiles, those who were afar off, and to the Jews, those who were near." [27]

Paul wraps up this portion of the Scripture with a glorious truth and a beautiful picture of the Trinity!

10. Write out Ephesians 2:18, then underline the persons of the Trinity and answer the questions below.

- Who can come to the Father?
- Through Whom do we come?
- Why are we able to come?

In the words of Paul, "Don't forget…" (Ephesians 2:11, NLT).

Never forget. Always remember. We are all outsiders apart from Christ. Now, because of the cross, "We are no longer Jews or Greeks or slaves or free men or even merely men or women, but we are all the same – we are Christians; we are one in Christ Jesus" (Galatians 3:28, TLB).

Day Four

Ephesians 2:19-22

If Paul could have fast-forwarded to 1979, I think he may have borrowed these lyrics from Sister Sledge: "We are family. I got all my sisters with me." [28] Perhaps he would have altered the last line to say "sisters and brothers" as he draws Ephesians 2 to a close. At any rate, I'm pretty sure the tune is now playing in your head. ●

DID YOU KNOW?

The word *Gentile* is "an English translation of the Hebrew word *goyim* ('people, nations') and the Greek word *ethne* ('nations, people groups, people'). The Latin Vulgate translated these words as *gentilis*, and this word was then carried over into English as 'Gentile.'" The term most often refers to a person who is not a Jew. [29]

The theme of Paul's closing words is unity. He is wrapping up this portion of Scripture by showing us what the church should look like. He has reminded the Gentiles that they are no longer outsiders, and there is no distinction between them and the Jewish people when it comes to a saving knowledge of Jesus Christ. Now, Paul speaks to the unity of believing Jews and Gentiles in His church.

As you read these closing verses, be mindful that these words apply to us today, to every Christ-follower on the planet. If you have accepted the grace gift of Jesus Christ on the terms of repentance and faith, you are a part of God's family. No other characteristic about you makes a bit of difference when it comes to being a child of God. And any teaching that says differently is a lie – a lie straight from the pit of hell.

Read Ephesians 2:19-20.

If the church today (meaning all who have called on the name of the Lord for salvation) would let these truths sink deep into their souls and live by it, the world would take note, and we would experience a vastly different way of life. Furthermore, our interactions with each other would be transformed.

1. What does Paul say the believing Gentiles "no longer" are? What are they? (v. 19)

Wiersbe elaborates on what it means to be a part of the family of God: "Through faith in Christ, we enter into God's family, and God becomes our Father. We are all brothers and sisters in the one family, no matter what racial, national, or physical distinctions we may possess." [30]

2. Upon whose foundation are we built? (v. 20a)

A sure and steady foundation is pivotal to a house standing the test of time. Just as a faulty foundation contributes to a crumbling structure, so will a shifting foundation (spiritually speaking) lead to the same in the house of God. The *Life Application Study Bible* notes the importance of this foundation: "The church is not built on modern ideas but rather on the spiritual heritage given to us by the early apostles and prophets of the Christian church." [31]

3. What is Jesus' role in God's "house"? (v. 20b)

In Bible times, every well-built structure with a firm foundation had a cornerstone, a "principal stone, usually placed at the corner of an edifice, to guide the workers in their course. The cornerstone was usually one of the largest, the most solid, and the most carefully constructed of any in the edifice." [32]

Jesus is referred to as the Cornerstone throughout Scripture (Psalm 118:22, Isaiah 8:14, Mark 12:10). He binds us together. He is the solid Rock on which we stand.

Then, Paul goes on to share a powerful truth about what we become as children of God.

Read Ephesians 2:21-22.

4. How are we "fitted" together? (v. 21)

In Him. This is the focal point of our entire study. Yes, we must believe and operate in the truth that Jesus lives <u>in us</u>. This is a necessary principle on which to stand in our Christian faith. But we also must grasp the power of living *In Him*. This allows us to be united as the body of Christ and to experience the abundant life for which Jesus died to give us.

5. What is the result of being joined together in Christ? (v. 21b)

Wiersbe explains this would have been a thought-provoking statement for both the Jews and Gentiles: "The Jews would think of Herod's temple in Jerusalem, and the Gentiles would think of the great temple of Diana. This temple [of which Paul speaks] is 'fitly framed together' as the body of Christ, so that every part accomplishes the purpose God has in mind." [33]

Paul concludes by telling the Gentiles that they are "being made part of this dwelling where God lives by His Spirit" (v. 22, NLT).

I can only imagine the soothing balm these words must have been to the Gentiles as they considered their past status as "outsiders." They are now discovering that they are a part of this holy temple for the Lord.

Have you ever felt excluded or left out? For different reasons, we have all felt like an outsider a time or two in our lives. It is not a feeling we wish to relive. The relief that comes when someone waves you over to their group or comes from across the room to say hello and reach out for a hug...we know and love that warm feeling, do we not?

The Gentiles were no different. They must have found such sweet relief in hearing these declarations made by Paul. They have been grafted into the family of God, joined in with every other believer, and are becoming a dwelling place for the Holy Spirit of God. And the same is true for us.

Max Anders expounds on the shift that has taken place in Christ:

> The stones are forming a living, spiritual temple to glorify the Lord. In the Old Testament, the presence and glory of God inhabited a literal stone building. Now God dwells not in a stone building but in the hearts of believers. Christ is the unifying factor that takes the separate stones and creates a temple. This temple is holy, set apart for God. In this temple God receives worship and praise. The hearts of believers is thus the basic worship place in God's Kingdom on earth. [34]

As you close out today, consider the rich truth of being a part of the family of God: God as your Father, every Christian your brother and sister, and all of us living as a dwelling place for the Lord Himself.

Everything rests on Jesus Christ. Faithfulness to Him determines all actions and decisions.
Jesus is the ultimate equalizer. In a world where we are proud of what makes us different/better than others, Jesus offers a place where we meet as equals. He declares the walls we build are irrelevant – and He wants to remove them. Jesus doesn't offer an alternative; He comes to us with the original plan and a way to get back to it. He is the way. [35]

~ Max Lucado

6. How does this reflection speak to your heart and how should it impact your daily life?

Day Five

Satan's strategy: Destruction

It has always been God's plan not just to forgive you but to restore you. [36]
~ John Eldredge

Just as you can be sure that God's plan for you has always been redemption and restoration, you can be as equally sure that the enemy's plan has always been, and continues to be, **destruction**.

1. Read the following verses and make a list of the names used to describe Satan.

Scripture	Names of Satan
Ephesians 2:1-2	
John 8:44	
John 12:31	
2 Corinthians 4:3-4	

2. Read John 10:10 and note the difference in God's plan for your life versus Satan's plan.

We know we cannot be snatched from the Father's hand (John 10:28), and we know that it is the Lord God who numbers our days (Psalm 139:16); but we must also be aware – not afraid, but aware – that the enemy of our souls is determined to bring destruction into our lives any way he can. And he will stop at nothing.

3. What are some of the ways Satan has attempted to bring destruction into your life?

If he can cause us to doubt the truths of God's Word, he will get a foothold in our lives, opening the door to his destructive ways.

So, let us do a quick recap of our study this week. These are truths we can stand upon:

- We were dead. But in Christ, we are now alive. God, in His great love and mercy, gave us life through Christ's death and resurrection.
- We are seated in Heaven and united with Jesus. Only His grace can give us new life. We do not have to earn it; it is a free gift!
- We are His masterpiece, created to do good things He planned for us.
- We are all one – a part of the family of God – and He, our Cornerstone, has brought us peace.
- We are reconciled to God because of Jesus Christ, and we can all come to the Father through the Spirit because of the Son.
- We are joined together as a holy temple for the Lord!

Another one of the devil's methods of bringing destruction is tempting us to question the reality of a new heart. By doing so, he lures us into living under condemnation. While we remain imperfect this side of Heaven and continue to sin while living on this earth, the Bible tells us that when we accept Jesus, He changes us. The old becomes new (2 Corinthians 5:17). The overall theme of Ephesians 2 is being made alive *In Him,* which brings us new life, unity and peace, and the indwelling power of the Holy Spirit. Paul's words in Romans proclaim a similar message, "Just as Christ was raised from the dead through the glory of the Father, we too may live a new life…In the same way, count yourselves dead to sin but alive to God in Christ Jesus" (Romans 6:4a, 11, NIV).

Consider this insight from John Eldredge on the reality of a new heart:

> Something pretty dramatic must have happened in our hearts, then, to make them fit to be the dwelling place of a holy God…What would happen if you believed it, if you came to the place where you knew it was true? Your life would never be the same. It would change our lives. It would change the face of Christianity. This is the lost message of the gospel, lost at least to a great many people. Small wonder. This is the last thing the Enemy wants the world to know. It would change everything. [37]

4. What specific changes do you sense the Lord leading you to make to combat the lies and schemes of the enemy to bring destruction into your life?

Take a few moments and ponder these lyrics from the hymn, *Come, Thou Fount of Every Blessing*. Pray these words as a commitment to stay close to the heart of God. Drawing near to Him and Him drawing near to you is your best weapon against the tactics and schemes of the evil one (James 4:7-8).

> *O to grace how great a debtor, Daily I'm constrained to be.*
> *Let Thy goodness like a fetter, Bind my wand'ring heart to thee;*
> *Prone to wander, Lord, I feel it, Prone to leave the God I love.*
> *Here's my heart, O take and seal it. Seal it for Thy courts above.* [38]

Nothing will protect your heart more than the truth of God's Word. Read it. Believe it. Meditate on it. Pray it. Stand on it.

Eldredge offers these cautionary words: "Our hearts do matter to God. Now, the enemy will tell you this is foolish…Remember: he fears you – fears your heart's coming alive and full and free. Caring for your heart is an act of obedience. It is an act of love, an act of faith, an act of war." [39]

5. In what other ways has God spoken to you through His Word in Ephesians 2?

Jesus died to give you life. Live it abundantly. *In Him.*

405 Come, Thou Fount

ROBERT ROBINSON

JOHN WYETH

Filled up to all the fullness of God

Ephesians 3

"Filled up to all the fullness of God"

Ephesians 3

Many do not advance in Christian progress because they stick to penances and particular exercises while they neglect the love of God – and the love of God is the purpose for which we live. [1]
~ Bro. Lawrence

The letter to the Ephesians teaches us some of the most crucial principles surrounding our position in Christ. In Ephesians 1 and 2, Paul reminds his audience of not only who they are in Christ, but Whose they are – and what that means for the power at work within them. In Ephesians 4, he will challenge his audience to use the power available to them to go deeper in their walk with Christ. But first, Ephesians 3 records a heartfelt reminder of the love of Christ.

If we are honest, most of us doubt that we are worthy of being used by God. And I would venture to say nearly all of us think we don't have what it takes to do big things for God. But none of that matters in the presence of Jesus. His mighty power is at work in our lives in even our darkest moments.

Paul's goal as he writes Ephesians 3 is to assure the believers in Ephesus of one thing: That they are deeply loved. But not loved by just anyone - loved by their Creator. And he doesn't want them to simply have knowledge of this love – but to know it by experience. And not just through any ordinary experience – but to experience it in ways that are abundantly beyond all they could ever even think to ask.

Why would Paul ask for these things for believers? Because it is through this knowledge that we "grow up" in Christ. It's how we are "filled up to all the fullness of God." It's how we look into the face of our Creator and receive the love He desires to pour out on us. And when we receive that love, we glorify Him and move forward in our calling.

As we will discover, Ephesians 3 contains great mysteries to be revealed. And perhaps the greatest mystery of all is the ability to comprehend the breadth and length, the height and depth of the love of Christ.

Let's begin our study by asking God to open the eyes of our hearts to His Word, so that we can know and experience His love in a deeper way.

Father, thank You for the immeasurable love You have shown me through Christ. Please strengthen my heart by Your Spirit so that I may truly grasp how wide and long and high and deep Your love truly is. Help me not just to know it in my mind, but to experience it deeply in my soul. May Your love shape how I see myself, how I see others, and how I live each day. Teach me to rest in the fullness of Your presence – to be filled with all the fullness of God. Let Your love be the foundation of my life, transforming me from the inside out.
In Jesus' name, Amen.

Day One

Ephesians 3:1-6

Read Ephesians 3 in its entirety to help you get a general idea of Paul's message in this chapter.

1. As you read, underline the key words and then write them in the chart below. Use a purple pen to mark every instance of "In Him," "In Christ," or the equivalent.

Key Words in Ephesians 3

2. Who does Paul appear to be addressing specifically?

3. How would you describe Paul's tone toward the Ephesians in this chapter?

4. How would you describe Paul's affections toward Christ in this chapter?

Now, let's zoom in on this rich section of Scripture as Paul encourages the growing congregation in Ephesus toward a deeper union with Christ.

Ephesians 3 opens with an introductory phrase that causes us to look back at what Paul has just written to the Ephesians in Chapter 2. Paul is getting ready to pray for the Ephesian believers, and he wants them to have fresh in their minds the reason behind his prayer. He starts his thought – "For this reason" – then gets sidetracked for 11 verses, before beginning to pray in verse 14.

As a bit of review for where Paul is headed, take a look back at Ephesians 2:17-22.

5. Based on what you just read in Ephesians 2:17-22, why has Paul devoted his life to serving the Gentiles?

From a legal standpoint, Paul is imprisoned because the Jews abhor the message he has been touting – Jesus as the Messiah and salvation for non-Jews. They have pressured the Romans to arrest Paul, claiming that he is causing a rebellion, something the Romans definitely do not want to deal with. [2] But Paul does not consider himself a prisoner of Rome. He sees the reason for his imprisonment from a divine perspective.

6. Who does Paul say he is a prisoner of? (3:1)

Whether he is freely roaming about the country, on house arrest, or chained to a Roman guard, Paul knows that everything he does is for Jesus. He is a servant of Christ. Long before Paul becomes a prisoner of Nero, he is taken captive by the grace of Jesus. And from that moment on, he considers himself a "prisoner" of Christ Jesus, a title he uses often (Ephesians 3:1, 4:1; Philemon 1:1, 1:9).

What about us? Can we use those words to describe ourselves? Can we say that Jesus has captured every part of us? As paradoxical as it may seem, being a "prisoner of Christ Jesus," willing to do whatever is needed to carry out His calling, is where Paul finds true joy. And the same should be true for us.

Read Ephesians 3:2-6.

This is where Paul begins to digress before later returning to his "for this reason" thought in verse 14. This entire section is dedicated to the Gentiles. Paul is speaking directly to an audience who would have once thought they were excluded from the gospel: The unclean ones. The rejected ones. The outsiders. This gospel is for them! This message is Paul's mission.

7. What phrase does Paul use to refer to his ministry calling to the Gentiles? (v. 2)

The *Life Application Bible Commentary* gives unique insight into Paul's assignment:

> "The administration of God's grace" refers to the special stewardship, trust, or commission that Paul had been given, and the grace and authority he had been given in order to fulfill it...God had given Paul this special stewardship for the sake of others, not just for Paul's own benefit. God had assigned Paul the special work of preaching the Good news to the Gentiles. [3]

8. Read Acts 9:15. What does this tell us about God's call on Paul's life?

What must this have meant to this Gentile audience? In our modern-day, western culture, we may not readily understand the level of brazen hostility the Jewish religious leaders felt toward the Gentiles. All their lives, the Gentiles have heard that they would not and could not be saved. Imagine the looks on their faces and the burning in their hearts when the Apostle Paul freely invites them in, based on the authority of the risen Messiah.

9. What word does Paul repeat in Ephesians 3:3-4?

The meaning of this word is a little different from how we understand it today. John Stott explains the richer understanding the Greeks of the day would have had for what Paul is saying:

> In English, a "mystery" is something dark, obscure, secret, puzzling. What is "mysterious" is inexplicable, even incomprehensible. The Greek word *mysterion* is different, however. Although still a "secret," it is no longer closely guarded but open...More simply, *mysterion* is a truth hitherto hidden from human knowledge or understanding but now disclosed by the revelation of God. [4]

This mystery is given to Paul, but not as new information. That's why understanding this meaning is important. Salvation for all people has always been God's plan.

Charles Swindoll explains that Paul has been given special insight into this mystery:

> The revelation of this mystery was...unheard of prior to its unveiling to the New Testament apostles and prophets (3:5) – recipients of those foundational ministries established by Christ through the power of the Holy Spirit for the first generation of the church (2:20). Previous generations had been told of a coming Messiah, but they had assumed He would be a Messiah for the Jews only. They had no idea that the salvation promised through their Davidic King would cross the boundaries of Israel to be offered to the Gentiles. [5]

10. Read Genesis 22:18. Who did God say would be blessed by Abraham?

This promise was first given to the Jews, but it was always intended for the Gentiles – for all nations (Romans 1:16). Paul's message, while revolutionary to his audience, was not actually something new. The "mystery" he spoke of was the fulfillment of a promise God had made long ago to Abraham. It wasn't until after Christ's death that this promise was fully revealed and understood – no longer hidden, no longer a mystery.

11. How has this "mystery" been revealed to Paul? (v. 5)

God has entrusted Paul with the stewardship of the mystery, calling him to share it with the Gentiles. Warren Wiersbe expounds on Paul's responsibilities to the Gentiles, "It was not enough simply to win them to Christ and form them into local assemblies. He was also to teach them their wonderful position in Christ as members of the Body, sharing God's grace equally with Jews." [6]

The "mystery" involves three ways that the Gentiles are united with Jews (v. 6).

12. From what you've learned so far, what do you think these three phrases mean?

Phrase	Meaning
Gentiles are "fellow heirs."	
Gentiles are "fellow members of the body."	
Gentiles are "fellow partakers of the promise in Christ Jesus."	

DID YOU KNOW?

Why was this "mystery" so revolutionary? And why was this so difficult for the Jews at the time to understand? Here is a helpful insight: "While the early prophets had written of the inclusion of Gentiles with Jews (Isaiah 49:6; 56:6-7), their writings were interpreted to mean that the Gentiles could become proselytes. The extent of this inclusion and the radical change – the Jews and Gentiles becoming one body under Christ's headship – was not even considered." [7]

To say that the Jews and Gentiles are now one *In Him* is radical indeed! Paul wants to assure the Gentiles that his message is not some special provision for them or that they were going to be given some hand-me-down, lightweight version of the gospel. No – this is the <u>same</u> promise.

Why does this matter today? Because, whether you're Jew or Gentile, no matter your background, even if you're "far off," this gospel is for you. You haven't been given a hand-me-down gospel or some leftover grace. *In Him*, all that is God's is yours – and as we'll continue to see, His power is going to work on your behalf in ways you could never imagine.

Day Two

Ephesians 3:7-13

In this section, Paul continues the aside he began in verse 2, elaborating on the mystery that has now been made known through the gospel and how he has been entrusted to share it with others. Paul takes no credit for his prominent role among the believers of his day. In fact, he views his mission with great humility, knowing that in and of himself, he is totally unqualified for the task.

If you know much about Paul, you may be thinking, "More than just about anyone, with all his knowledge and religious prestige, he would've been the superstar God was looking for!" But God isn't looking for superstars. He's looking for "jars of clay" (2 Corinthians 4:7, NLT) He can shine through. And that is exactly how He used Paul.

Read Ephesians 3:7-8.

1. To what does Paul attribute the assignment given to him for preaching to the Gentiles? (v. 7)

Paul isn't "able" to fulfill his calling all on his own – it's not the result of his knowledge or persuasive skills, though he certainly has those in abundance. He is empowered through the gift of God's grace and the working of His power. God is the One who will accomplish the spread of the gospel. The only thing Paul brings to the equation is his willingness.

2. According to verse 8, how does Paul view himself?

Charles Spurgeon notes, "While Paul was thus thankful for his office, his success in it greatly humbled him. The fuller a vessel becomes, the deeper it sinks in the water. A plenitude of grace is a cure for pride." [8] By worldly, and even religious standards, Paul might have room for boasting, but not when he sees himself in view of the cross. This isn't false humility or self-deprecation. And the cross certainly did not create shame over his past. But Paul is self-aware. He knows the life he has been saved from. He has a similar sentiment as King David when God had promised him the kingdom: "What more can I say to you? You know what your servant is really like, Sovereign Lord" (2 Samuel 7:20, NLT).

Do you identify with Paul and David? Do you feel like the least useful of all the saints? Do you wonder how or why God would use you when He, more than anyone else, knows what you are really like?

Then take a moment to wonder at the gospel. Because that's exactly what Jesus does. He came as the least of these, died as the least of these, and was raised so the least of us could be brought in by His grace. Yes, He knows what we are really like, but He chose to save us anyway. And then use us anyway.

Isn't that an amazing phrase in verse 8: "the unfathomable riches of Christ"? The "endless treasures available…in Christ" (NLT). "The unsearchable riches of Christ" (ESV). Spurgeon speaks to these "unsearchable riches" of God's grace:

> I am bold to tell you that my Master's riches of grace are so unsearchable, that He delights to forgive and forget enormous sin; the bigger the sin, the more glory to His grace. If you are over head and ears in debt, He is rich enough to discharge your liabilities. If you are at the very gates of hell, He is able to pluck you from the jaws of destruction. [9]

3. Take a moment to write a prayer of thanksgiving for the "unfathomable, "unsearchable," "endless treasures" that are yours *In Him.*

Read Ephesians 3:9.

4. What does Paul say his role is in relation to the mystery? (v. 9)

Paul's responsibility includes more than merely defining the mystery. He is called to explain how God is globally expanding the gospel to include every person. Wiersbe helps us to understand the significance of Paul's calling:

> Certainly the Old Testament clearly states that God will save the Gentiles through Israel, but nowhere are we told that both Jews and Gentiles will form a new creation, the Church, the Body of Christ. It was this mystery that the Spirit revealed to Paul and other leaders in the early Church, and that was so difficult for the Jews to accept. [10]

Read Ephesians 3:10.

When I first read this verse, my mind screeched to a halt. Let me encourage you to read it once again, this time aloud, so that you can fully understand what Paul is saying.

5. Write Ephesians 3:10 in your own words.

Isn't that astounding? God is going to use the Church to reveal His "manifold wisdom to the rulers and the authorities in the heavenly places." You would think it would be the other way around, that God would commission His angels to reveal His wisdom to us. But that's not what the Bible says. We are the ones now being entrusted with that task. The Greek word for "manifold" is *polypoikilos,* which conveys the idea of something being variegated or multifaceted. [11] Wiersbe explains that "manifold" implies "the beauty and variety of God's wisdom in His great plan of salvation." [12]

And "the rulers and the authorities in the heavenly places" are not just God's angels. Paul is referencing the entire invisible world, including the evil powers. The *Life Application Bible Commentary* sheds more light on what Paul is saying:

> All powers in the heavenlies, whether good or evil, will receive their understanding of God's great mystery from humans. God builds his church on earth from saved sinners, who, through God's grace and mercy, received their salvation through Jesus Christ's death on the cross. No angel or demon can comprehend what God has done. [13]

Peter says something similar in 1 Peter 1:12, "It was revealed to them that they were not serving themselves, but you, in these things which now have been announced to you through those who preached the gospel to you by the Holy Spirit sent from Heaven – things into which angels long to look." Swindoll observes that Peter is talking about the "good angels who had to catch up to understand what God had planned to do through Christ in the Church," [14] and then comments,

> If angels of God had a steep learning curve to master, surely the wicked spirits were left in the dust! In fact, Paul says that if the rulers of this world – likely the demonic powers working through human earthly powers – had understood the plan of God in advance, "they would not have crucifed the Lord of glory" (1 Corinthians 2:8). [15]

God had hidden His great plan since the beginning of the world because if the forces of darkness had known that Jesus was God, here to die and rise again so that man could escape the curse of death and be restored to God, they wouldn't have fallen for it.

But now, all believers, every one of us, is a steward of this great truth!

Read Ephesians 3:11–13.

Verse 11 reminds us that all of this was God's purpose from the beginning – and it was accomplished through Jesus. A united church, all nations bowing before God and giving Him glory, was always the plan. And it's Jesus who makes this possible. All who come to faith *In Him* will experience this. But wait, there's more.

6. What does Paul say believers now have in Christ? (v. 12)

Because of our faith *In Him*, we are able to actually approach Jesus and boldly talk to Him with confidence.

7. Read Hebrews 4:16. What does it mean to you that you are able to approach God with <u>all</u> that is on your heart?

When the grace of God got hold of Paul, he began to have "tribulations" (v. 13). We're not sure what these "tribulations" were. It could've been his living conditions, his physical state, or even just his anguish over the lost.

8. Why does Paul tell the Ephesians not to "lose heart" over his sufferings? (v. 13)

We don't think often about the implications of Paul's actions toward us. As he obeyed God's call on his life, he made an eternal impact on his audience – and we are part of that audience. If you're a Gentile reading this, Paul was suffering "for your glory." In other words, he was suffering for the sake of your salvation. Because of what Paul and other members of the early church were willing to endure, the gospel made it to you and me.

Who is God calling you to "suffer" for so they may experience God's glory? Your "tribulation" may not look like imprisonment or persecution. It may mean a seemingly awkward conversation in which you introduce someone to Jesus for the first time. It may mean serving someone in need in such a way that it impacts your comfort or your bank account. But rest assured, God will use every bit of your suffering.

So don't lose heart. Just as Paul's suffering had purpose, so does yours. Every act of obedience, every sacrifice, every step outside your comfort zone has the potential to echo into eternity. You never know how God might use your willingness to endure for the sake of someone else's salvation. Let Paul's example remind you: Glory is on the other side of the cost. And someone's story with Jesus might begin because you were willing to carry the weight of grace.

Day Three

Ephesians 3:14-19

Paul has just devoted the last 11 verses to expounding on the revelation given to him by God on behalf of the Gentiles, the unity between Jews and Gentiles, and the glorified position all believers have because of their faith in Christ. But all of that is an aside to where he was originally going with his statement in Ephesians 3:1. You might remember that we started this week with Paul's statement, "For this reason…." And now he repeats that opening phrase as he picks back up to resume his prayer over the church at Ephesus.

Read Ephesians 3:14-19.

Having just explained our ability to go to the Father with boldness and confidence, Paul does exactly that as he begins praying. Much like his earlier prayer in Ephesians 1:15-21, this is a deeply Trinitaritan prayer: Each Person of the Godhead – the Father, Son, and Holy Spirit – is intimately involved in the things Paul asks on behalf of believers.

1. To Whom does Paul kneel before and direct his prayer? (vv. 14-15)

This kneeling posture represents humility and reverence in contrast to the common practice of standing to pray (Mark 11:25; Luke 18:11,13).

As Paul prays, he makes six heartfelt supplications on behalf of the Ephesian believers. As we consider each request, fill in the blanks on the headers:

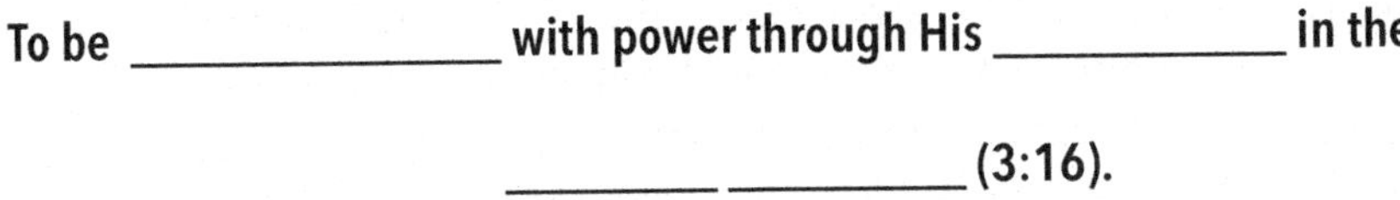

To be _______________ with power through His ____________ in the

________ _________ (3:16).

DID YOU KNOW?

English majors beware: In verses 14-19, Paul once again uses one of his favorite writing techniques: the run-on sentence. In these six verses, we won't see a period until the end of 3:19. But Tony Merida points out the importance of this section: "The first three chapters are about who we are in Christ. The next three chapters are about how we are to live. Understanding both is essential for Christians, but you need more than knowledge of these things. Sandwiched between these two sections is this prayer for power." [16]

The *English Standard Version* (ESV) uses the word "grant" in this verse – that the Father "may grant you to be strengthened…" The source of our power is unmistakable. We are powerless without the mercy of God and His willingness to grant us His power.

In Ephesians 4–6, Paul is going to place a high calling on the believers in Ephesus. He is going to challenge them to take the information he's just given them and act on it – to utilize the power available to them. It's been said that the Holy Spirit is the electricity, and all we have to do to shine for God is plug into our Power Source. We can't muster this power on our own. Paul is praying for believers everywhere to be granted this power "according to the riches of His glory."

The power Paul is talking about is not physical power. This is not the "when the going gets tough, the tough get going" type of power. This isn't God making us physically strong necessarily, though He can if He wants! Paul specifies that he prays they will be strengthened in their "inner being."

2. Why do you think it's more important for you to be strengthened in your "inner man" versus simply physical strength?

Paul's prayer for inner spiritual strength leads to his second request:

So that ____________ may ____________ in your hearts through ____________ (3:17a).

Paul is not praying for Christ to come and dwell in our hearts. He is writing to believers. What Paul is praying for is spiritual depth, something more than the faith that takes up residence in our hearts at the time of our salvation. Merida makes this observation:

> Paul is speaking about something more than just Christ dwelling in our hearts. Paul is talking about Christ ruling in the heart. Paul's choice of words for dwell is important. He uses a strong word. He could use the word that means "to inhabit," but instead he uses the word that means "to settle down." It carried the idea of a permanent resident, not a short-lived resident. [17]

In *My Heart Christ's Home*, Robert Munger compares the Christian life to a house where Jesus moves room by room. In the library of the mind, He replaces worthless thoughts with His Word. In the dining room, He exchanges sinful cravings for godly virtues. He continues through each area – the living room of fellowship, the workshop, the hall closet of hidden sins – cleansing and transforming as He goes. Only when every space is surrendered can Christ truly be at home. For Christ to dwell in our hearts through faith means allowing Him full access to every part of our lives, because we trust Him and therefore become obedient to His Word. [18]

Third, Paul prays for love to become a dominant quality in their lives:

That you, being ____________ and ____________ in ____________ (3:17b).

Wiersbe draws attention to imagery behind the verbs Paul uses:

> The verb rooted moves us into the plant world. The tree must get its roots deep into the soil if it is to have both nourishment and stability, and the Christian must have his spiritual roots deep into the love of God. Psalm 1:1-3 is a perfect description of this word, and Jeremiah 17:5-8 is a good commentary on it. One of the most important questions a Christian can ask himself is, "From what do I draw my nourishment and my stability?" If there is to be power in the Christian life, then there must be depth. The roots must go deeper and deeper into the love of Christ. Grounded is an architectural term; it refers to the foundations on which we build. [19]

Together, these two verbs point to love as both the source and foundation of life for the believer. This kind of love only comes through Christ. R.C. Sproul notes, "The form of these verbs indicates past action that has taken place and is continuing." [20] In other words, it is Christ's love that has rooted and grounded us, and it continues to hold us fast. Through His death and resurrection, Jesus paid for our sin once and for all. That's why He cried, "It is finished!" (John 19:30) from the cross. His completed work remains the anchor of our souls (Hebrews 6:19), offering steadfast security for every believer.

3. Why do you think it's important that love is what roots us and grounds us in our faith?

4. How is this different from good behavior or religious works being our foundation?

Paul's fourth request is that somehow, some way, we may be able to grasp how loved we are by Jesus:

May be able to __________________ with all the saints what is the ____________ and _______________ and _____________ and _______________ (3:18).

When my dad lost his battle to cancer in 2022, people kept telling me, "You are so loved." Of all the words of comfort people could've given me, it was interesting how often people gave me that particular reminder. But when you're grieving that deeply, sometimes all a girl needs to know is that she's loved. And that's what Paul is essentially saying here. He's telling them and us, "Hey look. It's going to get tough out there. The battle is going to be hard. You're going to have good days and bad days, and you're going to want to quit. That's why you need to know – you are more loved than you could ever imagine."

Fifth, Paul prays for believers:

To know the ____________ of Christ which _________________ __________________ (3:19a).

Does this sound a bit like an oxymoron? Is Paul praying that believers will know something that can't be known? The *Amplified Bible's* expanded paraphrase helps us out: "[That you may really come] to know [practically, through experience for yourselves] the love of Christ, which far surpasses mere knowledge [without experience]…." Paul's desire, knowing what they really need, is that they will come to know the love of Christ, not through mere knowledge and facts, but by their own personal experience. As Sproul says, this knowledge "goes beyond head and comes into the heart."[21] Just like gushing water cannot be held back, so it is with the love of Christ. His love overflows every boundary we try to put around it. It's not measured, rationed, or reserved – it pours out on us in abundance.

Sometimes, experiencing the love of the Father comes through moments of affliction. It's not always the warm sunshine on a summer day that causes you to feel His love. Sometimes it's His presence in the darkest storm that reminds you He loves you and He will never forsake you. That is the type of awareness Paul is praying for.

5. Describe a time when you have experienced the love of Christ. If you are struggling to remember a time, write a prayer asking Him to help you experience this love. He longs to show it to you.

Paul's final request is a prayer for God's fullness:

That you may be ____________ _________ to all the _________________ of ____________ (3:19b).

Let's think about the progression of Paul's prayer. The inner strength of the Holy Spirit, which God gives to those who seek Him in prayer, allows Christ to dwell fully in our hearts. When Christ is at home in us, we become rooted in His love, secure, confident, and able to love others. This deepening love leads to the fullness of God in us: His presence, power, and life filling every part. This is what it means to be "filled up to all the fullness of God."

Ultimately, Paul's prayer is a call to spiritual maturity, to grow in Christlikeness. And that won't happen by accident. It begins with a daily surrender to the Spirit's strengthening work, a growing trust in Christ's love, and a willingness to let that love shape how we live and love others.

What step can you take today to move deeper into the fullness of God?

Day Four

Ephesians 3:20-21

The difficulty with writing about Ephesians 3:20-21 is: What more is there to say? In the middle of this letter, at what turns into the hinge point of his entire message to the church in Ephesus, Paul bursts into praise. And this outburst has become one of the most beloved passages of hope and encouragement to Christians for centuries.

Take a moment to read Ephesians 3:20-21. Whether you're reading it for the first time or the millionth time, stop to read it slowly and take in these God-breathed words.

Let's take a look back to remind ourselves what led Paul to this outburst of praise.

1. Read Ephesians 3:18-19 again. What aspect of God's character inspires worship in Paul?

As he says in his letter to the Corinthians, "Christ's love compels us" (2 Corinthians 5:14). We can't overstate the importance of understanding the love of the Father. We can't truly comprehend it, but when we think on His love, it should drive us to worship – and it should inspire us to have courage.

2. What does God's power accomplish? (v. 20a)

3. What does Paul disclose about the power of God? (v. 20b)

DID YOU KNOW?

These verses are what many refer to as one of Paul's doxologies. If you've never heard the word "doxology," it simply means words of praise to God. "The word *doxology* comes from the Greek *doxa*, ('glory, splendor, grandeur') and *logos*, ('word' or 'speaking')." [22]

When I was first discipled and God's Word began coming alive to me in new ways, there were three words I felt I couldn't escape from: He. Is. Able.

To me, that phrase covered a multitude of sins - literally. But it also took the pressure off of me. He is able. It's not up to me. None of it. My righteousness, my achievements, my purpose, my "influence" on this world - are not dependent on me. It requires my cooperation and obedience, but not my power. And thank goodness, because I fail a lot. Every day, in fact. But He is able, and His power works in me – and in you.

This theme of "power" is key in Paul's letter, and his point is that God's power dwells within us. Sproul reminds us, "Paul keeps coming back to that theme in Ephesians. That power by which God creates the universe and displays His operations in all the realm of nature is the same power that God has caused to indwell the believer." [23]

4. As a follower of Jesus, how does it encourage you to know that right now, in this very moment, the power of God is at work in you?

The power of God is an amazing thing to ponder. We can't fathom all that God can do as He works on our behalf. Paul had it right: He is able to do "far more abundantly beyond all we ask or think." I love how the NIV phrases it, "Now to him who is able to do immeasurably more than all we ask or imagine." But perhaps nobody nails it on the head better than the *Amplified Bible* that says He is "able to [carry out His purpose and] do super abundantly, far over and above all that we [dare] ask or think [infinitely beyond our highest prayers, desires, thoughts, hopes, or dreams]."

5. What are you daring to ask God for? What are you thinking about asking for but fear it's too much? What is your "highest prayer, desire, thought, hope, or dream" that you've been hesitant or fearful to pray? Write a prayer boldly asking God for that, knowing He can do even more than you can ask or think. In fact, immeasurably more.

Read Ephesians 3:21 again.

Paul's doxology is that of worship, but it's also a call to action.

6. Where is God's glory displayed? (v. 21a)

"To Him be glory in the church…." With these words, Paul reminds us that the Church is not just a place we go – it's the people of God living for the glory of God. In Ephesians 3:10, we saw that God's wisdom is made known through the church. That means our lives, our worship, our service, and our love all have one purpose: to glorify the Son of God. And when our hearts are set on His glory, God gladly pours out His power to do more than we could ask or imagine. He uses ordinary people – people like us – to accomplish His extraordinary purposes.

7. How far does God's glory extend? (v. 21b)

For centuries, Satan has sought to snuff out the church. But, because of the power at work within us, the church cannot be stopped. Because of Christ Jesus, the church will carry on "to all generations forever and ever. Amen." What a promise! You are part of something eternal, something bigger than yourself, something that reaches beyond your lifetime.

8. As part of the Church, how is God calling you to bring glory to Him?

Take a moment to reflect before you answer. What gifts has God placed in you? What passions stir your heart? If you're unsure, ask someone close to you – a friend, a mentor, or a family member. Sometimes others see in us what we struggle to see in ourselves. As you discover your gifts, remember: God gave them to you for a reason – so that you can point others to Him and bring Him glory.

You were created to know God and to make Him known. His glory is not just something we admire, it's something we reflect. May your life, joined with the life of the Church, shine brightly for His glory, for this generation, and those to come. "To Him be glory!"

Day Five

Satan's strategy: Discouragement

One of the most subtle and effective weapons Satan uses against believers is **discouragement**, and because it is so successful, it's one he uses on all of us. But often, we fail to recognize it because it doesn't always look like an obvious attack. Sometimes it shows up like exhaustion. Or silence. Or frustration that something <u>still</u> hasn't changed. The enemy knows he cannot take away our salvation, but as we discussed in Lesson Two, he will try to make us ineffective by discouraging us with his persistent lies. He says things like:

> "You're not making a difference."
> "Why isn't this changing?"
> "God must be disappointed in you."

You see, the enemy doesn't have to pull you off course in one big leap. He just needs to plant enough doubt and discouragement to slow you down, wear you out, or make you question if God is even paying attention. And he knows exactly <u>when</u> to aim these fiery darts:

- When prayers go unanswered.
- When progress feels invisible.
- When comparison creeps in.

1. Is there an area where Satan is trying to discourage you? Name the lie and expose it to the light by writing it down.

Satan's strategy is to strike when we are vulnerable so that we are caught off guard and begin to listen to his lies. Then he keeps on and on until it begins to "feel" like what he is saying is the truth, so we start to believe his lies. And before we realize it, we've disconnected from the very Source of our strength. But that is not the way God has called us to live. In Galatians 2:20a, Paul reminds us: "I have been crucified with Christ; and it is no longer I who live, but Christ lives in me."

You don't walk alone. You don't fight in your own strength. <u>Jesus lives in you.</u> That means your identity is secure even on your worst days. The weight is not on your performance; it's on His presence.

Several years ago, I co-taught a class at our church for women who had struggled with addictions. I felt totally unqualified to lead this group of courageous women. But week after week, God showed up, and something beautiful happened. We built a sisterhood grounded in honesty, healing, and God's Word.

Everyone in the group, including the teachers, had deep needs that only Jesus could meet. One night, in an exercise similar to question 5 in yesterday's homework, we challenged everyone to write a specific prayer request, something that fell into the category of "exceeding abundantly beyond all that we ask or think." The requests were raw and real:

- "Mend my son and daughter-in-law's relationship."
- "Healing and staying sober."
- "A better relationship with my son."
- "Clear direction in ministry."
- "A job and a place to live."
- "To ease my ex-husband's anger toward me and love me again."

Then, we added a slight twist to the exercise and asked them to end their prayer request with "...or something better." [24]

- "Mend my son and daughter-in-law's relationship… or something better."
- "Healing and staying sober… or something better."
- "A better relationship with my son… or something better."
- "Clear direction in ministry… or something better"
- "A job and a place to live… or something better"
- "To ease my ex-husband's anger toward me and love me again… or something better."

Those three words, "or something better," changed everything. They became a statement of surrender. A way of saying, "God, I trust You more than I trust my plan. And even if it doesn't look the way I want, I believe You can do something better." We placed those requests in envelopes decorated with the words "Exceeding Abundantly Beyond" from Ephesians 3:20, the verse that anchored our group:

> Now to Him who is able to do exceeding abundantly beyond all that we ask or think, according to the power that works within us (NASB, 1977).

That's the God we're trusting: Not One who simply meets expectations, but One who exceeds them. The God "who causes all things to work together for good" (Romans 8:28). The God who is "good "and only does "good" (Psalm 119:68). The God who dispatches "goodness and mercy " to follow us all the days of our lives (Psalm 23:6, NKJV).

Surely we can trust this One, our Father, to answer our request or to do something even better than we can ask or think!

2. Write yesterday's prayer request from question 5 again below. This time, end it with "... or something better."

3. How does praying in this way reframe your trust in God's character and plan?

Over the months in our group, when discouragement would creep in over a prayer yet unanswered, the words "or something better" would remind us that although God's timeline and outcomes might not match ours, His ways are always higher (Isaiah 55:9). Always wiser. Always rooted in love.

Recently, I realized something that revolutionized how I look at extended seasons of pleading, those times when we feel like we've asked God for the same thing over and over and over. It could be healing, restoration of a relationship, deliverance from crippling sin, forgiveness – it could be many things! Whatever it is, if we don't witness a breakthrough, we get tired of asking. And we assume God gets tired of hearing. Then, discouragement settles in. But what if the "something better" is that the intimacy of our relationship with Christ is deepened? What if we know Him better in the end from simply placing our requests before Him in humility, knowing He is equal parts sovereign and good?

That's what Paul meant when he talked about his "thorn in the flesh, a messenger of Satan to torment me" (2 Corinthians 12:7). While we don't know exactly what his "thorn" was, the enemy used it to discourage Paul. The apostle pleaded for God to take it away. But God didn't. Instead, God told him, "My grace is sufficient for you, for power is perfected in weakness" (2 Corinthians 12:9). Paul didn't get the answer he wanted, but he got more of Jesus!

Fanny Crosby, the renowned hymnwriter, understood this too. Crosby was blinded by an incorrect treatment for an illness when she was only six weeks old. Though she never received physical healing, God did "something better." He used her pain to bring glory to Himself. And even now, generations later, we still sing her hymns. Somehow, knowing her story makes the lyrics even richer: "And give Him the glory, great things He hath done!" [25]

Friend, Satan is clever, but he's not creative. He reuses the same tactics over and over. Discouragement. Doubt. Delay. But when those fiery darts come, we don't stand in our strength, we stand in God's. When you are discouraged, let the promise of Ephesians 3:20-21 call you back to the truth:

> Now to Him who is able to do far more abundantly beyond all that we ask or think, according to the power that works within us, to Him be the glory…forever and ever. Amen.

As we seek Him and experience His love working within us, as we live *In Him*, we will not only be filled with courage, we will "be filled up to all the fullness of God."

Heavenly Father, who are we that You would be mindful of us? Like David said,
"You know what Your servant is really like." And yet, You choose to use us anyway.
Thank You for Your grace and the immeasurable power You give us to live for You.
We couldn't do it on our own. Thank You for loving us more than we can even comprehend
and for working on our behalf in bigger ways than we could ask or imagine.
God, please draw us closer to You and let us see Your power at work.
In Jesus' name, Amen.

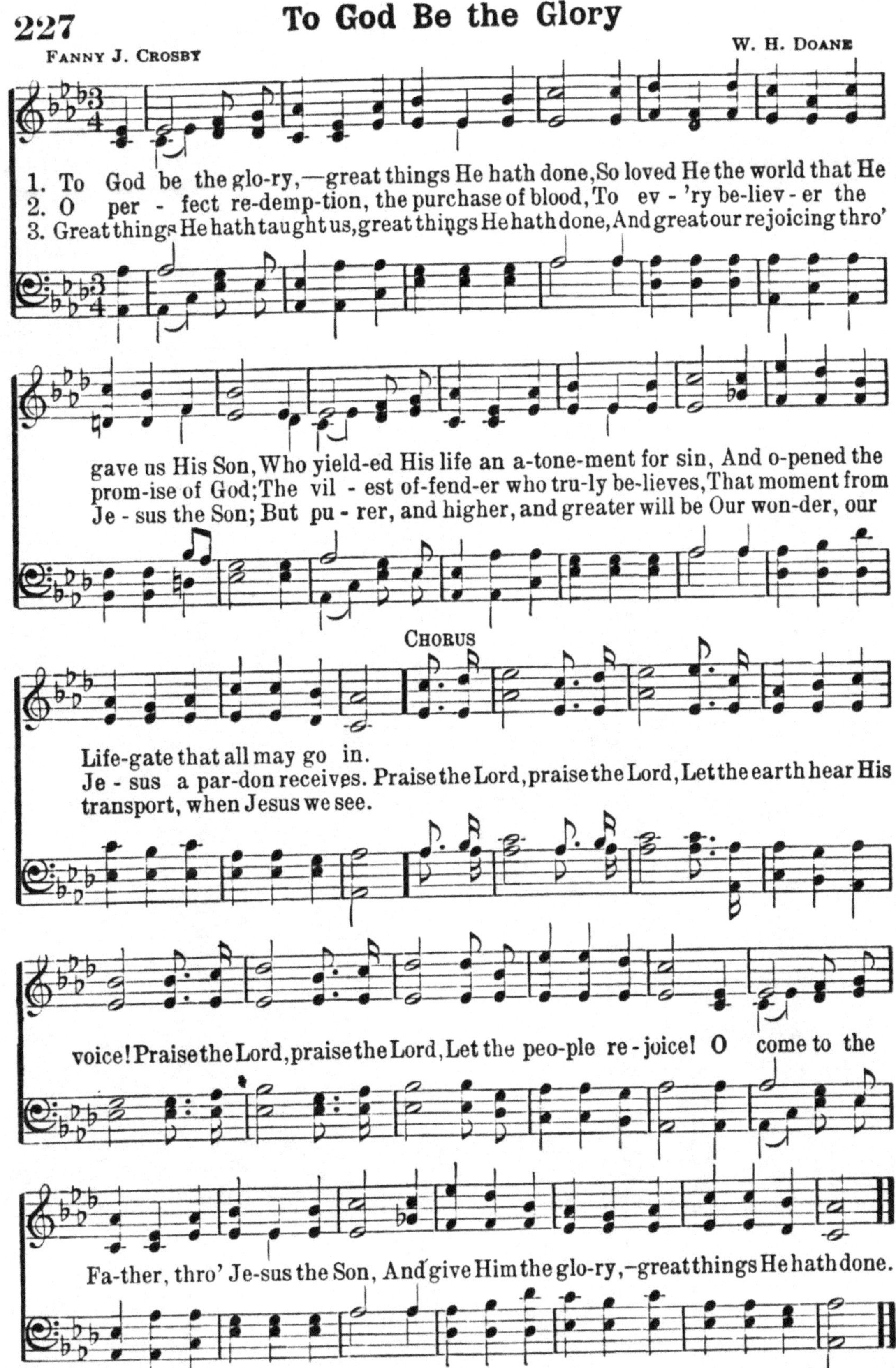
227
To God Be the Glory
Fanny J. Crosby
W. H. Doane
1. To God be the glo-ry,—great things He hath done, So loved He the world that He
2. O per - fect re-demp-tion, the purchase of blood, To ev - 'ry be-liev - er the
3. Great things He hath taught us, great things He hath done, And great our rejoicing thro'
gave us His Son, Who yield-ed His life an a-tone-ment for sin, And o-pened the
prom-ise of God; The vil - est of-fend-er who tru-ly be-lieves, That moment from
Je - sus the Son; But pu - rer, and higher, and greater will be Our won-der, our
Chorus
Life-gate that all may go in.
Je - sus a par-don receives. Praise the Lord, praise the Lord, Let the earth hear His
transport, when Jesus we see.
voice! Praise the Lord, praise the Lord, Let the peo-ple re - joice! O come to the
Fa-ther, thro' Je-sus the Son, And give Him the glo-ry,—great things He hath done.

Walk in a manner worthy

Ephesians 4:1–16

"Walk in a manner worthy"

Ephesians 4:1-16

Tidbit #1: My husband owns a pickup truck. Don't they all? It's usually his vehicle of choice. But for the past two years, while he has been recovering from a broken back, I've done most of the driving – a major role reversal in our marriage. And even when he does drive, he opts for my car because it's easier to get into and far more comfortable than his truck.

Tidbit #2: In 2021, I was diagnosed with cancer. By God's grace, I'm now cancer-free, though I still take medication to help prevent its return. One of those meds, in its infinite wisdom, convinced my way-past-menopausal body to revisit that stage, just for fun. As a result, I now suffer from relentless hot flashes, regardless of the temperature around me. It's as if I am creating my own personal weather system.

Now, with those two details in mind, let me tell you about something that happened recently:

I was speaking at a Bible conference and was well into my message – totally all-in, with my full-on sanguine mode activated. Then, right as I was honing in on an important point, a mega hot flash hit. It felt like someone flipped the internal combustion switch inside me, triggering a nuclear meltdown. Beads of sweat began to roll down my face, cutting rivulets through my makeup and dripping off my chin. I'd love to say I was merely "glowing" – that genteel Southern euphemism for perspiration – but no, friends, I was all-out sweating. My hair quickly plastered to my head, sweat literally began dropping onto the platform, and my clothes fused to my body like a second, soggy skin. I looked like I'd just run a 5K… in August…here in Tennessee… wearing a wool blazer.

To add to the drama, the sanctuary was freezing. Women were bundled in scarves, sweaters, and shawls like they were sitting inside the crisper drawer of a refrigerator. Meanwhile, there I was, creating my own microclimate – somewhere right in between tropical rainforest and lava flow. Now, I've gotten used to this regularly occurring event. Not thrilled about it, but used to it. However, I could feel the room shifting. The sweet women in the audience were exchanging worried glances, whispering, nudging their neighbors, probably wondering if they should call 911 or grab a mop. When I paused to explain, the older ladies gave me the "we've been there" nod, while the younger ones looked like they'd just witnessed a science experiment gone terribly wrong, and were seriously reconsidering their life choices…and maybe their seat location.

When the conference was over, my husband arrived in my car to pick me up. Noticing my obvious heatwave aftermath, he immediately began trying to cool down the interior of the car. While I was occupied with attempting to unstick my clothes and do something with my drenched hair, he kept fiddling with the knobs on the dashboard, without any success. After several minutes of battling the uncooperative air conditioner, he said "I think your air conditioner is broken."

In the South, between the heat and the humidity, those words create an emergency. So, we scheduled a repair, drove an hour to the auto shop, and dropped my car off. It wasn't long before we received a call back from the service mechanic. We braced ourselves, assuming the worst. With a bit of a chuckle, he said, "We found the problem. All the vents were shut off." See, I usually close them when I'm driving, something my husband didn't know. The air conditioner was working just fine. We were relieved...and slightly embarrassed.

In our upcoming lesson, Paul urges us to "walk in a manner worthy of the calling with which you have been called" (Ephesians 4:1). It's a high calling, and one we can only live out by depending on the indwelling power of the Holy Spirit.

The truth is, we have a choice. We can walk in step with the Spirit, allowing the life of Jesus to flow through us, or we can shut off that flow (like the air conditioner in my car) by slipping back into the flesh. Beloved, may we walk in such a way that others recognize we are *In Him*.

Day One

Ephesians 4:1-3

The turning point in Paul's carefully crafted letter to the Ephesian believers comes at the beginning of Ephesians 4. In the first three chapters, Paul has been expounding on our position in Christ, who we are *In Him*. He has been explaining that because of the life, death, resurrection, and ascension of Jesus, things have changed. As believers:

- We've had a change of address: We are now in Christ, located in the heavenly places.
- We've moved into a new community: We are adopted into God's family, where the language spoken is grace, redemption, and forgiveness.
- We're living in a different country: Once dead in sin, we are now alive with Christ, raised with Him, and seated with Him in the heavenlies.
- In fact, we're part of a brand new universe:
  - where the Spirit of God has moved in, right in the center of our being;
  - where God's love infiltrates our entire existence;
  - where we're being filled up with the fullness of God Himself.

With Ephesians 4, Paul begins explaining how to live out the new life we have received in Christ. While salvation is the free gift of God (Romans 6:23), true surrender calls us to personal holiness and practical righteousness.

So, what do we do? Enter in. Live like it's all true (because it is!). Mature *In Him*.

Before we begin to unravel Ephesians 4:1-16, prayerfully read through the entire passage. As you read, mark any instances of "In Him," "In Christ," or the equivalent in purple. Don't rush through. Read with an open heart. God is speaking. Let's be ready to listen.

1. How would you title this passage?

2. What verse is the most meaningful to you? Write it out here and include how it is speaking to you.

3. Making note of key words or phrases is a good habit for every Bible student to apply to their spiritual disciplines. This helps train your mind to look for repeated themes the writer is emphasizing. It will also help you string together the metanarrative of Scripture. Make a list of the key words in Ephesians 4:1-16.

Key Words in Ephesians 4:1-16

God's Word is unlike any other book. After all these years, I still open the Bible with a sense of wonder, and have never gotten over how fresh and "new" it is every time I read it. I love the way the writer of Hebrews describes Scripture, "For the Word of God is living and active and sharper than any two-edged sword, and piercing as far as the division of soul and spirit, of both joints and marrow, and able to judge the thoughts and intentions of the heart" (4:12). God's Word speaks with precision. It speaks with love. And it always speaks with purpose.

So as we turn now to our study of Ephesians 4, let's do so with open hands and soft hearts, ready to receive whatever the Lord wants to show us. He's not just teaching us – He's transforming us.

Read today's focal passage, Ephesians 4:1-3.

Paul begins this chapter with the word, "Therefore." While no one is certain of its origin, a common quote fits here, "When you see a 'therefore' in the Bible, you need to see what it is 'there for'." In this case, the "therefore" marks Paul's transition from positional truth to practical truth, from doctrine to duty, from principle to practice.

4. How does Paul describe himself? (v. 1)

This is the second time in his letter that Paul has refered to himself as a prisoner (3:1). John Phillips explains how Paul turns his prison into a pulpit:

> With these words Paul dignified his chains. He was not the prisoner of Nero. He was the prisoner of the Lord. A mere caesar could not arrest an apostle without God's permission. Paul was undaunted. Since he had to wear a chain, he wore it like a chain of office. If every move he made had to be accompanied by the rattle of fetters, he made each clank of iron a note in a melody of praise to God. He converted his prison into a palace. He considered himself shut up with God. [1]

By mentioning his imprisonment, Paul is reminding his readers of the high cost of following Christ. And the fact that Paul is in chains gives further weight to his words.

5. What does Paul "implore" his readers to do? (v. 1)

Chuck Swindoll explains the passionate urgency in Paul's words, "It's the Greek word *parakaleo*, which could also be translated 'urge' or 'exhort.'" [2] Paul is earnestly exhorting, even pleading with believers to lead a life "worthy" of their calling. The verb he uses is "walk." Not just exist. Walk. Life with the Living God is a step-by-step, daily, deliberate, forward-moving walk.

In light of all Paul has written in the first three chapters, we are, therefore, to walk out our faith in a manner that is pleasing to God and demonstrates we are *In Him*. Exposure to solid Biblical doctrine through a Bible-believing church where we will hear great preaching and teaching, as well as our own personal Bible study, is how we develop a working knowledge of God's Word. It is impossible to live a godly life without it. Right thinking leads to right living; right orthodoxy leads to right orthopraxy.

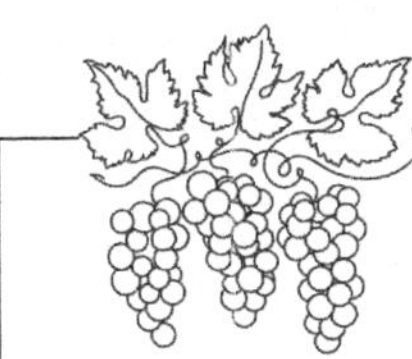

DID YOU KNOW?

The word "walk" is frequently used in the New Testament to refer to daily conduct. That is, as we go about our day, doing the tasks the Lord has assigned to us at home, at school, at work, in the church, and in the community, we are to walk worthy of Him.

6. What word does Paul use to describe the way believers are to walk? (v. 1)

How do we live "worthy" of our calling? The Greek word for "worthy," *axios*, paints a picture of what the worthy life is like. *Axios* refers to a balance, as on scales. In other words, what is on one side of the scales should equal the other side. So, "believers are to live 'in balance' with their calling. How they act should match what they believe." [3]

When my husband had his own business, for a brief time I served as his assistant and took on the task of answering his phone. On one such call, I spoke with a sub-contractor my husband knew well. To be honest, the man was rude and just plain ornery. When I told my husband about the challenging phone call, he replied, "I am shocked. That man is a Christian." I could not hide my surprise that the contentious caller professed to be a brother in Christ. Beloved, no one should ever be surprised to find out that we are believers! Walk worthy! We are *In Him*.

Paul then gives us a snapshot of what a "worthy" walk looks like in Ephesians 4:2-3.

7. Using the chart below, list the five qualities that describe how to walk in a worthy manner (vv. 2-3). Then look up the definitions for each word and summarize what each quality means.

Walking Worthy Qualities	Qualities Defined

Walking Worthy Qualities	Qualities Defined

In Galatians 5:19-23, Paul lists deeds of the flesh and the fruit of the Spirit:

> Now the deeds of the flesh are evident, which are: immorality, impurity, sensuality, idolatry, sorcery, enmities, strife, jealousy, outbursts of anger, disputes, dissensions, factions, envying, drunkenness, carousing, and things like these, of which I forewarn you, just as I have forewarned you, that those who practice such things will not inherit the Kingdom of God. But the fruit of the Spirit is love, joy, peace, patience, kindness, goodness, faithfulness, gentleness, self-control; against such things there is no law.

8. In the passage above, use two different colors (other than purple), to mark the deeds of the flesh with one color and the fruit of the Spirit with another. You will notice there is some overlap with Paul's list of the fruit of the Spirit in Galatians and the qualities of a worthy walk he lists in Ephesians 4:1-3.

In light of the gracious riches we have in Christ and the glorious reality of being part of the family of God, there are accompanying responsibilities. Swindoll laments that many Christians never seem "to move from the talk to the walk, from faith to life, from calling to commitment." [4]

Dear sister, let's not settle for just knowing the truth, we need to walk it out in a way that reflects the high calling we have received in Christ. May everyone around you today, believers and unbelievers alike, see that you are walking *In Him.*

Thank You, Lord, that I am in Christ. I desire to live a crucified life, being dead to sin and alive to Christ.
I want others to be able to see Christ in me, my hope of glory. I deliberately set my mind on things above and not on the chaos around me, because I have died and my life is hidden with Christ in God.
Lord, I ask You to help me walk worthy of the calling with which I have been called.
This is my sincere desire to go deeper with You. More of You, Jesus, and less of me.
In Jesus' name, Amen.

Day Two

Ephesians 4:4-6

In 1991, we built a home in Fayette County. Every day or so, we would drive out to the house to check on the progress. We quickly learned that everything takes longer than expected and costs more than promised. So there is that. But the entire construction process was fascinating to me: The foundation was poured. The structural pieces were set in place. The brick was set. Plumbing was installed. The sheetrock was nailed in place and plastered. Cabinetry was brought in. Little by little, a house emerged on what once was a pile of dirt.

Likewise, in the brief passage we are dissecting today, Paul writes about seven aspects of the faith that, like massive pillars of truth, support the framework of the universal Church.

Read Ephesians 4:4-6.

1. How many times is the word "one" used in these verses?

2. Read 1 Corinthians 3:11. Who is the foundation of the church?

3. The Church, built on the foundation of Christ, is supported by the seven pillars upon which the unity of the Church is built. Fill in the diagram below (Ephesians 4:4-6).

Paul makes it clear that all believers, regardless of denomination, worship preferences, location, ethnicity, race or any other things that might divide orthodox, Bible-believing, evangelical churches, hold to these seven truths. Tony Merida notes that Paul may be citing an early Christian creed and then goes on to help us understand the oneness we are to have:

> One Body. We share a common existence in Christ's church. We are diverse in background and gifting, but we are united as one.
>
> One Spirit. We share a common origin in the Holy Spirit's work. The Spirit is the One Who creates unity and empowers us to maintain it.
>
> One Hope. We share a common hope in Christ. Formerly, we were "without hope" (Ephesians 2:12, NIV) until we were called to Christ. Now we have hope, and we must live in a manner worthy of our calling.
>
> One Lord. Believers confess and proclaim, "Jesus Christ as Lord" (2 Corinthians 4:5, ESV). When the early Christians said, "Jesus is Lord," they were saying, "Caesar is not lord." When Jewish Christians said this, they were boldly identifying Jesus with the God of the Hebrews Scriptures (Deuteronomy 6:4). So, this was not merely an empty creedal affirmation for early believers. This confession could literally cause you to lose your head.
>
> One Faith. The creed reminds us that we embrace the essential truths together, for "faith" here seems to refer to the body of truth we believe.
>
> One Baptism. We share a common experience of being spiritually baptized into Christ. We are united with Him. The act of baptism into water pictures this reality. This ordinance may be in view here.
>
> One God and Father. As His adopted children, we share the same Father (Ephesians 1:5). He is the God over all and the Father of all His children – regardless of their ethnicities. We are one big, adopted family. [5]

4. Which of the seven "ones" do you feel most grounded in, and which one do you struggle the most to live out?

The New Testament church united believing Jew and Gentile, slave and free, male and female, rich and poor, young and old, educated and illiterate, and people from "every tribe and people and tongue and nation" (Revelation 13:7) into one body. Just imagine how this new dynamic in Christ impacted these groups who had been at odds for centuries. Paul makes it clear that this new community, called the church, needs to be "diligent to preserve the unity of the Spirit in the bond of peace" (Ephesians 4:3).

5. Read the following passages. Why is unity among believers so important?

- 1 Corinthians 12:12-13 –

- John 17:20-23 –

6. Read Ephesians 4:4-6 once again. How is each member of the Trinity represented in these verses, and what does that teach us about Christian unity?

Swindoll reminds us why unity within the body of believers is imperative, especially in the splintered culture we are living in today, "In a divisive, warring hurtful world, the most powerful testimony the church can give is genuine unity prompted by true love and shown in the example of peace." [6] The unity we're called to as the Church isn't something we manufacture. It's something we receive – flowing from our shared relationship with the one God and Father of all. When we truly grasp that He is in all of us, it becomes harder to judge, dismiss, or divide. Instead, it compels us to see one another with humility, love, and honor.

7. How does the truth that we are all held together by the same loving Father (Ephesians 4:6) encourage you to live in unity with other believers?

Since I came to Christ in my early twenties, I didn't grow up singing the great hymns of the faith. But it didn't take long for me to fall in love with the sound of my church lifting their voices in worship. When I paused to listen, I could hear it all around me – strong baritones, wandering off-key voices, bright sopranos, rich harmonies, and the chirpy tones of little children. Each voice was different, yet together they formed a single song of praise to the Father. To me, it was a living picture of the truth Paul is proclaiming in Ephesians 4:4-6: Many voices, one heart. One hope. One Lord.

Early on, one hymn in particular moved me – "Be Thou My Vision." Originally a Gaelic poem later adapted into a hymn in the early 20th century, it gives voice to the unity that flows from a life centered on Christ. The words remind us that being one body is about more than doctrine, it is sharing a common focus, a common vision:

Be Thou my Vision, O Lord of my heart;
Naught be all else to me, save that Thou art.
Thou my best Thought, by day or by night,
Waking or sleeping, Thy presence my light.

We become one not by looking sideways at each other, but by looking upward, fixing our eyes on Jesus, the One who holds us all together:

Riches I heed not, nor man's empty praise;
Thou mine inheritance, now and always.
Thou and Thou only, first in my heart,
High King of Heaven, my treasure Thou art.

High King of Heaven, my victory won,
May I reach Heaven's joys, O bright Heaven's Sun!
Heart of my own heart, whatever befall,
Still be my Vision, O Ruler of all. [7]

As we close our study of Ephesians 4:4-6, may our prayer and our posture be: One Body. One Spirit. One Hope. One Lord. One Faith. One Baptism. One God and Father of all.

And one Vision: Jesus Christ.

Day Three

Ephesians 4:7-13

In this section of his letter to the Ephesians, Paul moves from describing the church's unity to addressing individual diversity. Within the unity of the Spirit, each of us has received a spiritual gift by the grace of God in order to serve the church, the body of Christ.

Read Ephesians 4:7-10.

While Paul is calling for unity with the church, he now makes it perfectly clear that unity does not mean the same as uniformity. As one person has said, "God in His wisdom did not make believers photocopies of one another." [8]

1. Define unity and uniformity.

- Unity –

- Uniformity –

The church benefits from the unity of the Spirit and the diversity of individual gifts. A spiritual gift is bestowed on each believer at the moment of conversion. Unlike natural talents, which are present in everyone at birth and develop with time and maturity, spiritual gifts are only available to believers in order to benefit the body of Christ.

2. To whom has grace been given? (v. 7)

The word "grace" is used in verse 7 in the same way it was in 3:2, 7-8; it refers to the privilege of having been called by God. This grace gift applies to every believer and is given in differing degrees "according to the measure of Christ's gift" (Ephesians 4:7). In His perfect wisdom, Christ has given different gifts to different people. But no one believer possesses them all.

Ephesians 4:7-10 is one of the key passages on spiritual gifts in the New Testament (compare with Romans 12:1-8; 1 Corinthians 12-14). Merida observes that what makes the Ephesians text on gifts distinct is its "exalted, Christ-centered focus. Paul highlights Christ's generosity and authority. Christ Jesus died, rose, and ascended in Heaven as the victorious King with all authority and gave gifts to His people, displaying extravagant generosity." [9]

In verse 8, Paul quotes Psalm 68:18, which celebrates God's gracious and powerful victories on behalf of Israel. This included the time in the wilderness as well as their conquest of the Promised Land.

3. Look up Psalm 68:18 and write it out.

4. Compare Ephesians 4:8 with Psalm 68:18. What difference do you notice in the wording between the two verses?

Rather than directly quoting Psalm 68:18, Paul gives more of a summary of the verse. The Apostle is not the only New Testament writer to use different wording when quoting the Old Testament. Phillips gives us a good working explanation of this seeming discrepancy:

> Paul saw in all this a fulfillment of Psalm 68:18, which he quoted in Ephesians 4:8 with a slight alteration. We find many amended quotations in the New Testament. The Holy Spirit, the Author of both the Old and New Testaments, certainly had the latitude to use His own material in whatever manner suited Him and to bring out shades of meaning He had in mind from the beginning. [10]

Because the authority and authenticity of the Scriptures have come under vicious attack, I thought it important to pause a moment and address this. The doctrine of biblical inerrancy (the belief that the Bible is without error in its original manuscripts) is a central tenet for Christianity. Currently, we have a variety of Bible translations available to us. Here is a helpful explanation as to why that is the case:

> That's the main reason we have different translations – for different uses of the Bible. Sometimes a stricter, more word-for-word translation of the original language is exactly what you need. But at other times, you want something a bit more readable, a bit more readily understandable, and so some translations offer a more phrase-for-phrase (or even thought-for-thought) approach, smoothing out word order, preferring English syntax over Greek or Hebrew syntax, and generally just rendering the thoughts of the original in a form that an English-speaking reader will better understand. To put it slightly more technically, every translation of the Bible has to aim, to one degree or another, at both accuracy and readability. Some translation committees take it as their mission to heavily privilege accuracy and (as we saw with Mark 10:50) necessarily sacrifice readability to a certain degree. Other translation committees set out to produce a version that is eminently readable, but that decision necessarily means the translators will have to rearrange some of the original language's word order so that the sentences will sound "right" to an English-language ear.
>
> I hope you can see the point in all this. Nothing in either the theory or the reality-on-the-ground of Bible translations introduces the slightest bit of doubt about whether we can really know what the Bible in its original languages says. In fact, we do know what it says, and the places where some scholars disagree are few and far between and ultimately of minor significance. The Bible can be and has been translated correctly, over and over and over again. [11]

Now back to the comparison of Ephesians 4:8 with Psalm 68:18.

Psalm 68 is a victory hymn. Historically, when a king won a significant victory, he would return back home, bringing the spoils of war with him. In Ephesians 4:8, Paul uses this picture from Psalm 68 to explain how Christ conquered his enemies, returned to Heaven, and then bestowed gifts on His Church. Swindoll walks us through what happened, "After His crucifixion and resurrection, Christ led His people to freedom and ascended in victory. He 'led captive a host of captives' (Ephesians 4:8), seating believers with Him spiritually in the heavens (2:6)." [12] What does this mean for us? Though we were once enemies of God, we have been brought into the family of God through the reconciliation of Christ. Though we were once bound by sin and held captive by Satan, we have now been taken captive by Christ! Colossians 1:13-14 says, "For He rescued us from the domain of darkness, and transferred us to the Kingdom of His beloved Son, in whom we have redemption, the forgiveness of sins." Hallelujah! What a Savior!

DID YOU KNOW?

The phrase at the beginning of Ephesians 4:8, "Therefore it says," is a "favorite rabbinic introduction to a scriptural quotation. It conveys and reaffirms the divine authority of Scripture." [13] In this case, it introduces the scriptural basis for spiritual gifts.

The mention of Christ's ascension in verse 8 leads Paul to a parenthetical thought in verses 9-10 in which he gives some of the details of what happened during this victorious event. In verse 9, Paul reasons that Christ's ascent infers a previous descent, which begs the question: How far did Jesus descend? As there are some differing views among Bible scholars, we cannot be dogmatic as to exactly what Paul is saying.

Some believe that the descent refers to Christ's Incarnation, when He left Heaven to take on human form and come to earth. Others propose that the descent is a reference to the descent of the Holy Spirit at Pentecost after Christ's ascension. Perhaps the most widely accepted view (and the one I lean toward) is that the descent denotes the time period between Christ's death and resurrection. Many believe that during this time, "Christ descended into the place of departed spirits, proclaiming victory over wicked spirits in bondage and leading Old Testament saints on a victorious ascent to paradise (1 Peter 3:18-20)." [14]

While scholars may differ in their interpretations of Ephesians 4:9, they agree in affirming the essential truth of verse 10: Christ ascended "so that He might fill all things." Christ's ascension was not to leave the world behind, but so that His influence and presence in the world would expand. As He said in John 16:7, "But I tell you the truth, it is to your advantage that I go away; for if I do not go away, the Helper will not come to you; but if I go, I will send Him to you."

In essence, Paul is declaring that through Christ's descent and ascent, He won the spoils of victory and the blessing of the Holy Spirit. In triumph, He poured out the gift of the Holy Spirit upon the Church. The Spirit now empowers the body of Christ by distributing a rich diversity of spiritual gifts, making Christ's presence manifest in and through His people.

Read Ephesians 4:11-12.

As Paul continues, he expands upon the thought he began in 4:7-8 concerning the gifts Christ gave. In this particular context, the gifts are actually people who are called to different functions.

5. What specific roles are mentioned in verse 11?

6. What is the purpose of these positions? (v. 12)

The gifts of apostles (those sent out as appointed representatives of Christ), prophets (proclaim and clarify truth), evangelists (those gifted to share Christ and see people come to faith), pastors (those who preach the Word and shepherd the flock of God), and teachers (those who nourish the saints with the Word and take profound Scriptural truth and make practical application for daily living) are given to the Church. [15] Their purpose is the equipping of the saints to do the work of the ministry and to bring the body of Christ to its full potential.

Many believers in the western church operate on the assumption that their pastor has been hired to do all the work of the ministry. These casual Christians attend church services and expect to experience good music, hear a brief Bible message that is flashy and entertaining, and toss a bill or two into the offering plate, all the while intending to slip out before the invitation, only to resume living as they choose. And they consider themselves to be active, involved church members. Nothing could be further from the truth. We have been saved in order to serve and act as "ambassadors for Christ" (2 Corinthians 5:20). Dr. Adrian Rogers captured this calling for all believers in this concise statement, "You have been 'sanctified' – set apart for the Master's purpose – not to sit, soak, and sour, but to be obedient to God for what He has for you to do." [16]

Sit, soak, and sour? That's not for me! My husband and I have determined, "As for me and my house, we will serve the Lord" (Joshua 24:15).

What are you doing with the gifts God has given to you? When members give, serve in the nursery, make meals for those who are sick, and minister to each other, the body of Christ is "built up" (v. 12). Serving is evidence that we are maturing in our faith. Consider what Paul Tripp says:

> Your life is bigger than a good job, an understanding spouse, and non-delinquent kids. It is bigger than beautiful gardens, nice vacations, and fashionable clothes. In reality you are part of something immense, something that began before you were born and will continue after you die. God is rescuing fallen humanity, transporting them into His Kingdom, and progressively changing them into His likeness – and He wants you to be a part of it. [17]

Beloved, there is no greater calling than to spend our lives serving Christ and His Kingdom. May we make the choice to serve in whatever way He calls us, because we are *In Him.*

Day Four

Ephesians 4:13-16

As Paul continues his message to the Ephesians in verses 13–16, he reveals the intended outcome of the church's unity and diversity: spiritual maturity.

Read Ephesians 4:13-16.

1. What is the ultimate picture of maturity in Christ? (v. 13)

The goal is for us to become like Jesus. A spiritually mature believer – and by extension, a mature church – reflects the character of Christ. Paul mentioned these Christlike qualities earlier in the chapter: humility, gentleness, patience, love, and unity (vv. 2-3).

2. What specific qualities are we meant to attain as we mature? (v. 13)

But what happens when we fail to grow into this kind of maturity? In verse 14, Paul answers this question. We remain like children, "tossed here and there by waves and carried about by every wind of doctrine, by the trickery of men, by craftiness in deceitful scheming" (Ephesians 4:14). As I read this verse, I was reminded of a trip our family took to the beach. Disclaimer: Things happen to me that don't happen to others!

A few years ago, our family headed to the beach for vacation. At my age, squeezing into a swimsuit qualifies as cardio, but I managed to wrangle all the spandex into place and hit the sand. My beach bag was stuffed for what usually amounted to about an hour-long stay: towel the size of Texas, sunscreen, sunglasses, a book, and a cold Coke. I settled in, cracked open my book, read a few pages...and got bored. The real show was in front of me – the turquoise waves crashing onto the shore. Lost in the majesty of God's creation, I sat gazing at the vast expanse of water in front of me.

DID YOU KNOW?

The Greek word for "mature" is *telios* which means complete, whole, or perfect. [18] Similarly, "the fullness of Christ" is also an expression of completion or perfection. Put together: Our spiritual maturity is measured by how fully Christ is formed in us.

As I was basking in the beauty of it all, I saw it: a dark fin just a few yards from the shore line slicing through the water! I pulled myself up on my knees to get a better look and make sure I wasn't just imagining things. Trust me, I have a vivid imagination and that has happened before. But no, there it was again. A dark fin. Dark. Dangerous. Deadly. In horror, I realized lots of mommas with little ones in tow were splashing in the shallows while a predator was just a short distance away. Teens were paddling on surfboards and lounging on inflatable rafts, totally unaware of the danger lurking nearby. Dads were diving into the surf without any idea of the monster gliding through the churning water. As I got up to my feet, I began to simultaneously pray, "Lord, if you want me to be the one who begins to run up and down this beach screaming, 'Shark, Shark' just say the word and I am on it, because I am your girl."

Just as I inhaled to fill my lungs to their maximum capacity in preparation of verbally sounding the alarm at full volume, about twenty dolphins joined their solitary friend. He playfully jumped out of the water, and I could clearly see that what I thought was a shark with malicious intentions was actually a curious dolphin. He had made his way near the shore for a closer look at the vacationers who yearly invade his watery domain.

The moral of the story is: Don't be like children who are tossed about by waves, and are tricked into believing dolphins are sharks!

Phillips elaborates on the meaning of the word "children" (v. 14) in the original language:

> The word translated "children"...is derived from a word that literally means "one not old enough to speak" – in other words, a small infant. A child who is not yet old enough to speak is helpless. He is picked up and put down at the will and whim of others. He has no vocabulary with which to express his wishes. The gifts to the church are designed to get us past the highly vulnerable stage of infancy in our Christian lives. [19]

3. Paul warns us of the dangers of remaining spiritual infants. What are they? (v. 14)

Children are naturally impressionable, indecisive, easily deceived, and open to exploitation. Like small, rudderless boats that are tossed about by waves and blown off course by contrary prevailing winds, they are easily deceived as every fresh gust of doctrine seems reasonable to them. This makes them easy prey for false teachers.

4. Read 1 Corinthians 13:11. In context, Paul is describing the behavior of believers.

- In this verse, he is making allowance for a baby Christian. How does Paul describe childishness? (v. 11a)

- There is a legitimate season for a young Christian to be spiritually immature. However, this should be a brief season. What should follow? (v. 11b)

Failure to "grow in the grace and knowledge of our Lord and Savior Jesus Christ" (2 Peter 3:18) generates spiritual immaturity, instability, and gullibility. God's gifts to the church are gifted persons to preach, teach, and train up spiritually strong believers. However, every Christian is responsible for his or her own personal spiritual growth.

At the end of his three years in Ephesus, Paul was moved to tears when he addressed the elders of the church, in part because he knew of the dangers they would face in his absence.

5. Read Acts 20:28-31. What warning did he give the overseers of the church? (vv. 29-30)

6. In Acts 20:32, Paul pointed them to the only source available to be built up in the faith. According to this verse, how does God accomplish the process of sanctification in our lives?

Paul then contrasts the immaturity in Ephesians 4:14 with a picture of spiritual maturity in verses 15-16.

7. How are we to grow according to verse 15?

8. What should we do as we grow? (v. 15)

Truth in love causes spiritual growth, which results in the whole body being built up to spiritual maturity. The love of God "has been poured out within our hearts through the Holy Spirit who was given to us" (Romans 5:5). God's love, demonstrated in and through us, validates the reality of Christ in us. It remains an enigma to those outside the faith but is often the catalyst for gospel conversations.

9. In Paul's return to the body metaphor, who is the "Head" (v. 15b) and what is His role in verse 16?

We are dependent on Christ, the "Head" of the church, for our spiritual growth. But as members of the body, we are also reliant on each other: "Each part...working properly, makes the body grow so that it builds itself up in love" (v. 16, ESV).

10. What role are you playing in the body of Christ?

We need each other! In the body of Christ, every member is important and is to contribute, using whatever gifts he or she has. And as each part of the body does its work, we grow up – together – into Christ, our Head. Embrace your God-given role in the Church. Whether you're a teacher, encourager, helper, or quiet intercessor, what you do matters. The whole body depends on it.

Beloved, press on toward maturity. Stay anchored in the truth of God's Word, walking in love, and building one another up. In doing so, we will reflect Jesus to the world – not as scattered individuals, but as one unified, thriving body, *In Him.*

Day Five

Satan's strategy: Division

As a child, I stepped into the role of peacemaker in my family because I did not like conflict of any kind. Avoiding any situation that made me or someone else uncomfortable became a part of my coping mechanism. Obviously, this was not a healthy habit, but pretending all was well became my mode of operation.

Then, as a young adult, I met Jesus. Praise God for His unfailing mercy! Psalm 40:2-3 says, "He brought me up out of the pit of destruction, out of the miry clay, and He set my feet upon a rock making my footsteps firm. He put a new song in my mouth, a song of praise to our God; many will see and fear and will trust in the Lord." I was so relieved that now, as part of the family of God, I would never again be faced with conflict. After all, we all loved Jesus, didn't we? Surely, there would be no reason for disagreements? So, imagine my surprise the first time someone did not agree with me. My eye began to twitch and I stood there, wide-eyed and blinking at my dissenter, unable to think of anything to say to counter her challenge.

In light of all that Paul has said in Ephesians 4:1-16, if we are all a part of the body of Christ, why is there **division** among believers?

Don't misunderstand me. There are issues worth standing for. We call these tenants essentials of the faith, and we hold them with a tight hand. The essentials include the Bible (The Word of God is inerrant), the Blood (Christ shed His blood to pay the sin debt held against us, and He is the one and only way to be reconciled to God), and the Blessed Hope (Jesus is coming back for His church, and we will reside with Him forever in the new Heaven and new earth). These are essentials of the faith that we must not compromise.

But the things that are considered non-essentials are to be held loosely. And let's face it, most of the things that divide us are non-essentials. The color of the carpet in the sanctuary, the style of worship music we should sing, what the thermostat should be set on in the church, and the list goes on and on – these things are all mere preferences and not essentials of the faith. Jonathan Pokluda gives us valuable insights:

> Disunity in the church is almost always a sign of immaturity. Somewhere in disunity there is usually someone given to pride, wanting to win, wanting their preferences to win out, or not taking the time and patience to see an alternative perspective from the other side. When we're in it to win, it causes a wedge between us and other believers. The longer the conflict lasts, the larger that divide becomes. [20]

And apparently, division among believers is not a new concept, or why else would Paul urge his first-century readers to be "diligent to preserve the unity of the Spirit in the bond of peace" (Ephesians 4:3)? Division and dissension plagued the early church and continues on today.

It doesn't take much investigation to discover Satan's fingerprints all over the issue of division in the church. He knows that separating the body of Christ into warring factions weakens the whole. Here are four examples of the way Satan sows seeds of division as he attempts to disrupt the ministry of the body of Christ in the local church.

Church Conflict

Satan loves a good church fuss. As Eugene Peterson writes, "The devil does some of his best work behind stained glass." [21] Let a business meeting go awry, and he is thrilled. Be it a trivial matter, like choosing a new paint color for the nursery, or an issue of big consequence like adding an additional worship service, the enemy is delighted when church members get all riled up. He is especially pleased when parts of the congregation take sides, because that really elevates the potential for a church split, one of Satan's true coups.

1. What are some examples of non-essentials that can potentially cause a rift among the membership of the church?

2. Read the following verses. What mindset can help us avoid being drawn into disagreements over personal preferences at church?

    - Hebrews 11:8-10 –

    - Hebrews 13:14 –

If we truly believe that we have been "raised...up with Him, and seated...with Him in the heavenly places" (Ephesians 2:6), then the things of this world will grow strangely dim!

Gossip and Rumors

The enemy loves a gossiper and the rumors that result. The more rapidly the gossip spreads, the greater the details grow, until the story is so inflated that it barely resembles the original tale. What may seem to be a harmless pastime, is designed by the enemy to dismantle reputations, cause division, and destroy Kingdom purposes.

3. Read Proverbs 20:19. What does the Bible have to say about someone who gossips?

Doctrinal Error

Satan enables false teachers to use slick techniques and charming personalities to make inroads into the church. The enemy is cunning enough to introduce a lie with enough truth wrapped around it to make it seem plausible. In this way, he is able to do damage in the church before being discovered.

4. Read 2 Timothy 2:15. How can we avoid falling victim to doctrinal error?

Differences

Inside the church, there are lots of uniquely created people made in the image of God. They all have their own stories, backgrounds, giftings, and differences. When we lose sight of that, we give the enemy an edge.

As we saw in Ephesians 4:15-16, the New Testament describes the church using the metaphor of a body: many parts, yet one whole. Each part has a unique role, but problems arise when the parts begin to compare or compete. The hands may grow frustrated that the feet can't grasp things, while the feet take pride in carrying the body's weight. In the church, we're each wired differently, shaped by the Spirit with distinct gifts and perspectives. These differences are by design. But when we assume our way is the only right way, and others are simply wrong, resentment can take root, and the body begins to work against itself. When we fail to appreciate each other's differences, we stop believing the best about each other. And Satan and his demons love it!

5. What is a way you can show appreciation to someone in the church who serves differently and is wired differently than you?

A healthy church is a church where everyone uses their gifts together for the glory of God. That is how we pursue unity in diversity. That is maturity.

Keep in mind, these four tactics are only some of the ways that Satan, the slippery serpent, is able to slither into the midst of church, wreaking chaos and havoc. And sometimes, his most effective methods are not loud or obvious, but subtle – using strained relationships, bruised egos, and unresolved conflict to accomplish division.

Toward the end of his letter to the church in Philippi, Paul mentions Euodia and Syntyche and urges them "to live in harmony in the Lord" (Philippians 4:2). These ladies were leaders in the church, perhaps teachers in women's ministry. Yet, the enemy had sown seeds of discord between the two. Paul writes and implores the congregation to help repair the broken relationship and restore them to Kingdom service:

> I urge Euodia and I urge Syntyche to live in harmony in the Lord. Indeed, true companion, I ask you also to help these women who have shared my struggle in the cause of the gospel, together with Clement also and the rest of my fellow workers, whose names are in the book of life (Philippians 4:2-3).

We know nothing about these women other than what is recorded in these two verses. What a bummer! Having your names recorded in the Scripture for being involved in a catfight is a good reminder of how damaging division can be.

6. In His High Priestly Prayer, Jesus speaks to the Father concerning unity among His people. Look back at John 17:20-23. The Lord sets His church on the world's stage as a living testimony to reveal the truth about Jesus.

   - What will the world believe about Jesus? (v. 21)

   - What will the world know about Jesus? (v. 23)

Doesn't it seem possible that the reason the devil produces strife and division among believers is that unity in the church teaches the world about the relationship between God the Father and God the Son? Doesn't it stand to reason that what might seem like a bit of bickering among the saints can quickly escalate into a Euodia and Syntyche moment? The damage the devil can do to the Church is incalculable when the body is not standing in unity against his schemes.

Beloved believer, may we be "diligent to preserve the unity of the Spirit in the bond of peace" (Ephesians 4:3). We are *In Him*, and the life we now live, we live by faith in the Son of God through the power of the Holy Spirit. All glory to the King of kings and Lord of lords!

Sweet Jesus, may we walk worthy as ambassadors of Christ. May we seek unity and peace in You. Lord, help us to invest in the lives of young believers to establish them in the faith. Teach us to speak the truth in love. Show us how harsh words and judgmental attitudes lead to division and do not serve Your Kingdom well. May we "attain to the unity of the faith, and of the knowledge of the Son of God, to a mature man, to the measure of the stature which belongs to the fullness of Christ" (Ephesians 4:13).
Amen and amen.

Be Thou My Vision

352

Irish hymn, 8th cent.
trans. Mary Elizabeth Byrne, 1905
vers. Eleanor Hull, 1912, alt.

SLANE
10 11 11 11

Irish folk melody

1. Be Thou my Vi - sion, O Lord of my heart; be all else but
2. Be Thou my Wis - dom, be Thou my true Word; be Thou ev - er
3. Be Thou my Breast-plate, my Sword for the fight; be Thou my whole
4. Rich - es I heed not, nor man's emp - ty praise, be Thou mine in -
5. High King of heav - en, Thou heav-en's bright Sun, O grant me its

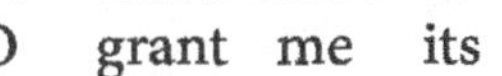

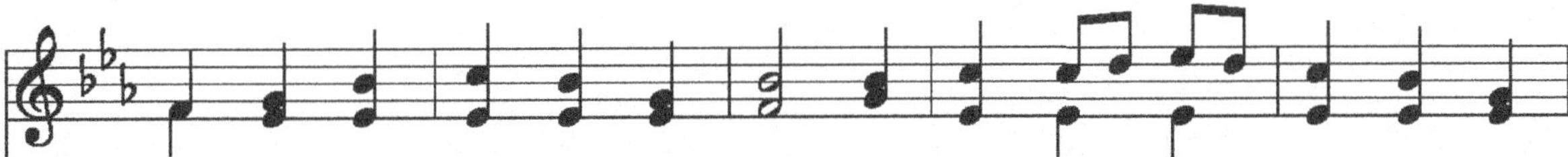

naught to me, save that Thou art; be Thou my best thought in the
with me and I with Thee, Lord; be Thou my great Fa - ther, and
Ar - mor, be Thou my true Might; be Thou my soul's Shel - ter, be
her - i - tance, now and al - ways; be Thou and Thou on - ly the
joys, af - ter vic - t'ry is won; Great Heart of my own heart, what-

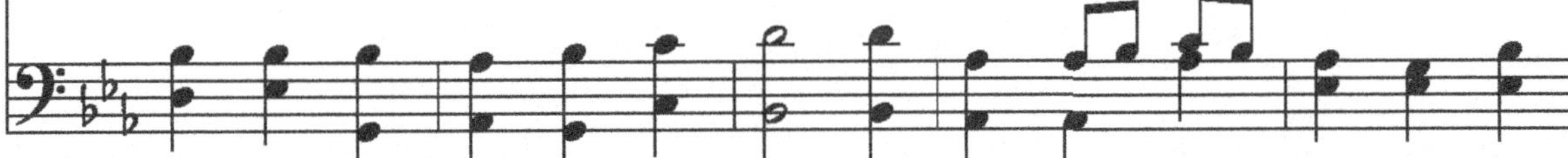

day and the night, both wak - ing and sleep - ing, Thy pres - ence my light.
I Thy true son, be Thou in me dwell - ing, and I with Thee one.
Thou my strong Tow'r, O raise Thou me heav'n-ward, great Pow'r of my pow'r.
first in my heart, O High King of heav - en, my Trea - sure Thou art.
ev - er be - fall, still be Thou my Vi - sion, O Rul - er of all.

Put on a new self

Ephesians 4:17-32

"Put on the new self"

Ephesians 4:17-32

If you are still wrapped in grave clothes...it is time for you to dare to rise and in sweet faith in the risen Jesus Christ declare: "I will not take this any longer. I am a child of God!" [1]
~ A.W. Tozer

On April 23, 2013, Geraldine "Gerry" Largay set out to fulfill a dream, to hike thru the Appalachian Trail, a journey of more than 2000 miles. An experienced hiker, the 66-year-old from Brentwood, Tennessee spent months training and planning for the trek. Her route would begin in Harpers Ferry, West Virginia, go north to Mount Katahdin in Maine, then return to Harpers Ferry, before heading south to her final destination in Springer Mountain, Georgia. Her friend, Jane Lee, would accompany her on the northern half and her husband, George, would meet her along the way to replenish supplies.

Setting out, she had all the gear she needed to hike and camp for weeks on end, including maps, a journal, and a small compass. At first, things went according to plan. But then, nine weeks into the hike, on June 30, a family emergency forced Jane to return home. Gerry determined to press on, alone. For the next three weeks, things went well as she eventually crossed into Maine. But then on July 22, Gerry, who friends say did not have a good sense of direction, wandered off the trail and got turned around. It did not take her long to realize she was lost. She pulled out her cell phone but had no signal. She climbed higher to try to get one, but that only added to her disorientation.

When she failed to arrive at a pre-arranged meeting point on July 24, her husband reported her missing. Search teams were called in and began to look for her. Sadly, her body was not found until October 14, 2015, more than two years after the search began, less than 3000 feet from the Appalachian Trail. Investigators read through her journal to piece together what happened. The last entry was dated August 6, 2013.

How did someone with years of hiking experience get so turned around? Her biographer, Dee Dauphinee, says that although Gerry was trained for the rigors of the trail, she was not prepared on what to do if she got lost. She had a small compass with her, but did not know how to use it. The maps she had were useless without a way to gauge direction. If Gerry had known how to use a compass, it is possible that she could have found her way back to the trail and her tragic death could likely have been avoided. [2]

If we aren't careful, the same thing can happen to us in our walk with the Lord. After we are saved, we begin our journey well, but somewhere along the way, we can veer off the path, get entangled in old habits, and end up disoriented. It's as if we are still wearing the grave clothes of our old life – the remnants of who we were before Christ – even though we've been raised to new life *In Him*. That's why Paul writes with such urgency in Ephesians 4:17-32 as he pleads with believers not to walk the way of the old life any longer. Christ has given us not just a new destination, but a new mind, a new heart, and a new way to walk. And God has given us His Word – a compass, steady and true – that will guide us back to the path of righteousness and life until we arrive safely home, *In Him*.

Day One

Ephesians 4:17-19

As you begin this lesson, pray and ask God to reveal Himself to you in the way 1 John 5:20 tells us, "And we know that the Son of God has come, and has given us understanding so that we may know Him who is true; and we are in Him who is true, in His Son Jesus Christ. This is the true God and eternal life." Ask Him to open your eyes, shape your mind, and stir your heart to live out your new life *In Him.*

Read Ephesians 4:17-32.

1. As you read, underline the key words in this passage. Then write them in the box below.

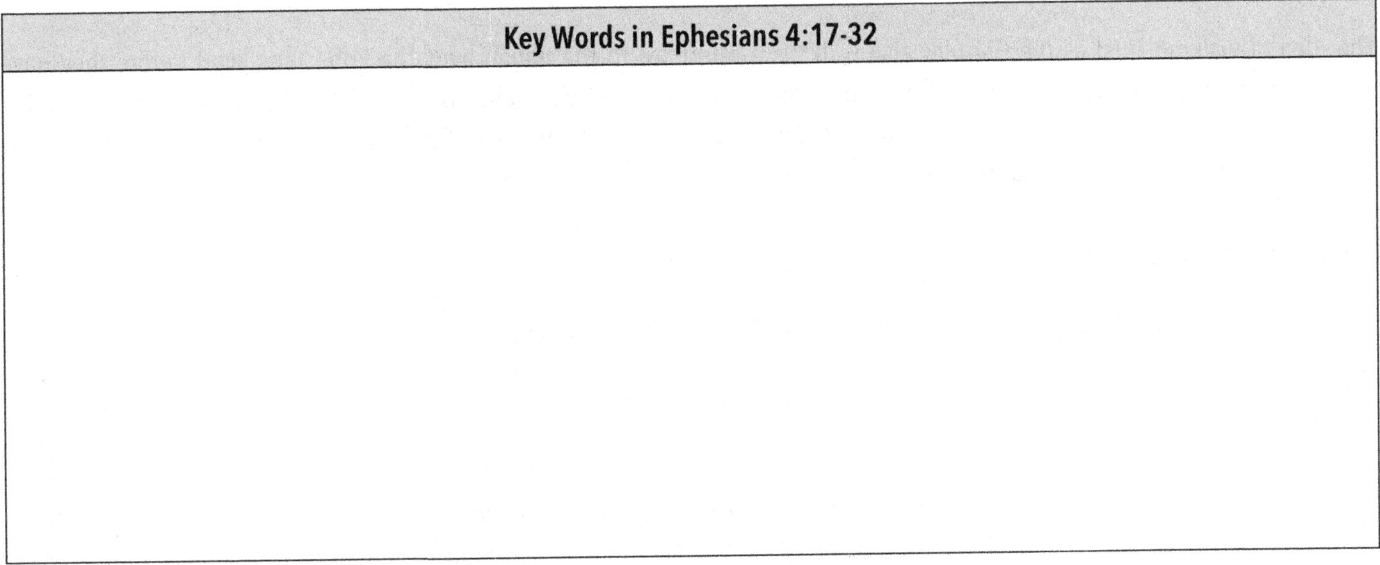

Key Words in Ephesians 4:17-32

2. What stands out to you about the way Paul contrasts the "old self" with the "new self"?

3. Summarize Ephesians 4:17-32 in one sentence.

In the first century, life in the Roman world revolved around pagan worship. In the city of Ephesus, this was especially true, as the city centered around devotion to Artemis, the Greek goddess of fertility, known to the Romans as Diana. The grand temple of Artemis was the focal point of religious activity, anchoring a system steeped in idolatry and immorality, with more than a thousand priestesses working as prostitutes. The area surrounding the temple, a radius of a quarter mile, was designated as an asylum for criminals. Anyone who could reach that zone was safe from prosecution, regardless of the severity of the crime committed. [3]

Yet, situated amid the vile worship practices and some of the most dangerous criminals of the ancient world, is a group of people who have placed their faith in Christ. Certainly, these new believers are experiencing intense strain as they struggle to live godly lives in the midst of such an ungodly culture. Writing to them, Paul wants to be clear: Following Jesus isn't just a minor lifestyle change. The Christian life is a radical way of living, involving a brand-new identity and a new spiritual heritage.

Now, read Ephesians 4:17-19 again.

In verse 17, Paul circles back to the instruction he began at the start of the chapter, his appeal for the Ephesians to "walk in a manner worthy of the calling with which you have been called" (v. 1). Only this time, he negates the opposite to emphasize what he is saying. Paul's opening phrase, "So this I say," is a signal to his readers that he is about to say something significant. The words, "affirm together with the Lord," give the basis for the authority of what he is about to say. His message is not a suggestion nor an option, but a mandate from Christ that must be obeyed.

4. What command does Paul give to the Ephesians? (v. 17)

The idea of walking "just as the Gentiles also walk" is a reference to the pagan lives the Ephesians lived before they gave their lives to Christ. But now, as believers, they no longer belong to that world and should quit acting like they do. To help the Ephesians clearly distinguish between their old life and their new identity in Christ, Paul gives them a vivid description of the mind, heart, and behavior of an unbeliever.

The Mind of an Unbeliever

5. What word does Paul use to describe the way an unbeliever's mind operates? (v. 17b)

DID YOU KNOW?

The term, "Gentile," can be used in an ethnic sense, referring to a person who is not Jewish (Ephesians 2:11). But it can also be used in an ethical or moral sense, as Paul does in 4:17, similar to the way we use the word "pagan," referring to an unbeliever.

The Greek word for "futility," *mataiotes,* means worthless, empty, devoid of truth, the product of a vain mind, meaningless. [4] Paul uses the same word in Romans 8:20 to depict the misery of nature removed from the bliss of Eden. Separated from God, man's reasoning is meaningless. He may conjure up all kinds of religions and belief systems in his mind, but they are useless and purposeless.

Not only is the mind of the unbeliever focused on things that are worthless and empty, but it is also "darkened in...understanding" and the "ignorance" of God (Ephesians 4:18), incapable of perceiving spiritual truth. It is not that unbelievers lack intelligence or the capacity to reason, what is missing is the ability to comprehend the things of God, things that are "spiritually appraised" (1 Corinthians 2:14). In writing to the Corinthians, Paul elaborates, "The god of this world has blinded the minds of the unbelieving so that they might not see the light of the gospel of the glory of Christ, who is the image of God" (2 Corinthians 4:4). In Romans 1:21, Paul expounds on the depravity of the

Gentiles, "For even though they knew God, they did not honor Him as God or give thanks, but they became futile in their speculations, and their foolish heart was darkened." Grant Osborne explains that Paul is emphasizing a deliberate choice to reject God:

> In a sense, sin has caused them to lose their minds. Their thinking process has been tainted by the dark forces of evil, called "the powers of this dark world" in Ephesians 6:12 (see also 2:2). Here the emphasis is on fleshly decisions; sinners deliberately prefer darkness to light. The rational process that should lead them to realize the truths of God is lost in the shadows of sin, and darkness prevails. [5]

Apart from God, the mind wanders aimlessly from darkness to darkness…in darkness…into deeper darkness, the root issue being the heart.

The Heart of an Unbeliever

6. What reason does Paul give for the unbeliever's alienation from God? (v. 18b)

When sin and darkness prevail, the heart bears the weight. As John Eldredge pointedly notes, "There is no greater disaster for the human heart than this – to believe we have found life apart from God." [6] The Greek word translated "hardness" is *porosis* which denotes a stony, petrified condition. [7] Sin has a petrifying effect. Think about a petrified tree that was at one time alive and growing, but as minerals seeped into the wood, it became hardened, keeping its form but losing the life within. The hardened heart mirrors this process: Desensitized by sin, it loses the ability to feel, to respond to truth. Just as the tree can no longer bend in the wind or draw nourishment from the earth, the heart, once tender, becomes impenetrable – present in form, but dead in spirit.

7. If someone continues to reject Christ, what do they become? (v. 19a)

What a word picture Paul gives here! A heart hardened to the things of God becomes "callous," the Greek word *apalgeo,* which means "to cease to feel pain or to be past feeling." [8] Such is the effect of repeated sin – the person loses the power to feel at all. Osborne makes this pointed comparison:

> Repetition anchors a practice in one's muscle memory. Great athletes have the touch because they have practiced moves thousands of times. In a similar way, when we sin repeatedly, the muscle of our mind learns to practice evil with a sense of impunity. That is the definition of a psychopath: one who feels no remorse for their terrible evils. [9]

The hardened heart doesn't feel the pain it causes, the grief of sin, nor the absence of God. Because, you see, the hardened heart is not just resistant to God, it is numb to Him. And when that happens, the inevitable result is that the soul plunges headlong into desire. The fruit of a darkened mind and a hardened heart is unrestrained behavior.

The Behavior of an Unbeliever

8. To what types of behavior do people with darkened minds and hardened hearts "give themselves over"? (v. 19b)

When the mind is alienated from the truth and the heart is closed to God, the natural outcome is a life without restraint. People begin to indulge in "every kind of impurity," as Paul says, and it becomes habitual. "Sensuality," "impurity," and "greed" – picture a lifestyle with no moral compass, just full surrender to whatever feels good in the moment. Paul's words well describe our contemporary, Christless culture, don't they? People indulge in unhindered lust, rampant promiscuity, and wanton self-indulgence because sin never satisfies. It always leaves them craving for more.

Paul's message leaves no room for ambiguity: As new creations in Christ, our minds, hearts, and actions should be different from the base world surrounding us. The good news in this passage is that God can transform anyone by His grace! Before Christ, the Ephesians, like all of us, were trapped in a cycle of empty thinking, hardened hearts, and sinful behaviors. Their lives were marked by separation from God, and that alienation showed up in their choices and actions.

9. What are three words that describe your life before Christ?

Through Jesus, we are not who we once were. The same people who once walked in "ignorance" and "impurity" are now new creations.

10. How has being *In Him* changed the way you think and live, compared to the way you walked prior to coming to Christ?

Ephesians 4:17-19 reminds us not just to avoid old sin patterns, but to remember what we've been saved from and who we've been called to become. When we allow God to renew our minds, we begin to live in a way that reflects the light and love of Christ.

Charles Swindoll notes that although Paul's words "refer primarily to unbelievers, the fact that he urges his readers to 'walk no longer' as the Gentiles do (4:17) indicates that even Christians can backslide into these conditions." [10] He goes on to say that when that happens, they will find "their minds shrouded in moral haze, their hearts increasingly hardened to the work of the Spirit, and their lives careening into a tangled jungle of immorality." [11]

Take a moment to reflect. Is there any part of your old life that is still trying to pull you back? Let this passage serve as a warning and a hope. We are no longer bound to the darkness we once knew, but we must stay vigilant, allowing the Holy Spirit to continually renew our minds and hearts.

As you go throughout your day, may His light flood your mind and your life reflect the beauty of a soul set free *In Him.*

Day Two

Ephesians 4:20-24

As I am writing, spring is in full bloom. The grass is turning green, birds are singing again, butterflies are emerging from their cocoons, and the azaleas are just starting to bud. This time of year, I spend most of my free time outside in our flower beds – pulling weeds, pruning roses, planting annuals, and putting out fresh pine needles. It's not at all unusual for me to get so caught up in my gardening tasks, that I completely lose track of time.

More than once, I've glanced at the clock, realized I was supposed to be somewhere, and had to rush to get ready in just a few minutes. But no matter how short on time I am, I've never once considered skipping a shower and simply putting clean, dressy clothes over my sweaty, stinky yard clothes. That would just be gross! But spiritually, that's what we often try to do, continuing to cling to our old way of life while attempting to step into our new identity in Christ.

In Ephesians 4:20-24, Paul talks about this very thing. He reminds us that knowing Jesus isn't only about believing differently, it's about living differently. It's about taking off the old self – our former habits, attitudes, and sinful patterns – and putting on the new self, created to be like God in true righteousness and holiness.

As you begin today's study, pause and honestly reflect: Are you trying to wear the "new" while still holding on to the "old"? Are there parts of your old life you still hang on to? How can you truly embrace the transformation Jesus offers – not just in theory, but in real, everyday ways?

Read Ephesians 4:20-24.

1. What pronoun does Paul use in these verses? (vv. 20-24)

In an intentional contrast, Paul switches pronouns from "they" to "you" as he turns from addressing the way unbelieving Gentiles live to focus on the profound difference that finding Christ makes. True transformation is only found *In Him.*

Reminding the Ephesians of what they already know, Paul writes, "You did not learn Christ in this way" (v. 20). The pagan lifestyle from their past, depicted in verses 17-19, no longer fits, as that life stands in direct opposition to the truth they've received through Paul's teaching.

Warren Wiersbe points out that Paul "did not say 'learned about Christ,' because it is possible to learn about Christ and never be saved. To 'learn Christ' means to have a personal relationship to Christ so that you get to know Him better each day." [12] Likewise, Paul omits "about" again in verse 21. Rather than saying "you have heard about Him," he says, "you have heard Him." Frank Thielman explains, "As with that expression, the implication is that Christ is alive and that when one hears the gospel preached, as Paul assumes his readers have, one is put in touch with a living person." [13] What Paul is describing is a daily encounter with the living Christ, a relationship and connection with Him like His original disciples experienced. While an unbeliever may have learned and heard *about* Christ, a believer "learns" Him and "hears" Him. In essence, Christ becomes both our School and Teacher.

2. What does Paul assure the Ephesians regarding what they taught *In Him*? (v. 21b)

3. What similar statement does Jesus make about Himself in John 14:6?

As Paul proceeds in verses 22-24, he tells them how to practically apply the "truth" by laying out a simple three-part process for spiritual growth: Lay aside the old. Renew your mind. Put on the new.

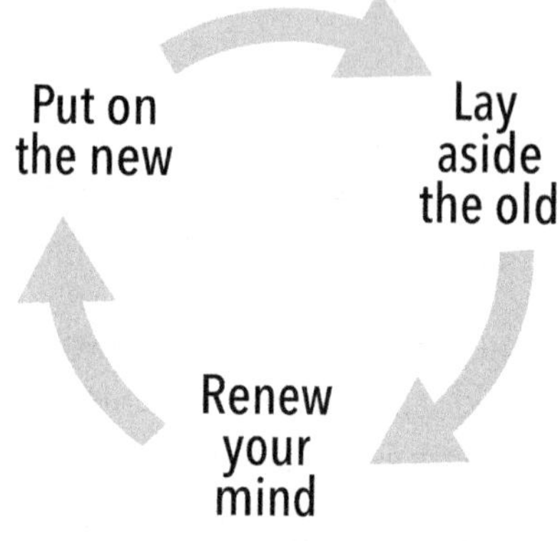

DID YOU KNOW?

While Paul often refers to "Christ," "Lord Jesus Christ," or "Christ Jesus" in his letter to the believers in Ephesus, Ephesians 4:21 is the only time that Christ is called "Jesus." Tony Merida asserts that Paul's choice here is intentional and explains, "Paul is talking about the historical person, Jesus. He lived, died, and rose from the dead in human history. Find Him and you find truth. Find Him and you find life." [14]

The image that comes to mind is taking off our old dirty clothes so that new clean clothes can be "put on."

Lay aside the old

The first step in our spiritual clothing exchange is "to lay aside the old" (v. 22). Just as a butterfly lays aside its cocoon, never to return, as new creatures in Christ (2 Corinthians 5:17), we must discard the old thinking and behaviors associated with our former life. In Christ, our hearts are made new as God promised in Ezekiel 36:26, "I will give you a new heart and put a new spirit within you; and I will remove the heart of stone from your flesh and give you a heart of flesh." But notice, Paul says our old nature doesn't change. It "is" (present tense) still "being corrupted" by "lusts of deceit" (Ephesians 4:22).

We can be followers of Christ and still struggle with the old nature. While we are redeemed once, our sanctification is an ongoing process. Osborne's comments help us to grasp what Paul is saying here:

> The old has been nullified and rendered powerless – has been "crucified with Christ" (Romans 6:6) – but while it is no longer an internal force controlling us it is still an external force tempting and deceiving us. It operates through the flesh, the sin nature that is still a part of us. It has been defeated but not destroyed, cast out of our new being but still operative as a threatening outside force. The battle still rages, and our victory must begin with a studied repudiation of the old nature and its ways. [15]

The NIV and ESV Bibles translate "lusts of deceit" as "deceitful desires." Sin, like Satan in the Garden of Eden, deceives. It promises fulfillment but produces emptiness.

4. What are some examples of "deceitful" desires that try to infiltrate our lives?

In the ancient world, people did not have closets full of clothes like we do. In fact, some might not have even owned a change of clothes. So, clothing would not be discarded unless it was completely unwearable. That is the picture here. Like filthy, ripped clothing, the deceitful ways of the old self are so totally beyond repair that the garbage is the only place they belong.

5. What pieces of your old life do you still need to take off?

As new creations in Christ, we are called to daily cast off the flesh and the sin that entangles us. This continual process, our sanctification, is how we mature and "grow up in all aspects" into our new identity *In Him* (Ephesians 4:15). And it all begins with surrendering and renewing our minds, bringing every thought under Christ's authority.

Renew your mind

As Paul continues, he gives the key ingredient for putting on the new self: "Be renewed in the spirit of your mind" (v. 23). He uses similar language when he commands the church in Rome to "be transformed by the renewing of your mind" (Romans 12:2).

6. In Romans 12:2a, what is the opposite of renewing your mind?

The renewed mind is the "polar opposite of the mind mired in futility," that Paul talks about in verse 17. [16] In the Greek, "be renewed" is present tense and refers to a continuous process. [17] This renewal, becoming like Christ, is a daily act that begins in the mind. Max Anders explains:

> You are what you think. You move in the direction of what you put into your mind and what you allow your mind to dwell on. So, if you are not what you want to be, then you must begin to think differently. If you are to think differently, you must put into your mind that which you want to become. If you do, the Holy Spirit will use it to change you to become what you want to be. If you don't, you will never be what you want to be. It all depends on what you put into your mind. This is what it means to be made new in the attitude of your mind. [18]

Swindoll likens renewal to "taking a shower every day that cleanses us and readies us to put on the Christlike clothes of our new wardrobe." [19] We will not be ready to put on our new clothing unless our minds have been reshaped to reflect God's truth instead of patterns of the world. This spiritual process parallels with the way neural pathways in the brain are restructured through repeated thoughts and behaviors. As old, destructive pathways of sin weaken, new, life-giving ones are strengthened that lead to Christlikeness.

7. Read Philippians 4:8-9 and 2 Timothy 3:15-16. What are some practical ways to renew your mind?

Since our mindset forms our identity, mind renewal prepares us for true transformation, putting on the "new self." As we deliberately choose to live out our new identity in Christ, we must put on what we are so that we can become who we are.

Put on the new

Paul's instruction to "put on the new self" is about living in alignment with who we already are in Christ. When we come to Christ, we are to begin living in a way that reflects Him.

8. What two qualities characterize the new self? (v. 24)

Righteousness describes the way we are to interact with others; holiness is our conduct toward God. As we put on the new self, our God-likeness will shine through: We will have a right relationship with God that produces right behavior towards others. That is the new self!

While I wish those two words described me 24/7, some days, they just don't. And I'm pretty sure I'm not alone. Reflecting on this gap in our lives, Rankin Wilbourne asks, "If Christianity is true in its promise of a new life, then why don't I feel more... new?" [20] If only our sanctification, like our salvation, was a one-time event! But it's not. Our journey to Christlikeness is more like a "three steps forward and two steps back" process. [21]

The word "process" is defined as "a series of actions or steps taken in order to achieve a particular end." [22] The "particular end" of our process is Christlikeness. The "series of actions" to achieve that end are: laying aside the old, renewing our minds, and putting on the new. While throughout the process, we may not always feel "new," the truth remains: God is faithfully forming us into the likeness of Christ, one intentional step at a time. That has always been His plan as Paul explains to the believers in Rome:

> God knew what He was doing from the very beginning. He decided from the outset to shape the lives of those who love Him along the same lines as the life of His Son. The Son stands first in the line of humanity He restored. We see the original and intended shape of our lives there in Him. After God made that decision of what His children should be like, He followed it up by calling people by name. After He called them by name, He set them on a solid basis with Himself. And then, after getting them established, He stayed with them to the end, gloriously completing what He had begun (Romans 8:29-30, MSG).

You are created in the image of God (Genesis 1:27). When He fashioned you, God had a specific person in mind to reflect His character. Although that image was marred by sin, through the redeeming work of Jesus Christ, He brought you back into relationship with Himself. And now, He is in the ongoing process of restoring you as He shapes your life into the image of Jesus. Transformation doesn't merely come by trying harder, but by surrendering more deeply to the One who is already at work within us. Will you do that today?

Jesus, thank You. Thank You for rescuing me, not just to save me from something,
but to bring me into a whole new life. You've given me a new heart, a new name, a new identity.
And yet, I confess I find it so easy to forget and slip back into old habits, old fears, old lies.

Holy Spirit, I invite You now to renew my mind. Restore the truth of who I am in You.
Help me to put off the old self. Awaken in me the desire, the courage,
and the strength to walk as the one You say I am.

Father, I want to live from my new self. Teach me how to wear my new spiritual clothing.
Shape me to look more and more like Jesus. I give You access to every part of my life.
Renew it, reclaim it, restore it. You are the Author of my story,
and I trust You to finish what You've started in me.

In the name of Jesus, my Savior, my King, and my Life, Amen.

Day Three

Ephesians 4:25-29

In Ephesians 4:25-29, Paul paints a picture of what transformation (becoming like Christ) looks like in everyday life. It's not just about what we believe. It's about how we live. Paul isn't just calling us to clean up a few behaviors. He's calling for a complete restoration, a new creation. Charles Wesley's prayer captures this well:

> *Finish then Thy new creation,*
> *Pure and spotless let us be;*
> *Let us see Thy great salvation*
> *Perfectly restored in Thee.* [23]

Read Ephesians 4:25-29.

1. With what word does Paul begin verse 25?

"Therefore" connects the principles of the Christian life (4:20-24) with the actual practice of living in Christ. Using specific examples, Paul encourages his readers to take off the rags of the old man and put on the robes of the new man.

2. Create a general overview of Ephesians 4:25-29 by filling in this chart with the old behaviors to take off, new actions to put on, and the reasons to do so.

Scripture	The Rags of the Old Man to Take Off	The Robes of the New Man to Put On	The Reason
v. 25			
vv. 26-27			
v. 28			
v. 29			

Now, let's dig in a little deeper into what a transformed life looks like. Paul examines four behaviors that should be on display in our new man: A Transformed Tongue, A Transformed Temper, Transformed Conduct, and Transformed Words. All four behaviors are relational: They not only impact our relationship with God, but also our relationships with others.

A Transformed Tongue (v. 25)

So stop telling lies. Let us tell our neighbors the truth, for we are all parts of the same body.
Ephesians 4:25, NLT

At first, it may seem surprising that Paul needs to tell believers not to lie, but is it really? Have you ever, in an unguarded moment, when someone put you on the spot, found yourself taking refuge in words that aren't completely true? As Paul told the Corinthians, we all have "things hidden in the darkness" that lie wait in our souls (1 Corinthians 4:5). Swindoll explains that the Greek word for "falsehood," *pseudos,* "includes all forms of lying, from out-and-out contradictions of known facts to carefully couched nuances intended to deceive and mislead. It includes everything from white lies to unbelievable whoppers." [24] Just like we would pull up weeds defiling our flower garden, all falsehood must be uprooted, and truthfulness sowed in its place.

3. Read some of the verses in Scripture that address lying: Exodus 23:1; Psalm 5:6; Psalm 34:13; Proverbs 6:16-19; Proverbs 13:5; Mark 7:21-23; Colossians 3:9; 1 Peter 3:10. What did you learn?

4. What does Jesus say about Satan in John 8:44?

5. What does Isaiah 45:19 say about God?

DID YOU KNOW?

Paul's words, "speak truth each one of you with his neighbor," refer to Zechariah 8:16, "These are the things which you should do: speak the truth to one another; judge with truth and judgment for peace in your gates." As a postexilic prophet, Zechariah was warning the Jewish remnant against repeating the sins that had gotten them exiled in the first place. Relating to each other in truth is one of the changes the prophet told God's people they must make to stay in the land.

Simply said: Satan's native language is the lie, God is truth. Truth identifies those who belong to God.

Sadly, we live in a culture that feeds on lies. Whether it's on social media, at work, or in conversations with friends, lying has become an accepted practice. In a day when everyone else seems to be stretching the truth or hiding behind half-truths, it can feel isolating to go against the norm. But Paul reminds us that truth isn't optional for believers, it's an indication of the new life we have in Christ. *In Him*, we're called to live differently: We are to speak the truth. Practice it at home. Keep it up at work. Make honesty and truth your habit with your friends and neighbors. One of the expressions of "new life" in Christ is a transformed tongue.

A Transformed Temper (vv. 26-27)

And "don't sin by letting anger control you." Don't let the sun go down while you are still angry, for anger gives a foothold to the devil.
Ephesians 4:26-27, NLT

Paul acknowledges that in a fallen world, anger will exist, and at times, it is even fitting. Jesus became angry when he saw the stubborn hearts of the religious leaders (Mark 3:5), and again when He saw sinful practices taking place in the temple (Matthew 21:12-13). The wrath of God regarding sin is a recurring theme in the Bible. When Paul says, "Be angry," the kind of anger he has in mind is not a temper tantrum or lingering hostility, but instead, righteous indignation. Here's the difference:

> Biblical, righteous indignation directs its anger at the appropriate object – sinful behavior, moral corruption, and unjust circumstances....Sinful anger, on the other hand, lingers. It holds a grudge. It seeks retaliation, revenge, and harm toward those who anger us. [25]

Paul is clear regarding the latter type of anger, "Don't do it!" The Greek word translated "sin" in verse 26 is *harmartano* which means "to miss the mark." [26] Quoting from Psalm 4:4a, "Be angry, and do not sin" (NKJV), Paul is saying, "Be angry, but don't miss the mark and sin." Although anger may be warranted, it is never an excuse to sin.

6. What makes anger sinful?

The way we prevent anger from spiraling into sin is by refusing to let it gain control of us. When anger does occur, we cannot allow it to remain in our hearts: "Do not let the sun go down on your anger." In other words, don't allow anger to continue festering from one day to the next, or it will give Satan an "opportunity" to take control in your attitudes, actions, and relationships. The word "opportunity" (NASB) or "foothold" (NLT) used in this text stems from the Greek word *topos,* which means "place." [27] *Topos* refers to a physical location. The picture here is of allowing the devil into our home and offering him a room. The longer we hold on to anger, the more opportunities we give the enemy to wreak havoc in our lives. And nothing is worth that!

The evidence of a changed heart includes a transformed temper.

Transformed Conduct (v. 28)

If you are a thief, quit stealing. Instead, use your hands for good hard work, and then give generously to others in need.
Ephesians 4:28, NLT

Paul doesn't just say, "stop stealing," he is calling for a total identity shift – the person who once took from others is invited to live with purpose and generosity. As John Phillips asks, "What greater proof of a changed heart and life could there be than for a former thief to seek honest employment, become concerned about those unable to work, and give of his own wages to alleviate the problems of the poor?" [28] Not only are believers not to steal any longer, we are to do just the opposite. The Christian life is not just about avoiding wrong, but actively doing good and blessing others.

From thief to philanthropist, that is the transformative power of the gospel!

Transformed Words (v. 29)

After confronting honesty, anger, and stealing, Paul continues to pound away at our old self by targeting our speech.

7. Define "unwholesome" and "edification."

The Greek word *sapros* translated "unwholesome," means rotten, bad, or putrid, and was used to describe something that was decaying. [29] When applied to words, it can mean cursing, vulgar talk, crude jokes, or even remarks that are unkind, flippant, or sarcastic. Our words have power (Proverbs 18:21). Instead of rotting words, we are to speak words that build up and encourage each other. The pass-fail test Paul shares with the Ephesians is simple. Is it unwholesome? Don't say it. Does it encourage and build others up? Then say it. If Ephesians 4:29 was consistently obeyed, think how many conflicts would be eliminated!

Our words display what is in our hearts. Jesus said, "A good person produces good things from the treasury of a good heart, and an evil person produces evil things from the treasury of an evil heart. What you say flows from what is in your heart" (Luke 6:45, NLT). Our "new self" should not continue speaking "old self" words. If our hearts are transformed, our words will follow suit.

As we wrap up today, let's circle back to the end of Ephesians 4:27: "Don't give the devil an opportunity" or "foothold." Although Paul links the sin of anger with this admonition, the wider application is to any sin. When we choose to sin, we open the door to the enemy. Even a tiny crack is enough for him to start working his way in. Just like a rock climber only needs a small crevice to get a grip and pull themselves up, the devil only needs a little space – one unchecked attitude, one bit of bitterness, one secret compromise.

Every time we give in to sin and leave it unconfessed, we're handing the enemy a place to stand – and he won't stop there. He'll use that foothold to gain ground. Take a few minutes to examine your heart. Ask the Holy Spirit to reveal to you any area in your life where you have left a door open to the enemy. Confess. Repent. Stand firm. Close the door...Then lock it.

If we confess our sins, He is faithful and righteous to forgive us our sins and to cleanse us from all unrighteousness.
1 John 1:9

Day Four

Ephesians 4:30-32

In Ephesians 4:25-29, Paul has just explained what a transformed life in Christ looks like: speaking truth, controlling anger, working honestly, and building others up with our words. All of these are relational commands. Now, as he continues in verses 30-32, Paul clarifies that our relationships aren't only horizontal, they are also vertical. Our behavior doesn't just impact people around us; it affects God Himself.

Read Ephesians 4:30.

1. What emotion is associated with the Holy Spirit in verse 30?

As the third Person of the Trinity, the Holy Spirit is a personal being with emotions. Scripture tells us that He feels joy (Luke 10:21), can be outraged (Hebrews 10:29, ESV), and experiences grief (Ephesians 4:30).

The word translated "grieve" is *lypeo,* which means to cause pain, sorrow, or distress. [30] Grief is an emotion that finds its roots in love. Only someone who truly loves us can be grieved by us. Like the other two Persons of the Trinity, the Father and the Son, the Holy Spirit loves us. And that is why we can grieve Him.

What grieves the Holy Spirit? Our sin. Anything in our lives that is inconsistent with the Spirit's own nature causes Him sorrow. H.A. Ironside elaborates, "As a divine Person and heavenly guest, He is listening to everything you say and is taking note of everything you do. All that is said and done contrary to the holiness of Christ and to the righteousness of God, grieves the indwelling Holy Spirit." [31] Like parents who want their children to make wise choices, the Holy Spirit's desire for us is to live according to our new self. And when we fail to do that, it causes Him pain and sorrow.

Paul's command not to grieve the Holy Spirit is a reference to Isaiah 63:10 which addresses the rebellion of Israel on their way to the Promised Land: "But they rebelled and grieved His Holy Spirit; therefore He turned Himself to become their enemy, He fought against them." Paul is warning his readers, who have been "sealed" by the Holy Spirit, of the serious consequence of grieving Him by repeatedly rebelling against God. In Ephesians 1:13, Paul has already cited the work of the Holy Spirit in our lives in sealing us at the time of our salvation. Here, in 4:30, Paul wants us to understand that although our sealing by the Holy Spirit is permanent, our sin dishonors His indwelling presence in our lives. Let's look at this verse in *The Message*:

> Don't grieve God. Don't break His heart. His Holy Spirit, moving and breathing in you, is the most intimate part of your life, making you fit for Himself. Don't take such a gift for granted.

Before you go any further in today's lesson, stop and ask, "Holy Spirit, is there anything in my life that is grieving You?" If He reveals anything to you, repent, and determine to walk in the opposite direction, in a way that honors Him and causes Him delight. Don't take the gift of His presence for granted.

After Paul's exhortation regarding the presence of the Holy Spirit, he then adds to the catalog of attitudes and behaviors that have no place in the lives of believers.

Read Ephesians 4:31.

2. List and define the six characteristics believers are instructed to "put away." (v. 31)

Behaviors to "Put Away"	Definition

Then, sticking with his message to "lay aside the old" and "put on the new," Paul tells the Ephesians to exchange these six vices with three virtues.

Read Ephesians 4:32.

3. List and define the three new behaviors that are to replace the sinful habits of our old lives.

Behaviors to "Put On"	Definition

Did you notice the order of these three virtues? Kindness leads to compassion. Compassion proceeds to forgiveness. All three are an outworking of love.

4. What reason does Paul give for us to forgive each other? (v. 32b)

Paul's words at the end of Ephesians 4:32 sound familiar to the way Jesus taught us to pray in the Lord's Prayer: "And forgive us our debts, as we also have forgiven our debtors" (Matthew 6:12). It is interesting to note that the only part of the Lord's Prayer that Jesus expounded on was the forgiveness segment: "For if you forgive others for their transgressions, your heavenly Father will also forgive you. But if you do not forgive others, then your Father will not forgive your transgressions" (Matthew 6:14-15). Osborne correlates the two passages:

> The motivation clause [Matthew 6:14-15] is in keeping with "just as in Christ God forgave you." We will never have to forgive as often or as much as God has. We forgive one sin at a time, but God forgives our lifetimes of sin. When we have experienced the unbelievable mercy and grace of God and realize that Jesus took our place on the cross to forgive our sins, it should be easy for us to forgive others. [32]

5. How does remembering God's forgiveness help you to forgive others when it is hard?

Forgiving like Him is becoming like Him.

When we come to Christ, we replace the tattered clothing of our past with a brand-new wardrobe, one that is clean and fitting for our new identity *In Him*. As we daily put on our new clothing, we "reflect the holiness of God, follow the example of Christ, and avoid grieving the Holy Spirit of promise." [33] But just like with any new outfit, it's possible for stains to appear – moments of anger, careless words, or slipping back into old sinful habits. When that happens, don't ignore the stain or pretend it's not there. Take it to God, confess it, and let Him cleanse you again.

For You, Lord, are good, and ready to forgive,
And abundant in lovingkindness to all who call upon You.
Psalm 86:5

Day Five

Satan's strategy: Desensitization

One of the most deceptive tactics the enemy uses against us is **desensitization** – making us numb to the effects and consequences of our sin. In Ephesians 4:17-32, Paul warns us not to live like people who have "lost all sensitivity" (v. 19, NIV). His point is that if we have placed our faith in Christ, we can't live like the pagans do, with hardened hearts that are indifferent to the things of God. Instead, we're called to throw off the old ways, put on the new self in Christ, and live the way Jesus taught us to live.

You're probably familiar with the story about the frog in the pot. If you throw a frog into boiling water, it'll jump out immediately. But if you put it in cool water and slowly turn up the heat, the frog won't notice the danger. It will just sit there, getting more comfortable, until it's too late. That's exactly how desensitization works in our lives. Drifting away from God rarely happens in a one swoop crash and burn. More often, it's like a slow boil, a steady dulling of the soul – a little compromise here, a little numbing there – until our hearts aren't as sensitive to God as they once were. By the time we realize it, the temperature around us has risen, and we're in real danger.

Imagine that C.S. Lewis' characters from *The Screwtape Letters* have a new modern-day "patient." With apologies in advance to Professor Lewis, here is how a text thread between Screwtape, the senior demon, and Wormwood, his apprentice, might go as they attempt to desensitize their human to sin and draw him away from God (who they refer to as the Enemy), one small degree at a time.

Wormwood: Quick update. Patient doing fine. No big sins, just small stuff. Ignoring prayer. Doomscrolling daily. Calls it "self-care" and "staying informed." Faith cooling off nicely. No alarms. No leaps. Just drifting. Temp rising slowly. She doesn't feel a thing. Will update you when she's fully cooked.

Screwtape: Good. Comfort is the anesthesia of hell. Keep it gradual. Sudden shocks wake them up. Temperature report?

Wormwood: Heat's up. She binges Netflix until 2 a.m. Wakes up late. Skips her quiet time. Too rushed to pray. Spends more time scrolling news feeds than seeking the Enemy. Calls it "staying connected."

Screwtape: Good work! Numbness is better than rebellion. Has she started explaining away her compromises yet?

Wormwood: Yep! Missed church? "Busy season." Gossiping? "Just venting." Clicking on websites she shouldn't? "Everyone does it."

Screwtape: Perfect. When our patients begin thinking of sin as personal freedom, they marinate beautifully. Any danger of her noticing the rising temperature?

Wormwood: Small scare last night. She felt "off" after zoning out for 3 hours on TikTok. Almost prayed. But I hit her with a YouTube rabbit trail of people deconstructing their faith and she forgot.

Screwtape: Well played! Doubt wrapped in postmodern thinking is one of our best tools. Keep her convinced she's smarter and wiser than she used to be. Her past zeal? "Immaturity." Her old convictions? "Narrow-minded."

Wormwood: Exactly! She still thinks she's in control. ● Meanwhile, we're basically slow cooking her soul.

Screwtape: Remember: No quick moves. Just keep her centered on herself. By the time she notices, she'll have no strength left to jump out. Carry on. Turn up the heat, just a notch.

Just like in this text thread, the devil and his demons are always playing the long game, subtly nudging us toward spiritual numbness. The drift is gradual, which makes it all the more dangerous. Slowly, and without realizing it, the enemy's influence over us creeps in, then it becomes normalized. The question for us is, how do we recognize when we're headed down the same path?

1. What are some warning signs that someone has become desensitized to sin and drifted in their relationship with God?

2. In Ephesians 4:19, Paul paints a picture of people who have become "callous," emotionally numb to sin, one small choice at a time. What are some examples of small compromises that can begin to harden our hearts?

3. In verses 20-21, Paul contrasts the old self with the new self. How does our conscience play a role in the ongoing battle between these two selves?

4. How does ignoring or suppressing the conviction of the Holy Spirit (Ephesians 4:30) lead to spiritual desensitization?

One of the best ways to stay sensitive to God is by keeping a short leash on sin. Repent quickly. Don't let sin pile up. One moment of true repentance can undo weeks, or months, of slow drifting. It's like hitting a spiritual reset button.

Let's check out what happens behind enemy lines when the two demons realize their human target is beginning to wake up:

> **Wormwood:** 911! The patient seems suspicious. In a weird moment of clarity she said, "Feels like I'm drifting."
>
> **Screwtape:** Awgh! How did you let her notice?? Don't botch this up! She needs to be too numb to feel the drift.
>
> **Wormwood:** It was that podcast she stumbled on. Some pastor talking about "slow spiritual death." Actually mentioned the frog-boiling story. Patient literally stopped mid-scroll. Sat there thinking.
>
> **Screwtape:** Thinking is dangerous. Feeling is disastrous. Quick: Flood her with urgent distractions. Emails. Notifications. News alerts. Keep her too busy to deal with those "feelings" the Enemy calls conviction.
>
> **Wormwood:** I tried. But you won't believe this. She actually turned off her phone. Then she prayed. Like, really prayed. For the first time in months. Started confessing sin.
>
> **Screwtape:** This is an utter disaster! Real prayer is spiritual oxygen. It clears their heads like a plunge into cold water. She might as well have jumped out of the pot.
>
> **Wormwood:** What do I do now?? Is it too late?? Should I make her feel ashamed for drifting so far?
>
> **Screwtape:** Yes. Shame is our last weapon now. Whisper: "You've failed too much." "You can't go back." "It's too late to start over." If we can't keep her in the pot, maybe we can convince her she's too far gone to be healed.
>
> **Wormwood:** On it. Guilt trip underway. Will report back.
>
> **Screwtape:** If she believes the Enemy's mercy and grace is still running after her, you're finished. Keep her looking at her failures – not at the cross.

Beloved daughter of the King, guilt and shame are some of the enemy's favorite weapons. He'll throw lies at you – about who you are and what you've done. Don't listen. Resist his lies. Surrender fully to God (James 4:7). When you do, it won't just ruin the enemy's day – it will crush his schemes beyond repair. Just ask Wormwood and Screwtape:

> **Wormwood:** Bad news. Patient didn't just pray. She repented. Full surrender. Asked the Enemy to "wake her up" and even said, "Lord, pull me out of whatever pot I'm sitting in." Cried. Worshiped. Feels alive again. Should I tell her it's just a temporary emotional high that will go away?
>
> **Screwtape:** It's too late, you numbskull. She's tasted real grace. The pot is shattered. The water is drained. The frog has leaped – and now she's back in the stream of life. You better hope you are not reassigned to the Department of Lower Vermin for this…although, frankly, you deserve it.

Have you started drifting toward desensitization without realizing it?

Just like the frog in the pot, we don't always notice when we're slipping into spiritual numbness. It's not something that happens overnight. We compromise a little here, get distracted a little there. One day at a time, we move further and further away from the heart of God. All the while, the enemy is turning up the heat. As Eldredge insightfully writes, "The story of your life is the story of the long and brutal assault on your heart by the one who knows what you could be and fears it." [34]

It's time to wake up! We are at war and the battle is real. The enemy fears who you are becoming in Christ, and he will do anything to keep you from that. You were not made for passivity. You were made to walk in power, to love with boldness, to live in the fullness of God. Rise up, warrior daughter! Fight. Abandon the old self and embrace the new, live fully alive to the Holy Spirit. You don't belong in the enemy's boiling pot. You belong to the King.

83 Love Divine

CHARLES WESLEY — JOHN ZUNDEL

Be imitators of God

Ephesians 5: 1-20

"Be imitators of God"

Ephesians 5:1-20

*The gospel is this: We are more sinful and flawed in ourselves than we ever dared believe,
yet at the very same time we are more loved and accepted in Jesus Christ
than we ever dared hope.* [1]
~ Tim Keller

With Ephesians 5:1-20, Paul moves us deeper into the practical part of his letter, where theology gives birth to transformation. He will take us through some difficult spaces as we traverse these verses. In fact, the very first line of the chapter opens with a weighty invitation: "Be imitators of God." With these four breathtaking, yet daunting words, Paul gives us a glimpse into the high calling on the church in Ephesus – and the Church today.

How do we as sinful, flawed people even begin to reflect a sinless, flawless God?

The answer lies in what we've already learned in Ephesians 1-3, Paul's treatise on our position in Christ. We are chosen, redeemed, sealed, and seated with Christ. We are His. Our identity *In Him* provides the foundation for us as we face some of the more challenging topics in the epistle.

Make no mistake, this is a difficult section. I won't sugarcoat it. Paul doesn't shy away from uncomfortable truths about sin, nor does he minimize their weightiness. But neither does he speak with condemnation. Instead, he reminds us who we are: beloved children, already accepted in Christ, already made new. He speaks not to shame us, but to shape us - to call us into a deeper relationship with Christ, the kind of life that reflects the One who saved us.

As we navigate what it means to "imitate God," Paul will give us three signposts directing us on our journey:

- Walk in love (v. 2)
- Walk in light (v. 8)
- Walk in wisdom (v. 15)

These aren't just checklists. They paint a picture of the kind of life that naturally flows from knowing who we are in Christ.

And the good news? We're not left to figure this out on our own. We're not feeling our way through the dark, just hoping we're headed in the right direction. We are walking with Jesus: The One Who is love, Who is light, and Who gives us wisdom for the journey.

Day One

Ephesians 5:1-2

By now, studying Ephesians might feel like standing beneath a powerful waterfall with truth after truth pouring over you. Let's pause for a moment, step back, take in the view, and remind ourselves of the big picture. Chapters 1-3 show us our wealth in Christ – all that God has given us *In Him*. Chapters 4-6 turn to our walk in Christ – how to live *In Him*. Our walk flows from our wealth, and our wealth should always shape our walk.

We'll cover just two verses today as we go deeper into this theme of "walking" in Christ. But first, let's get an overview of the passage for this lesson.

Read Ephesians 5:1-20, and answer the questions below.

1. Make a list of the key words from Ephesians 5:1-20. Use a purple pen to mark "in the name of our Lord Jesus Christ" in verse 20.

Key Words in Ephesians 5:1-20

2. What major themes jumped out to you as you read through these verses?

3. What tone do you detect from Paul in this section? Does it seem the same or different from previous chapters?

4. What, if anything, might feel difficult to digest about Paul's instructions?

Now, let's dive into our passage for today.

Read Ephesians 5:1.

One of my dearest, most prized possessions hangs on the wall in my living room. It was a simple gift from someone in my family – probably costing no more than about $30. So what makes this such a valuable item? It's an 8x10 photo of my Dad wrapping me in a bear hug while we stood on the back deck of a cabin in the fall of 2021, a moment my sister captured, not knowing our Dad would be with the Lord by the next fall.

But it's not really the grief or loss that makes this photo so dear. Even if Dad were still with us, I think I'd still love it just as much. Because when I look at that photo, regardless of what else is going on or how down on myself I may feel, I see the essence of Paul's words in Ephesians 5:1.

5. Fill in the blanks here for 5:1, "Therefore be imitators of God, as ______________ ____________________."

6. Why do you think it is important that we remember this portion of the verse as we strive to imitate God?

The photo I have of Dad hugging me always reminds me how much he loved me. But my earthly father's love is merely a shadow of the love my heavenly Father has for me as His adopted daughter.

It's a joke in our family that I, being the youngest of three girls, was a "happy surprise" for my parents. So "happy," in fact, that my mom cried when she found out she was pregnant with me – not exactly happy tears, but the tears of an exhausted mom who was already pouring herself out for a two-year-old and a five-year-old. (Don't worry, Mom's tears soon turned to happy tears. If I know nothing else in this world, I know that I'm loved by my mom.) But I was certainly an unexpected "gift" to the family!

Why do I tell you that? Look back at Ephesians 1:4-5.

7. As believers, how did we become God's children?

Do you see the difference? I was a surprise to my parents – ready or not, here I come! But we were no surprise to God. He chose us. He wanted us, even in our worst moments. He saw us before we were made and wrapped us in His arms as His "beloved children." Tony Merida explains, "An appropriate application of Ephesians 1:5 is Ephesians 5:1. These two verses belong together. Amazingly, the Father has loved us in the Beloved (1:6). We share in the love the Father has for the Son."[2]

That is our position as we're called to imitate God.

R.C. Sproul elaborates on the connection between the Father and His children:

> It is interesting that Paul conjoins the idea of imitation with the link that we have to God as His beloved children. Remember that the Apostle has spelled out in detail the glorious inheritance that is the Christian's, of having been adopted into the family of God. As the sons and daughters of God, we are to reflect the character of our parent, our heavenly Father. [3]

Read Ephesians 5:2.

With verse 2, we come to the first of the three instructional signposts: **Walk in love.**

8. Who is our example for walking in love, and how did He show His love? (v. 2)

We often say things like, "I'd do anything for the people I love, even die for them." And we might truly mean it. But when we read verses like this, do we pause to realize that Christ actually did that for us? He gave Himself up completely, walking the road of suffering, shame, and death – for us. His love wasn't symbolic. It was sacrificial.

That is the kind of love we're called to as we imitate God – the kind of love for one another that is "an offering and a sacrifice to God as a fragrant aroma" (5:2b). Merida explains, "In the Old Testament, sacrifices were placed on an altar. A 'pleasing aroma' was an Old Testament description of God's acceptance of a sacrifice given from a sincere and wholehearted worshiper (Genesis 8:21)." [4] For a long time, I struggled to articulate why Jesus had to die for our sins. But here it is, tucked right in the middle of this letter to the Ephesians: We needed a pleasing sacrifice. Jesus was it. The final sacrifice. That's how much God loved us, and we're told to love others the same way.

This command didn't just come from Paul. This directive came from a much higher authority, some thirty years before Ephesians was ever written.

9. Read John 15:12. Is the following statement true or false?
   Jesus was giving them a suggested way to live. Explain how you arrived at your answer.

   A. True B. False

DID YOU KNOW?

When you visit Israel and see the site where most scholars believe Jesus was crucified, you learn some background about the location. Jesus wouldn't have been crucified on a peaceful hill overlooking Jerusalem. No. The Romans prided themselves on their barbaric crucifixions, and it was all in the name of intimidation. Jesus' body didn't hang in a remote place, removed from the crowds. His bloodied body was on display for any passersby on the Damascus Road, a major thoroughfare just outside Jerusalem's city walls. Today, that site is a parking lot. Jesus knew all of this would happen when He gave Himself up for us.

As we wrap up today, and as we think on what it means to "imitate God," let's look at God's own description of Himself.

10. Read Exodus 34:6-7.

- Which characteristic of God means the most to you in your current season of life? Why?

- How does the character of God reframe your view of what it means to "walk in love"?

Meditate much on the love of Christ, and may it compel you to love like the Savior. [5]
~ Tony Merida

Day Two

Ephesians 5:3-7

To set the stage for today's study, let's first revisit the two verses we examined yesterday.

1. What two commands are given in Ephesians 5:1-2?

   •

   •

As we move forward, keep two key insights in mind:

> First, where your Bible likely says "Be imitators of God," the original Greek carries the sense of "Become imitators of God." The word "become" denotes a process, a progression, something we grow into over time. As the *Life Applicaton Bible Commentary* notes, "Paul understood this is a process."[6]
>
> Second, the Greek word for "love" in verse 2 is *agape* – a faithful, sacrificial kind of love. One definition puts it this way: "Agape love, as modeled by Christ, is not based on a feeling; rather, it is a determined act of the will – a joyful resolve to put the welfare of others above our own."[7]

Now, hold both of these things in your mind as you complete today's study.

Read Ephesians 5:3-4.

2. In the chart below, list the six sins believers must be free from and what one thing should replace them.

Remove from yourselves (5:3-4)	Replace it with (5:4)

These six behaviors that are not "proper" for believers fall into three broad categories: Immorality and impurity, greed, and corrupt speech.

Let's take a closer look at the first two – **immorality and impurity**. The word translated "immorality" in the Greek translated is *porneia*, from which we get the word "pornography." [8] An entire lesson could be written on the devastating impact the pornography industry is having on our families. But the immorality Paul is pointing to is broader than what we see with our eyes. As followers of Christ, those who are imitators of God and walk in sacrificial love, our actions with our bodies should reflect purity and self-giving love, not any type of self-gratification. Let's say it plainly: illicit sex of any kind stands in stark contrast to the love of Christ, because it is self-serving and can be emotionally, mentally, and even physically damaging.

The Greek word for "impurity" here is *akatharsia*, meaning unclean or defiled. Charles Swindoll notes that this word is related to the English word "catharsis," but in a negative sense:

> Just as something cathartic cleanses us, something "akathartic" pollutes us. Thus, *akatharsia* refers to the effect of immorality on our hearts, minds, and bodies – moral uncleanness that leads to guilt, shame, habitual sin, obsessions, addictions, and a life that spirals out of control...Sexual immorality only degrades our humanity; it never enhances it. It turns humans created in the image of God into objects created for gratifying our own selfish desires. [9]

See, our bodies were designed to be satisfied by the good gifts our Creator provides. In our modern culture, the idea of "satisfaction" has been fractured by sin and by an enemy whose chief desire is to "steal, kill, and destroy" (John 10:10). Merida explains this further,

> Your sexual sin is fundamentally a worship problem. To be clear, the Bible is not anti-sex. Rather, it is pro-intimacy within the covenant of marriage. But if you do not get the worship problem solved, you will never enjoy the beautiful gift of sex the way God intended. [10]

God has so much more to give His children than the empty things we chase after in the dark.

The next category of sin on Paul's list is **greed**. The Greek word for "greed" here is *pleonexia*, meaning covetousness – always wanting more, more, and more. [11] The tenth commandment addresses this sin: "You shall not covet your neighbor's house; you shall not covet your neighbor's wife, or his male servant, or his female servant, or his ox, or his donkey, or anything that belongs to your neighbor" (Exodus 20:17).

3. Read Colossians 3:5. What does Paul link greed to?

He will make the same connection in Ephesians 5:5, because greed "makes a god of what it seeks to possess." [12] Greed is idolatry, a sin of the heart. It places the desire for something else above our desire for God, breaking the very first commandment: "You shall have no other gods before Me" (Exodus 20:3).

Paul then moves to the third area of sin: **corrupt speech.**

4. What kinds of speech are listed as "not fitting" among believers? (v. 4)

Regarding our speech, James 3:10 says, "And so blessing and cursing come pouring out of the same mouth. Surely, my brothers and sisters, this is not right!" (NLT). Other translations complete his sentence with "this ought not to be so" (ESV) and "these things should not be this way" (NASB). In other words: This just doesn't fit! Square peg, round hole. For those of us who proclaim Jesus as Savior, we cannot also speak as the world speaks or joke as the world jokes.

Let's take just a moment and consider the three types of corrupt speech Paul targets in Ephesians 5:4:

- Filthiness is a reference to "shameful, disgraceful talk, including degrading obscenities that rob people of their dignity." [13]
- Silly talk is one compound word in the Greek language, *morologia,* from which we get the English word, "moron." [14] *Morologia* denotes useless, pointless words that have no value.
- Coarse jesting comes from the Greek word, *eutrapelia*, which means "able to turn easily." Warren Wiersbe notes, "The gift of wit is a blessing, but when it is attached to a filthy mind or a base motive, it becomes a curse. There are quick-witted people who can pollute any conversation with jests that are...out of place." [15]

But to be clear, Paul's censure of filthiness, silly talk, and coarse jesting is not condemning a good sense of humor. "A joyful heart is good medicine" (Proverbs 17:22). At the time I'm writing this, one of the most popular comedians in the U.S., and maybe the world, is a man who has decided to keep his comedy clean and appropriate for family audiences. Talk about a culture clash! It's nearly impossible to find comedians whose language is clean and wholesome. But based on his ticket sales, his type of comedy may be a lot more of what the world is looking for.

5. Why do you think people today, Christians and non-Christians alike, might find "clean" comedy so refreshing?

Immorality and impurity, greed, and corrupt speech indicate a self-centered person who is solely focused on the gratification of their own sinful inclinations.

As one person has rightly observed, "It is impossible to give thanks and sin at the same time." [16] Once again, the issue is worship. Thanksgiving is a posture of the heart, an "attitude of gratitude" that declares:

Thank You, Father, for Your generous heart. You've provided everything I truly need.
I don't have to chase after lesser gods for joy or fulfillment.

When you turn to Christ with a heart devoted to thanksgiving, the pull of lesser things fades away.

6. In what ways can thanksgiving be an antidote for sin? (v. 4)

Read Ephesians 5:5.

Here, Paul repeated the list he gave in 5:3, but this time he gives a sobering outcome for those who persist in these behaviors.

7. What is the consequence of this type of behavior? (v. 5)

This proclamation from Paul, an appointed messenger of God, should get our attention. But Paul's words here are not referring to someone losing their salvation. As we'll see later, Paul is speaking to believers – those who were "formerly darkness" (5:8). Kent Hughes gives some clarity on Paul's language, "Do Christians fall into these sins? Of course! But true Christians will not persist in them, for persistence in sensuality is a graceless state." [17]

If you've been in a spiral of sin or returning to old sin patterns, Hughes' clarification may not have made you feel much better. But to that I would ask: How did those sin patterns make you feel? Were you happy? Were you free? Did you walk with your head held high? If you are in Christ, I can safely assume the answers to those questions were "no, no, and no." Sin ensnares us (Hebrews 12:1) and enslaves us (John 8:34). But in Christ, we are free indeed (John 8:36), and the Spirit within us can no longer tolerate captivity.

Read Ephesians 5:6-7.

8. What warning does Paul give? (v. 6)

9. What correlating command is given in verse 7?

Paul is basically warning against "running around with the wrong crowd" in these verses. Paul cautions the Ephesians not to be deceived by empty words that make light of sin. God's judgment is real, and those who persist in rebellion will face it. As children of light, we're called to separate ourselves from such influences, not out of some form of spiritual pride, but out of a deep desire to walk in the truth.

Ephesians 5:3-7 invites us to take a heart inventory and ask the hard question: Are we settling for substitutes - chasing after fleeting pleasures - or are we living in the fullness of what God has already provided? When we fix our eyes on Christ and fill our hearts with gratitude, the noise of counterfeit things is silenced. May we walk in the light of His love, choosing each day to reflect His purity, His joy, and His grace. That, my friend, is life *In Him*.

Day Three

Ephesians 5:8-14

Today, we come to the second "walk" signpost in this week's passage: **Walk in light.**

1. Do you remember the first way we're to "walk" that we studied this week? (Hint: see Ephesians 5:2.)

Read Ephesians 5:8-10.

When Paul first wrote this letter, there were no chapter numbers or verse breaks. Those were added later by Bible translators to help us find our way around. But honestly, if you're like me, sometimes it feels like they interrupt the flow, especially when they land in the middle of a sentence like in 5:8. To help us stay on track, let's back up for a second and get our bearings.

2. At the end of yesterday's lesson, what had Paul just told the Ephesians not to do? (5:7)

He follows this command with a positional statement, reminding them of their new identity.

3. Fill in the chart below describing the believer's journey in Christ and our call (5:8).

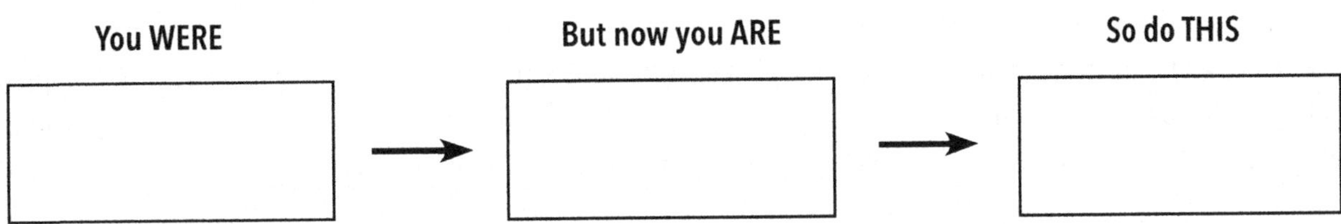

Here's the thing: We used to "partake" with these "sons of disobedience" (5:6-7). That's who we used to be. But the key word in verse 8 is "were." That is our old self, apart from Christ. Notice the word choice here – Paul didn't say "you were formerly in darkness;" he said "you were darkness." And he didn't say "you are in the Light of the Lord;" he said "you are the Light in the Lord." Paul is pointing to an exchange that goes deeper than behavior – it's a transfer of identity. It's not just about what we do, but about who we are now. He's saying that light has no place in darkness.

The *Life Application Commentary* reinforces Paul's idea:

> This darkness is part of every believer's past; all Christians were once darkness. But when they heard the gospel message and received salvation through Jesus Christ, they became light in the Lord. Christians are not merely "enlightened" to God's truth; they are also filled with light. [18]

Because believers are filled with Light, they should walk in light.

Read Ephesians 5:9-10.

Throughout Scripture, "Light" is used as a reference to God and His presence.

4. Read the following verses and record what the Light is doing in each passage.

Scripture	Light's Action
Genesis 1:3-4	
Exodus 13:21-22	
Psalm 27:1	
John 1:4-5	
John 8:12	
2 Corinthians 4:6a	

Then as we read in Ephesians 5:9, Light produces fruit. Think about it for a minute. Things don't grow in the dark, do they? Fruit is dependent upon light to ripen and mature.

5. What is the fruit of Light? (v. 9)

Wiersbe gives us a helpful description of this fruit, "Goodness is 'love in action.' Righteousness means rightness of character before God and rightness of actions before men. Both of these qualities are based on truth, which is conformity to the Word and will of God." [19]

In 5:10, Paul goes on to say that part of what we're called to do as children of Light is to "learn what is pleasing to the Lord." This goodness, righteousness, and truth is a good filter as we discern how to please the Lord. It's similar to Paul's list in Philippians 4:8, "Finally, brethren, whatever is true, whatever is honorable, whatever is right, whatever is pure, whatever is lovely, whatever is of good repute, if there is any excellence and if anything worthy of praise, dwell on these things."

6. How might dwelling on "these things" in "all goodness, righteousness, and truth" change the way you "walk" as a child of Light?

7. How can walking as a child of Light keep you from falling back into the path of darkness?

Read Ephesians 5:11-13.

As Paul continues, he doesn't just tell believers to stay away from the darkness, he calls us to "expose" it. That probably sounds a little intimidating. After all, who wants their worst thoughts or actions dragged into the light? And the idea of confronting someone else's sin? If you're like me, that feels equally daunting. So, let's pause here to consider the whole counsel of God's Word.

8. Look back at Ephesians 4:32. In what manner are we to relate to one another – even as we expose sin?

And in case it bears repeating, the first manner that Paul urged us to walk in is love. Sin must be taken seriously, and as we see a brother or sister stumbling back into darkness, the loving, kind, tenderhearted thing to do is to gently guide them back toward the Light. Remember, Jesus instructed us to "first take the log out of your own eye…" (Matthew 7:5). Many a church-goer has been irreparably hurt by someone who was quick to judge them without first examining their own heart. The goal isn't shame. The goal is healing. Light doesn't humiliate – it illuminates. It shows us where we've wandered so we can find our way home.

While it's important to handle fellow believers with tenderness and forgiveness, remember that the context here is actually how we should handle those who walk in darkness. There is much darkness and injustice in this world, and the Church must not be afraid of exposing it:

> The believer is called to expose the darkness in the corrupt places of our world – like where young children are trafficked, enslaved, and forced to work against their will, and where power is abused in other ways. We must bring the light of justice, exposing shameful, secretive sins, and bring the transforming light of the gospel to everyone – including the guilty enslavers themselves. [20]

Read Ephesians 5:13-14.

9. What happens when something is exposed to the light? (v. 13)

When believers share the gospel, we flip the light switch on for a world that is groping in darkness. God's light makes everything visible – it "exposes everything for what it is. Nothing can hide from the light." [21] As we share the light, we expose the lies of the enemy that keep people enslaved. We hold the flashlight that can help others leave their life of darkness and step into the Light.

10. Has there been a time when someone helped you see the darkness in your life? How did it feel at the time? How does it feel now?

DID YOU KNOW?

You may notice that the poem in Ephesians 5:14 likely does not have a cross reference listed in your Bible – or it may list several cross references pieced together – as it's not an exact quote from Scripture (though Paul is well known for quoting the Old Testament). This poem "may have been taken from a hymn well known to the Ephesians. The hymn could have been part of a baptismal hymn that was sung by the congregation for a new convert when he or she emerged from the baptismal waters. For the new believer, coming out of spiritual death is like awaking from sleep." [22]

Paul wraps up this powerful section with a wake-up call – literally. "Wake up, sleeper..." is not a command being shouted, but a song gently sung to a soul reborn. It's a poem about resurrection – about leaving behind the tomb of sin and stepping into the warmth of Christ's light. We were once darkness. But no longer. Now, like the hymn says, we rise...and the Light of the World greets us with open arms.

Dear friend, if you've been dozing in the shadows, today is the day to stop hitting the snooze button on your life in Christ. Allow the truth of God's Word to wake you up and call you back. Back to life. Back to light. Back to Him.

Day Four

Ephesians 5:15-20

Life moves fast. The days blur together. And if we're not careful, we can slip into neutral spiritually – drifting through life without direction or depth. But in Ephesians 5:15-20, Paul calls us to a higher plane. He urges us to live in wisdom – thoughtfully, intentionally, and filled with the Spirit. True wisdom isn't just about knowing more information, but about walking closely with the One who gives light to our path.

Read Ephesians 5:15-17.

Once again, Paul begins with the word "therefore," connecting verse 15 with what he said in the previous verse. Because you've been awakened, because Christ has shone His light on you, you are now called to live differently.

Paul then gives us the third "walk" signpost in verse 15: **Walk in wisdom.**

1. Quick review. Can you list the other two "walk" instructions we have covered in our lesson?

    -
    -

Connecting verses 14-15, Wiersbe makes an important observation:

> Paul appeared to be saying, "Don't walk in your sleep! Wake up! Open your eyes! Make the most of the day!" It is sad to see many professed Christians drift through life like sleepwalkers, never really making the most of opportunities to live for Christ and serve Him. [23]

Fun family fact: I used to sleepwalk a lot when I was a kid. My family has funny (and maybe a few scary) stories of things I would say or do while I wandered the house in a fog.

That's the kind of fog Paul is warning the Ephesians about. I imagine him clapping his hands in front of their faces to wake them up and get their attention. With verse 15, Paul begins the instruction on how to live now that you're awake. It's like he is saying, "Now that you've been brought into the light, here's what it looks like to walk in it."

2. What specific instructions does Paul give in verses 15-17?

3. How does Paul contrast wisdom and foolishness? (vv. 15-17)

Paul is clear: Those who do not walk wisely, will walk foolishly. There is no middle ground.

One of the ways wisdom shows up in our lives is the way we use our time. We all have the same 24 hours in a day, but not everyone spends them the same way. That's why Paul urges, "mak[e] the most of your time." The phrase carries the idea of buying something up before it slips away, like grabbing a rare treasure off the shelf before it's gone. Time is like that. Once a moment passes, it's gone. And in a world full of noise, distraction, and temptation, it's easy to lose whole days – or seasons – without ever realizing it.

4. What are some things that easily distract you from "making the most of your time"?

5. What are some practical steps you can take this week to use your time wisely?

The phrase "the days are evil" (v. 16) is similar to Paul's phrase in Galatians 1:4, "this present evil age" – it is the present time for the Ephesians and the present time for us as well. Merida makes the application, "We must passionately shine our light in the dark world while we have breath. When we see the King, we will not regret having spent our lives wisely." [24]

In verse 17, Paul urges us not to live thoughtlessly, but to pursue clarity about God's will. Foolishness, in this context, isn't about lacking intelligence, it's about living without direction, without purpose, and without reference to what God desires. Wisdom is found in aligning our lives with God's purposes rather than our own preferences.

6. Read Romans 12:1-2. How can we discern God's will for our lives?

Wiersbe notes, "God does not want us simply to know His will; He wants us to understand His will." [25] This type of understanding can only come from immersing ourselves in God's Word, keeping our minds set on Christ, and keeping our lives and our minds pure so that the Spirit can speak.

Read Ephesians 5:18-21.

7. What command does Paul give in Ephesians 5:18a?

8. In the table below, list three characteristics Paul gives of being "filled with the Spirit" in 5:19-20. In the second column, note what this can look like in your everyday life, in practical ways.

Characteristics of the Spirit	Practical Ways to Live it Out

Notice in 5:19, Paul's list of ways we're called to relate to one another. "Speaking to one another in psalms, hymns, and spiritual songs." Paul uses almost the same wording in Colossians 3:16, another passage on what it looks like to live as followers of Christ.

Frances Ridley Havergal, the writer of the hymn "Take My Life and Let it Be," understood what it meant to relate to each other in this way as children of God. As the hymn says,

Take my life, and let it be
Consecrated, Lord, to Thee;...
Take my moments and my days,
Let them flow in ceaseless praise,
Let them flow in ceaseless praise. [26]

Whether it's in our words, thoughts, or actions, we're called to conduct ourselves in such a way that our very lives pour out praise to God. This is what we were created for.

Ephesians 5:20 points us once again to thanksgiving – for all things. Gratitude is the overflow of a heart that is filled with the Spirit.

When we walked in darkness, our lives were marked by foolishness, confusion, excess, and wasted time. But now, as children of light, all of that is flipped on its head. We are called to walk wisely, to make the most of every opportunity, to seek the Lord's will, and to be filled with the Spirit. Our speech is to be life-giving, our hearts full of gratitude, our lives oriented around God's presence.

DID YOU KNOW?

The word "dissipation" or "debauchery" in Ephesians 5:18 is translated from the Greek word *asōtia* and, in this context, refers to "riotous living." One Bible study resource provides "wastefulness" as a synonym. [27] So we can read this verse as "Do not be drunk with wine, for that is wastefulness...." No wonder Paul gave this command in conjunction with verse 16, "make the most of your time."

This is the new way of living Paul invites us into, a life no longer shaped by the world's patterns, but by the Spirit's presence. Every moment becomes an act of worship. Every word a chance to build up. Every circumstance a reason to give thanks.

It's not about striving harder, but surrendering more deeply – allowing Christ to take our moments and our days and fill them with His wisdom, His joy, and His praise. This should be the daily life of the believer. As we walk forward from this passage today, may our lives sing the same prayer as Havergal's hymn: *Take my life, and let it be consecrated, Lord, to Thee.*

Day Five

Satan's strategy: Darkness

At this point in our study, we've looked extensively at what it means to be "in Christ" – how Christ is our identity, our power, and our salvation. Let's wrap up our week by taking a look at the contrast between what it means to be "in Christ" versus what it means to be "in the flesh."

The Bible refers to "the flesh" as sinful actions and desires. When we're "in the flesh," we're acting most like our natural selves instead of like the newly created beings we are "in Christ." And when we are in the flesh, it's like the light goes out. And instead of walking in light, we end up stumbling around in **darkness**.

Satan's favorite place to operate is in darkness. He loves to scheme and manipulate under the cloak of darkness, making us feel like the dark is the safest place to be.

Several years ago, I went for a run at the park near my house. I either misjudged how soon the sun was setting or how slowly I run. As I was jogging through a wooded area, a long way from my car, the last light of the sun dipped below the horizon. Not exactly ideal.

When I rounded the next corner, I saw a figure ahead on the side of the path. From a distance, it looked like a large dog with no owner in sight. As I got closer, I was almost certain that it was a large Doberman. It wasn't moving, which I hoped meant it was friendly...but then I realized – it wasn't moving at all. Heart pounding, eyes looking around for help in case this went south, I finally drew close enough to see the truth: it wasn't a dog at all. It was a broken tree stump.

I wasn't sure whether to be relieved or feel embarrassed. But one thought stuck with me: Darkness has a way of playing tricks on us.

1. Read 1 John 1:5 and write below what you won't find in Christ.

This is why abiding in Christ, being an imitator of God in how we walk, is actually our safe place. *In Him*, there is no deception. *In Him*, there is no regret. *In Him*, there is no manipulation. *In Him*, there is no condemnation. *In Him*, there is no fear. *In Him*, there is no darkness – at all.

No. *In Him*, we'll find quite the opposite of all those things. *In Him*, there is love, joy, peace, patience, kindness, goodness, faithfulness, gentleness, and self control (Galatians 5:22-23). And most of all, *In Him*, there is light.

2. Read the following verses and list the benefits of God's light:

- 2 Corinthians 4:6b –
- Psalm 119:105 –
- 1 John 1:7 –
- John 8:12b –

Satan's deceitful strategy is to convince us that darkness is safer than light – that light only exposes shame, that it burns rather than heals. And perhaps we've reinforced that lie with our "cancel culture" and our judgmental looks toward those who have stumbled. But that, too, is an agent of darkness. God looks upon every one of us, even in our darkness, and lovingly calls us to into the light. Because it's in the light that we begin to resemble Christ.

Remember, the lesson this week began with the challenge to "be imitators of God." And *In Him*, "there is no darkness at all." Do you believe this is possible? Do you know that it's possible to live without the constant shroud of darkness? Do you believe that you can live without the weight of hiding, pretending, and being fearful? We will only begin to taste that freedom when we step into Christ – when we stop striving and start surrendering – and allow His life to shine though ours.

3. Close this week by writing a prayer below, asking God to search your heart for any areas of darkness. Go to Him as a beloved child, and ask His forgiveness for what you've kept in the dark, and then rest in the comfort of the Father's love.

When you sin, don't give up. Let Him pick you up and put you on your feet again with fresh dignity.
He lifts your chin, looks you in the eye, and defines your existence:
"You in Me, and I in you (John 14:20)." [28]
~ Dane Ortlund

375 Take My Life, and Let It Be

FRANCES R. HAVERGAL — C. H. A. MALAN

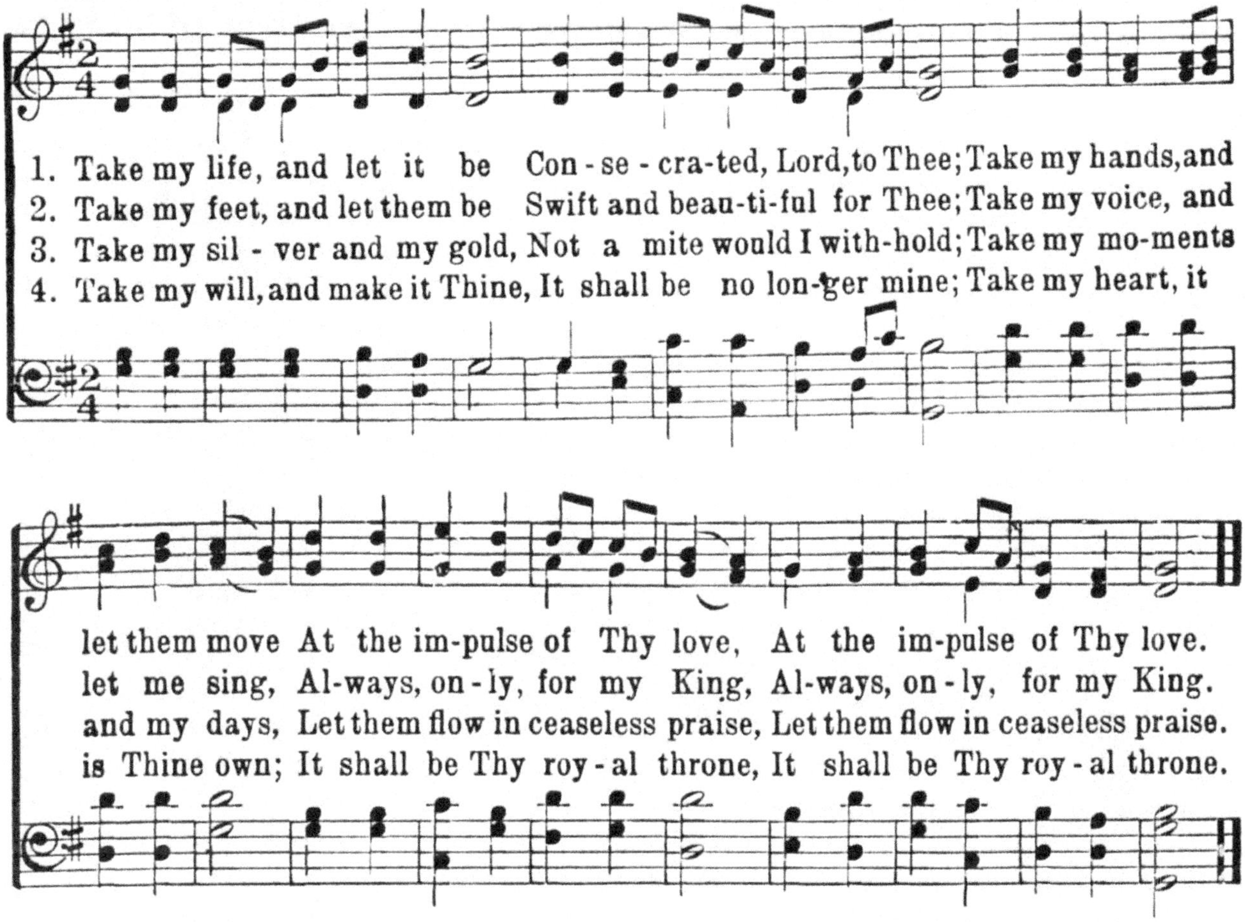

1. Take my life, and let it be Con-se-cra-ted, Lord, to Thee; Take my hands, and
2. Take my feet, and let them be Swift and beau-ti-ful for Thee; Take my voice, and
3. Take my sil - ver and my gold, Not a mite would I with-hold; Take my mo-ments
4. Take my will, and make it Thine, It shall be no lon-ger mine; Take my heart, it

let them move At the im-pulse of Thy love, At the im-pulse of Thy love.
let me sing, Al-ways, on-ly, for my King, Al-ways, on-ly, for my King.
and my days, Let them flow in ceaseless praise, Let them flow in ceaseless praise.
is Thine own; It shall be Thy roy-al throne, It shall be Thy roy-al throne.

Be subject to one another

Ephesians 5:21 - 6:9

"Be subject to one another"

Ephesians 5:21-6:9

Submission has nothing to do with the order of authority,
but rather governs the operation of authority, how it is given and how it is received. [1]
~ Warren Wiersbe

As you begin this week's study, the passage heading in the *New Living Translation* (NLT) and the opening verse in *The Message* translation help set the tone for the relationship dynamics we'll explore together. The *NLT* labels this section "Spirit-Guided Relationships," while *The Message* begins with the simple but solemn phrase, "Out of respect for Christ..." (Ephesians 5:21). Two key themes emerge right away: First, we need the Holy Spirit to guide us in our relationships. Second, our motivation in how we treat others should flow from our reverence for Christ. If those two truths shape our mindset, we will find ourselves entangled less in the daily struggle with our selfish and sinful nature.

Husbands and wives, parents and children – can you think of any other relationship dynamic that requires the aid of the Holy Spirit more than these? (If you are the parent of a teenager, you just gave a hearty "Amen!") And then consider the often complicated association between employers and employees (masters and servants in Paul's day). While these relationships can be filled with blessing, encouragement, joy, favor, and fulfillment, they can also be the source of our deepest wounds and greatest challenges. In our passage this week, Paul invites us to bring even the most difficult parts of our relationships under the Spirit's leadership.

Perhaps you are single, widowed, or do not have children. Maybe you do not currently hold a conventional job outside the home. Please do not check out if you find yourself thinking, "This does not apply to me." God's Word is alive, active, and applicable to you! Perhaps it speaks to what may be coming in your future. The Lord may put a woman in your path in search of godly counsel or wisdom from above – not just what the culture says is "normal," but what God says is true. Jennie Allen asks two pertinent questions for us to lay before the Lord as we begin our study this week:

God, what do you want me to know?
God, what do you want me to do? [2]

To prepare your heart for how God wants to speak to you, take a moment to sit in His presence and pray:

Holy Spirit, be my Guide. In marriage, in parenting, in my work, and in every relationship in which You have placed me, be my Teacher. In all these areas, I commit my words, my actions, my perspective, and my beliefs to be surrendered to You. Strengthen me to be submissive where You have called me to be submissive. Fill my heart with love for every person with whom I am in a relationship. May I serve You as I serve those in my life and may I fulfill every role as unto You, Lord.

Day One

Ephesians 5:21

Begin today by reading Ephesians 5:21-6:9 in its entirety. As you read, underline the key words in the chapter. Don't forget to use a purple pen to mark the one equivalent of "In Him" in this passage.

1. Make a list of the key words from Ephesians 5:21-6:9.

Key Words in Ephesians 5:21-6:9

2. What is Paul's general idea in this text?

Now, read Ephesians 5:21 aloud.

3. Why do you think submission ("being subject to one another") is such a difficult subject?

Before we walk through the rest of this passage verse by verse, let's pause to consider the broader idea of submission. Few topics are more misunderstood – or more misrepresented – in today's culture. But what Paul teaches here isn't oppressive or outdated. It's deeply spiritual, profoundly countercultural, and beautifully freeing when rightly understood. A biblical view of submission can transform our relationships and reshape any misconceptions we may carry. It's also important to keep in mind: Paul is writing to believers. These instructions are meant for those who have already surrendered their lives to Christ – people who are learning to live under His loving authority.

A quick side note: I know that some women have a negative view of submission due to abusive relationships. If this happens to be your story, first I want to say I am deeply sorry. As you open your heart to God's Word, my prayer for you is that your heavenly Father will reach into the depths of your soul and bring comfort, healing, and reminders of His perfect love. I want to encourage you to dig deep, to allow the Lord to renew and transform your mind in this area. The enemy would like nothing more than to use unjust and painful circumstances to keep you from knowing what God's Word really says about submission. Resist his foul intentions. Don't allow Satan to fill your mind with doubt about God's good and perfect plan for your life and your relationships.

I have a note written in my Bible that says, "Notice this follows the section entitled, 'Living by the Spirit's Power.' I cannot do this apart from being filled." You will recall, last week's lesson took us through the first part of Ephesians 5, which closes by cautioning us to be careful how we live, and then goes on to tell us to be filled with the Spirit, to live a life of praise and thanksgiving. Would you not agree that this is a prerequisite to having Spirit-guided relationships? Paul knew (by way of revelation) that to be submissive in a way that honors Christ, we would have to be filled with the Spirit, choose wisdom over foolishness, and have hearts filled with praise and gratitude. We cannot do this in our own flesh.

Warren Wiersbe reiterates, "By nature, we want to promote ourselves, but the Holy Spirit enables us to submit ourselves." [3] This truth fits well with our study, as we are learning the incredible reality of what it means to live *In Him*. It is only through the power of the Holy Spirit dwelling in us – and our ongoing choice to abide *In Him* – that we can truly understand and live out the kind of Spirit-empowered submission Paul describes.

4. What does it mean to yield or submit to someone?

5. Has your understanding of submission changed over time, and if so, why?

Submission is a God-appointed sequence. We see throughout Scripture that God is a God of order. The devil is a god of chaos. The world has distorted submission and given it a negative connotation, which plays right into the enemy's hand of causing us to doubt the heart and character of our good God.

6. Read Ephesians 5:22, 6:1, and 6:5 and make note of the repeated phrase/idea in each.

"As to the Lord." "In the Lord." "As to Christ." Our reason and our motive for submission in each of these situations should be out of fear of and reverence for God. He is the One to whom all glory and honor should be given. He is the One we should strive to please and honor in every relationship.

As a wife, a husband, a child, an employee – as a child of God – your primary reason for choosing to submit should come from a heart that loves God and lives to please Him.

7. In what ways does Jesus model submission for us?

- Luke 22:42 –

- John 4:34 –

- 1 Corinthians 11:3 –

8. How has the Lord spoken to your heart about submission through today's study?

So how do we live out this challenging call to submission? It begins not with willpower, but with resting in Christ. Watchman Nee puts it this way:

> The Christian's secret is his rest in Christ. His power derives from his God-given position. Forsake for a moment our place of rest in Him, and immediately we are tripped and our testimony in the world is marred. But abide in Christ, and our position there ensures the power to walk worthy of Him here. [4]

True submission flows not from striving, but from abiding – drawing strength from our position in Christ, not our own performance. When we stay rooted *In Him*, we find the grace to do what would otherwise be impossible.

Day Two

Ephesians 5:22-33

Contemplate the many-sided ways in which the truth about God Himself, and the truth about how we live out our most precious relationships, intertwine and create a God-given beauty the world never dreams of. [5]
~ N.T. Wright

When you think about husbands, wives, and marriage, do you ever consider that we're called – and empowered – to reflect a "God-given beauty," as N.T. Wright puts it? That's exactly what Scripture invites us to believe and pursue. Why? Because marriage was designed by God to portray the saving gospel of Jesus Christ.

When we, as Christ-followers, commit to living out marriage God's way rather than the world's, we become living, breathing, walking pictures of the gospel. But the opposite is also true: when we ignore God's design and follow culture's script instead, we risk presenting a distorted and perverted version of the gospel – one that misrepresents Christ's love and covenant with His people.

The eternal destination of souls can be affected by how we portray marriage in the Christian home. You might want to read those words again…and let them sink in.

As we begin, I want to gently encourage you to pause and examine your heart. I say this only because I've just done the same. Whether you're a wife, or a woman with assumptions about what it means to be a wife, this invitation is for all of us.

After sitting with this portion of Scripture for weeks, and now writing about it, I found myself needing to confess to my husband and sons. I don't tell you this to boast, or to try to sound "spiritual." Honestly, I would rather leave this part out, but I know how heavily the Lord impressed me to do this. Perhaps you need to do something similar – consecrating yourself prior to moving on through today's study.

If you are aware of specific ways you have been disobedient in this area, take a moment to give your husband a call, a text, or write out a note to say you are sorry. I had to specifically apologize for not always being respectful to my husband (leaving out any explanation or justification) and, in doing so, I was not setting a good example for my sons. Thankfully, they all offered a gracious response of love and forgiveness. Ok…now, I am ready to write!

Read Ephesians 5:22-24.

Paul first addresses wives. Yay! (If it makes you feel better, wives get two verses and husbands get nine.)

1. What instruction is given to wives? (v. 22)

2. How are wives to submit to their husbands? (v. 22)

How do we do this "as to the Lord?" J. Vernon McGee explains it this way, "The way we respond to the Lord is that we love Him because He first loved us. A very personal, loving relationship is the ground for submission." [6] Wiersbe adds:

> When the Christian wife submits herself to Christ and lets Him be the Lord of her life, she will have no difficulty submitting to her husband. This does not mean that she becomes a slave, for the husband is also to submit to Christ. And if both are living under the lordship of Christ, there can be only harmony. Headship is not dictatorship. [7]

3. What is the order of submission in verses 23-24?

Wright goes on to say, "The husband is to take the lead – though he is to do so fully mindful of the self-sacrificial model which the Messiah has provided. As soon as 'taking the lead' becomes bullying or arrogant, the whole thing collapses." [8]

The world often distorts Scripture, claiming that it calls for blind obedience from wives or suggests that women are inferior to their husbands. But that is <u>not</u> what Paul is teaching in Ephesians 5. Instead, God is giving us a beautiful and purposeful order for the Christian home – a structure rooted in love. Christ is the head of the husband, and the husband is called to lovingly lead his wife. The *Life Application Study Bible* explains, "According to the Bible, the man is the spiritual head of the family, and his wife should acknowledge his leadership." [9] This isn't about value or worth – it's about order, responsibility, and mutual devotion under the authority of Christ.

Think about a company, a volunteer organization, a non-profit ministry, a church, or even a high school club or college fraternity. All of these entities have a leader, someone who is in a position of authority. Why? Because without clear leadership, there is chaos, inefficiency, and ultimately, disorder. No company can function, much less thrive, without a CEO. For any group to work toward a common goal, someone must lead, and others must recognize and respect the position and authority of that leadership.

The Christian home is no different. Structure isn't about superiority; it's about unity and direction. Max Lucado offers this insight:

> Life presents decisions that must be made even if there is a disagreement. In a union of two, there can be harmony on most issues. But when there is a nonnegotiable disagreement, someone must have the responsibility of the deciding vote. This is the essential challenge and opportunity of love and respect. [10]

Wives, I encourage you (as I have been challenged) to see your role as a Christian wife as a sacred privilege and honor – to view your submission to your husband as an act of service, "as to the Lord," because that is exactly what it is. "As the church submits to Christ, so you wives should submit to your husbands in everything" (Ephesians 5:24, NLT).

Read Ephesians 5:25-33.

4. How should a husband love his wife and for what purpose? (vv. 25-26)

5. How does Christ's purpose for the church parallel a husband's role in marriage? (v. 27)

A husband is called to love sacrificially and with sanctifying intent. He is to love as Christ loves the church, laying down his life and taking spiritual responsibility for his wife's growth in holiness. This is no small task; it's a weighty calling. While wives are called to submit to an imperfect man, husbands are called to submit to a perfect God, and to love in a way that reflects the heart and character of Christ.

6. How else is a husband called to love his wife? (vv. 28-30)

How can we apply this section of Scripture to our lives?

- If you are a wife: Pray these verses over your husband. Thank the Lord if he obediently does these things, and if he does not, ask the Lord to move his heart to love you according to the Word of God.
- If you are a single woman: Look for, pray for, and expect these traits in a potential mate.
- If you are a mother or grandmother: Pray for these characteristics in your children and grandchildren.
- If you are a mentor or friend: Be knowledgeable about what God's Word says about Christian marriage as you teach and counsel women in your life.

Paul wraps up his exhortation by summarizing the purpose of Christian marriage, quoting Genesis 2:24.

7. What is the foundation for Christian marriage? (Ephesians 5:31)

One <u>man</u> and one <u>woman</u> joined together to become one flesh.

8. What does this union illustrate? (v. 32)

As husbands and wives fulfilling the roles to which God has called us, we have the distinct honor to present the relationship of Christ and the church to a lost and broken world. Ask God to help you see marriage as a display of Christ and the church, to tear down any worldly thought or belief contrary to His Word, and to give you opportunities to share the gospel through the gift of Biblical marriage.

Paul closes Ephesians 5 by reminding us again of our roles as husband and wife.

9. What is the husband called to do? What is the wife called to do? (v. 33)

Paul directs the wife to respect her husband. Paul instructs the husband to love his wife selflessly. But does this come naturally? For most of us, the honest answer is "no." Once again, we see the character of God on display, speaking directly into the places where we are prone to struggle. He doesn't ignore our weaknesses; He meets them with wisdom and grace. In commanding love and respect, God is not only guiding our relationships but also shaping our lives to look more like His Son.

Finish up today by pondering the quote below from Wiersbe. Read it slowly, contemplating each phrase. and take a few moments to journal your thoughts on how the Lord speaks to you about any change to which He is calling you.

If Christian husbands and wives have the power of the Spirit to enable them, and the example of Christ to encourage them, why do too many Christian marriages fail? Somebody is out of the will of God. [11]

Take a few moments to journal how the Lord is speaking to you, especially about any changes He is calling you to make in your life.

Day Three

Ephesians 6:1-4

"Because I said so."

Did you ever hear this as a child? Or say it as a parent? If you are like me, you despised hearing it as a child and promised you would never say it as a parent...right?

And I tried. I really did. I made a conscious effort not to use that phrase often, but I have to admit, it slipped out a time or two (probably accompanied by a pointed finger and clenched teeth). And frankly, in certain situations, it does serve as the best reason and is, in fact, true.

But when my boys were little, I purposefully turned to Scripture instead. Ephesians 6:1 became a familiar verse in our home. I would often have them say the verse to me. When those sweet little cherubs found themselves in trouble and needed correction, I would go over the offense and explain how they had been disobedient and then ask them, "What does the Bible say about children obeying their parents?" And they would respond by quoting Ephesians 6:1, which gave me the opportunity to remind them of the truth of God's Word.

Read Ephesians 6:1.

1. What is Paul's admonition? (v.1)

2. Why should children obey their parents? (v.1)

Have you found yourself at times reading a Bible passage that stumps you, one that may be a little difficult to understand or explain? Well, that is not the case here. Paul speaks clearly and to the point, and he offers a much better reason than "because I said so."

While it is true that my children should obey because I say so, it is much more important for them to obey because it is the right thing to do. This is the lesson I wanted to sear onto the hearts of my young children. I did not want them to obey me only because I told them to (and because it held down the embarrassment factor in public places). I wanted them to obey me because that is what the Lord wanted them to do, and it was right in His eyes. We do not want to teach our children to live to please us. We want them to live to please the Lord.

John Piper makes a powerful observation about the importance of this command:

> It makes no sense that God would require children to obey parents and yet not require parents to require obedience from the children. It is part of our job – to teach children the glory of a happy, submissive spirit to authorities that God has put in place. Parents represent God to small children, and it is deadly to train children to ignore the commands of God. [12]

This is strong language – but true. Children are not born knowing how or desiring to obey. That is the job of the Christian parent, to train them to obey because God has commanded it, and it is right.

Read Ephesians 6:2-3.

3. What command does Paul give and what promise is attached to it? (vv. 2-3)

Paul is quoting from the Ten Commandments when he gives the instruction to "Honor your father and mother" (Exodus 20:12). There is a distinct difference between obey and honor: "To obey means to do as one is told; to honor means to respect and love. Children are to obey while under their parents' care, but the responsibility to honor parents is for life." [13]

Have you ever wondered about the promise Paul attaches to the fifth commandment? I like the way Wiersbe explains it:

> This does not mean that everyone who died young dishonored his parents. He [Paul] was stating a principle: When children obey their parents in the Lord, they will escape a good deal of sin and danger and thus avoid the things that could threaten or shorten their lives. But life is not measured only be quantity of time. It is also measured by quality of experience. God enriches the life of the obedient child no matter how long he may live on the earth. Sin always robs us; obedience always enriches us. [14]

"Sin always robs us; obedience always enriches us" is powerfully true and a perfect summation of this text. Living a life of disobedience will rob us of God's favor and blessing. Living a life of obedience will enrich our lives with the abundance of God's favor and blessing. That is why we must teach our children to obey.

4. How can teaching obedience affect the lives of your children and your children's children? (If you do not have children, how can you teach this principle to those over whom you have influence?)

Read Ephesians 6:4.

While fathers are called to be the spiritual head of the home, this verse applies to Christian parents, both mother and father. McGee says, "The emphasis is on the father because the disciplining and training of the child is actually his responsibility, but it does include the mother also." [15]

5. What are parents commanded to do and not to do? (v. 4)

The purpose of discipline in the home is not to frustrate and discourage the children, but to train them up in the ways of the Lord. This can only be done in the "fullness of the Spirit so they can be sensitive to the needs and problems of their children." [16]

Raising children according to God's Word requires a Spirit-filled life, a life that is saturated *In Him.* A daily emptying of self and a fresh filling of the Holy Spirit is the only way to walk in obedience to the text we have studied today.

To discipline, train, admonish, and teach our children, we must be disciplined ourselves.

6. What areas of your life need to change so that you are equipped to pour into the lives of your own children or those whom God has placed in your life?

One of the greatest gifts you can give your children is the gift of prayer: to pray with them and over them. Luke 2:52 has always been one of my favorite verses to pray over my boys. I have prayed this for years and will continue all the days of their lives.

7. Read Luke 2:52 and make note of how Jesus grew.

DID YOU KNOW?

"Discipline" refers broadly to the whole process of training, but particularly in the form of discipline. "Instruction" is a word which literally means to put sense in the mind. It refers to encouragement by words and assurances if that is needed or admonishment if that is needed. [17]

What more could we ask of the Lord than for our children to grow just as Jesus did. This covers all of the bases: intellectual, physical, spiritual, and social.

Steven Cole emphasizes what our motive should be in following Paul's instruction: to follow the example of Jesus. He writes, "This is all about reflecting God's glory in Jesus Christ to a lost world. By obeying and honoring your parents, you are following the example of Jesus Himself, who although He was God in human flesh, 'continued in subjection' to His earthly parents (Luke 2:51). Go thou and do likewise!" [18]

Dear sisters, let's change the default in our parenting vocabulary from "because I said so" to "for this is the right thing to do" (Ephesians 6:1, NLT).

Day Four
Ephesians 6:5-9

As the servants of Christ, doing the will of God from the heart...
Ephesians 6:6b, KJV

William Carey, a shoemaker, applied to serve as a foreign missionary. During the process, someone, asked, "What is your business?", intending to belittle him because he was not an ordained minister. Carey responded, "My business is serving the Lord, and I make shoes to pay expenses." His simple but profound reply revealed the heart of a servant of Christ. His identity wasn't rooted in his trade, but in his calling. [19]

A servant of Christ. This language is consistent with what we have already studied this week. As we have explored the role of a Christian wife, husband, and child, the primary focus has been the attitude of the heart – choosing to be fully submitted and surrendered to the perfect design of the Father. And in most cases, the world's message stands in stark contrast to what the Word of God calls us to do in each of these roles.

Before we dive into our text, some clarification and context are in order. The Greek word for "slave" or "servant" (depending upon your Bible translation) is *doulos*, someone who belonged entirely to another. [20] These two words carry negative connotations as we consider those living in the days of the Roman Empire and the years prior to the Civil War in the United States. In both instances (and many other current day examples), slavery was and is wrong. McGee rightfully declares, "The very nature of the gospel condemned slavery." [21]

As he writes in Ephesians 6:5-9, Paul is not endorsing the abusive systems of human ownership, but rather using a familiar cultural reality to communicate a greater spiritual truth: the idea of total devotion and belonging. In the Christian life, a *doulos* is a picture of joyful surrender to Christ, a Master who is perfectly just, loving, and sacrificial.

DID YOU KNOW?

Some historians have estimated that upwards of one-third of the 180 million residents of the Roman Empire were slaves. They represented the lowest cast of society, and like women and children, they had no rights in society. Greeks and Romans thought of slaves as little more than "living tools." [22]

To be a "servant/slave of Christ" is to willingly place ourselves under His Lordship, not out of coercion, but out of love. It's not about oppression; it's about identity. In a world obsessed with autonomy, Paul reminds believers that true freedom is found in full submission to the One who gave everything to redeem us.

Paul's instructions here direct both master and slave in the areas of responsibility and integrity in their respective roles; and these same words apply to the Christian employee and employer today. The purpose of today's study will be to better equip us to work and oversee the work of others in a manner that honors the Lord Jesus Christ. As Carey well said, our "business is serving the Lord."

Read Ephesians 6:5-6.

Cole summarizes it this way, "Your relationship to Christ and the fact that you live primarily for Heaven should transform your relationships at work." [23]

1. What command is given to the slave (employee)? How and why should it be done? (vv. 5-6)

- v. 5 –

- v. 6 –

The goal here is a "right heart attitude on the job." [24] Serving your employer as you would serve Christ – even when no one is watching – is indicative of a heart that lives to please the Lord.

Paul is calling the Christian worker to see beyond an earthly boss and to work with the awareness that Christ Himself is the true authority. If we could view our employer as if he or she were Christ – even when they fall far short of acting like Him – and do our work as though Jesus were standing right beside us, it would radically change our attitude and actions. That's exactly the kind of obedience Paul is urging us toward: wholehearted, Christ-centered service in every task, big or small.

2. What is the first and greatest commandment according to Matthew 22:37?

Love God with all of your heart, soul, and mind. This instruction encompasses all of who we are. If we are living this way, we will work with our all – whether we are working in the presence of our boss or all alone.

3. What are some things that might keep you from working with "the right heart attitude"?

Read Ephesians 6:7-8.

4. How should we work and why? (v. 7)

5. How does Colossians 3:23-24 parallel this command?

We are serving Christ, not men. In the KJV, the language of Ephesians 6:5 reads "in singleness of your heart." One of my favorite verses to pray over myself and my family is Psalm 86:11, "Give me an undivided heart, that I may fear Your name" (NIV). If my heart is singularly focused on what God calls me to do and is not divided between the world and the Word, the area of work will fall in line with the will of my Father in Heaven.

Although it is often not easy, the Christian life really is simple. Love the Lord with all of me. Allow Him – only Him – to sit on the throne of my heart. Follow Him – only Him. Live to please Him – only Him.

6. Are you living as a slave of Christ?

7. What is the benefit of obeying Paul's instructions? (v. 8)

The Lord will reward us! Rather than the applause and approval of men, we should desire a heavenly reward from our heavenly Father.

Paul also has a word for the Christian employer as we close today's text.

Read Ephesians 6:9.

8. What is Paul's instruction for employers (masters) and the reasoning he gives? (v. 9)

The *Life Application Study Bible* offers this insight, "Although Christians may be at different levels in earthly society, we are all equal before God. He does not play favorites; no one is more important than anyone else." [25]

In our human reasoning, we tend to naturally view an employer as more important than an employee. In the days of the Roman Empire in which Paul lived, the master was undoubtedly viewed as a higher rank than the slave. Here, Paul shuts down the insignificance of any person or position. He assures his readers (and us) that the Master has no favorites and views every person the same. McGee reiterates, "In the presence of Christ, the master and the servant stand on the same footing. They are brothers in Christ." [26]

As we have discussed throughout our lesson this week, this perspective will set us apart from the world in a noticeable way. Today, we live in a society of "my rights" where people are quick to let others know what they will and will not tolerate. Paul's instructions encourage us to be most concerned with conducting ourselves as though we are working for the Lord, whether it be as a boss or a worker. This shows the world, even in unfair and imperfect circumstances, that we are choosing to live a life *In Him*. And only *In Him* are we able to live and work in the way God's Word calls us to.

Christian employees and employers should be the best on the job! Our identity as a follower of Jesus Christ should be the driving force behind everything we say and do. He must be at the center of our thoughts, words, actions, and reactions.

Choose today to work and serve as a slave of Christ – doing the will of God with all your heart.

Day Five

Satan's strategy: Dysfunction

God's intention for you is to live a life fully alive and abundant. Jesus' words in John 10 tell us just that – His purpose is to give us a "rich and satisfying life" (John 10:10, NLT).

Throughout his teaching in Ephesians 5:21-6:9, Paul has made clear the divine order as it relates to Christian households and relationships. We would be prudent to take Jesus' words from John 10:10 and apply them to these areas. In the relationships of marriage, parenting, and work, God has given us a design that ensures we can walk in this abundance.

However, the converse is also true. One of Satan's favorite tactics in these areas is to breed **dysfunction**. Why? Because dysfunction pulverizes any hope for abundance and fulfillment.

God's design → Delectation (delight, enjoyment) [27]

Satan's design → Dysfunction (impaired or abnormal functioning) [28]

As C.S. Lewis writes, "There is no neutral ground in the universe: every square inch, every split second, is claimed by God and counter-claimed by Satan." [29]

In our homes and in our relationships, this statement is unquestionably true. God has laid claim in His design over our homes, relationships, work, and service; but the enemy is on a relentless mission to destroy us and deceive us into a "better" and more widely accepted way of doing things – taking us back to the very definition of dysfunction.

In his book, *Experience Jesus. Really*, John Eldredge speaks to the importance of abiding in Jesus (John 15) and how, in doing so, we will experience refuge. He writes, "If we remain in him, the refuge and resources of God are ours. Here is the simple fact: You can choose to leave the protection of God. People do it all the time." [30] He goes on to say, "'Remain in me,' Jesus urges. You can almost hear the plea in his voice: Stay in Me; don't operate in anything outside of me." [31]

Operating outside of Jesus always leads to dysfunction – an impaired way of functioning.

To be certain, none of us would willfully choose dysfunction. But I believe I am safe to assume I am not the only one who has an element of dysfunction within my own family. Dysfunction is the result of sin entering into the world and perverting what God originally intended.

1. What are common ways Satan infuses dysfunction into marriages, parent/child relationships, and work situations?

2. How can you stand firm against the enemy's tactics to bring dysfunction?

As you reflect on this week's study, consider this insight from Watchman Nee, "If the life of a Christian is to be pleasing to God, it must be properly adjusted to Him in all things." [32]

3. What adjustments do you sense the Lord leading you to make to lessen dysfunction in your life?

As you close today, ponder this reflection of Watchman Nee.

> God never asks us to do anything we <u>can</u> do. He asks us to live a life which we can never live and to do a work which we can never do. Yet, by his grace, we <u>are</u> living it and doing it. The life we live is the life of Christ lived in the power of God, and the work we do is the work of Christ carried on through us by His Spirit whom we obey. [33]

We cannot do this alone. Jesus tells us that apart from Him, we can do nothing (John 15:5).

<u>Nothing</u>.

Outside of Him, you cannot be a submissive and respectful wife. Your husband cannot be a loving husband. You cannot be an encouraging parent or a child who honors your parents. You cannot be an honest worker or a generous boss.

But, *In Him*, you can walk in obedience and experience the abundance of His blessings.

Let us wrap up our study this week with praise – declaring the assurance we have because we are *In Him*. Pay close attention to these lyrics as you meditate on all the Lord has taught you this week. The words of this treasured hymn speak beautifully to the rest that come as a blessing to the submissive heart – rest like peaceful, still waters where the soul is quieted *In Him*.

> *Blessed assurance, Jesus is mine!*
> *Oh, what a foretaste of glory divine!*
> *Heir of salvation, purchase of God,*
> *Born of His Spirit, washed in His blood.*

Perfect submission, perfect delight,
Visions of rapture now burst on my sight;
Angels descending, bring from above
Echoes of mercy, whispers of love.

Perfect submission, all is at rest,
I in my Savior am happy and blest,
Watching and waiting, looking above,
Filled with His goodness, lost in His love.

This is my story, this is my song,
Praising my Savior all the day long;
This is my story, this is my song,
Praising my Savior all the day long. [34]

311 Blessed Assurance

Put on the full armor of God

Ephesians 6:10-17

"Put on the full armor of God"

Ephesians 6:10-17

God has objectively defeated Satan and his agenda.
He has delivered us from sin's penalty and power, and ultimately He will deliver us
from sin's very presence. In the interim, we are involved in guerilla warfare with demonic forces. [1]
~ Chip Ingram

As we have seen, the book of Ephesians follows a structure common to each of Paul's letters. Let's do a quick review. In the first three chapters, he lays a strong theological foundation, describing the believer's position in Christ. By grace, we are united with Him, raised with resurrection power, and seated in the heavenly realms, far above all rule and authority. This position is secure, unchanging, and eternally established. However, position is one thing; living it out is another.

So, in the final three chapters, Paul moves into the application of these positional truths in the daily arena of life.

Though we are seated with Christ in the heavenlies, we still live in bodies of flesh, battling desires we are not to give into. Instead, we are to walk in a manner worthy of God's calling on our lives. Paul outlines what this "worthy walk" looks like in our personal conduct, our relationships within the church, and in the home.

We are members of a new family – the family of God – that adds new members daily. Therefore, the family members are at varying stages of maturity. Unity in diversity is crucial, and that's why Paul urges us to walk in love. We must remember that we've put off the old self; we are not to participate in its unfruitful deeds of darkness. In every role – wife, mother, grandmother, daughter, employer, and employee – we should be filled with the Spirit and treat each other with honor.

And now, finally, Paul brings us to a sobering truth: the Christian life unfolds amid a spiritual war. In Ephesians 6:10-17, he pulls back the curtain on the ever-present warfare in the unseen realm, and tells us to stand firm in the Lord and put on the armor of God so that we can resist the enemy. You will notice as we look at the pieces of our armor, that in a very real sense, we are putting "on Christ." It is only as we are clothed *In Him* that we will be able to stand against our formidable enemy.

One reminder before we begin: The victory has already been won! What we face now is not a fight for triumph; it is just a mop-up operation. Jesus Christ is Lord, and we are In Him – fighting from victory, not for it.

Day One

Ephesians 6:10-11

As you begin today's lesson, read Ephesians 1-6 again (preferably aloud). Paul's letter was written to be read in its entirety. Each time you read it, you will become more familiar with its message, and its message will have a greater impact on your life.

1. Now, go back and read Ephesians 6:10-17. As you read, mark "in the Lord" (v. 10) in purple. With another color, underline the key words (including synonyms) or phrases that you see and list them below.

Key Words in Ephesians 6:10-17

2. Our focus passage today is Ephesians 6:10-11. Fill in the blanks in these verses:

   Finally, be ________________ in the Lord and in the strength of His might. Put on the full ______________

   of God, so that you will be able to ________________ ______________ against the schemes of the devil.

Paul begins with the command to "be strong in the Lord and in the strength of His might" (v. 10). The words Paul uses here are the terms he used in his first prayer for the Ephesians.

3. Look back at Ephesians 1:19-21 and describe the power that enables us to stand.

God empowers His people, but He does not send us into battle unarmed.

4. Whose armor are we commanded to put on? (6:11)

The Old Testament describes the armor of God several times in the book of Isaiah.

5. Read Isaiah 11:5; 52:7; and 59:17. List the pieces of armor described in these verses.

As Paul is writing, he is chained to a Roman soldier. It is possible that the soldier's armor is what brings this metaphor to mind. In light of this imagery, Paul urges believers to take a stand in a very real spiritual battle.

The phrase "stand firm against" is a military term that means to hold your ground, resist the enemy's advance, and refuse to surrender.

6. What are we told to "stand firm against"? (Ephesians 6:11)

DID YOU KNOW?

The *panoplia,* or full armor, means total head-to-toe protection, both defensively and offensively. This gear was not for appearances; it was for hand-to-hand combat. [2]

7. Define the word "schemes."

The schemes of the enemy are most often lies. Jesus said of the devil, "He was a murderer from the beginning, and does not stand in the truth because there is no truth in him. Whenever he tells a lie, he speaks from his own nature, because he is a liar and the father of lies" (John 8:44). Our ability to stand against him is dependent upon our use of the "full armor of God." The individual pieces are not to be used without the rest. If any part of the armor is left off, we are less than fully equipped for spiritual conflict.

Thomas Brooks, a Puritan pastor and writer, published his classic work on spiritual warfare, *Precious Remedies Against Satan's Devices*, in 1652. If you've ever thought spiritual warfare was a new phenomenon, this book proves otherwise. In fact, this battle has been raging since the Garden of Eden. And the lies the enemy uses are often disguised as our own thoughts.

Two of Satan's most effective tactics are temptation and accusation. In temptation, he distorts God's character by magnifying His love and grace while downplaying His holiness and wrath. In accusation, he does the opposite, overemphasizing God's wrath while diminishing His mercy and forgiveness.

One of the enemy's schemes that Brooks includes is: "Presenting God to the soul as One made up all of mercy." In other words, convincing us that because God is merciful, sin is not serious. But Brooks offers these wise remedies:

- God is as just as He is merciful. His mercy never cancels His righteousness.
- Sins against mercy will bring the greatest and sorest judgments on men.
- The saints now glorified regarded God's mercy as a most powerful argument against – and not for – sin. [3]

I have heard people casually address their own sin by saying, "God is a God of love and forgiveness." Yes, He is, and I am eternally grateful! But He is also Holy, Holy, Holy! (Isaiah 6:3). Without the shed blood of Christ, we would never be able to be in relationship with Him or anticipate an eternity in His Presence. We are commanded to "be holy, for I am holy" (Leviticus 11:44).

8. In what ways has the enemy tempted you to overemphasize the grace and love of God?

9. What practices and disciplines can you incorporate into your life to be holy and thus honor Christ?

Satan is a master counterfeiter; he is vile and manipulative. On our own, we cannot stand against his scheming ways. That is why we must wear the "full armor of God." Chip Ingram writes, "Satan comes to us in a multitude of ways. The serpent of Genesis 3 is crafty, the dragon of Revelation 12 will scare you to death, the angel of light in 2 Corinthians 11:14 will win you over, and the father of lies (John 8:44) is behind it all." [4]

Every day, we step onto a battlefield where the stakes are eternal. Satan is not only the father of lies, but also a master of distortion. Whether he's tempting us to take sin lightly under the guise of grace, or crushing us with guilt by obscuring God's mercy, his goal is always the same: to separate us from the truth that is in Christ.

But we are not left defenseless. God has given us His Word, His Spirit, and His armor. As we've seen, the key to resisting temptation and standing firm against accusation is to know Who God truly is and to live accordingly. His mercy is not permission to sin; it is power to live free from sin. His grace is not an excuse for compromise; it is strength for obedience.

So let us be women who live alert and equipped. Let us walk in the fear of the Lord, not in shame or fear of the enemy. Let us know and love the Truth so deeply that no counterfeit can deceive us. And let us put on the full armor of God – daily, prayerfully, and intentionally – knowing that victory is already ours in Christ.

Thanks be to God, Who gives us the victory through our Lord Jesus Christ.
1 Corinthians 15:57

Day Two

Ephesians 6:12

Read Ephesians 6:10-17.

1. Fill in the blanks for our focus verse today, Ephesians 6:12.

For our struggle is not against ______________ and ________________, but against the ______________, against the ________________, against the ________________ ____________________ of this darkness, against the ____________________ forces of __________________ in the heavenly places.

In any war, one of the most important units is the intelligence team. Why? Because you can't fight an enemy you don't understand. If we don't know who our enemy is, where he's operating, or what he's capable of, we're already at a disadvantage. Victory begins with insight.

2. Who is our struggle <u>not</u> against? (v. 12)

3. Who <u>do</u> we struggle against? (v. 12)

And Satan is a created being. That means he's not eternal, not all-knowing, not all-powerful, and certainly not everywhere at once. Only God holds those attributes. So how is it that the enemy seems to cause so much trouble in so many places at the same time? Simple – he's not working alone. He has an army. A highly organized network of helpers doing his bidding.

Charles B. Williams paraphrases Ephesians 6:12 this way: "Our contest is not with human foes alone, but with the rulers, authorities, and cosmic powers of this dark world; that is, with the spirit forces of evil challenging us in the heavenly contest" (WMS). This points to a real, well-structured army of demonic beings that work under Satan's command. *The Bible Knowledge Commentary* gives us insight:

> Though the ranks of satanic forces cannot be fully categorized, the first two (rulers and authorities) have already been mentioned in [Ephesians] 1:21 and 3:10. Paul added the powers of this dark world (2:2; 4:18; 5:8) and the spiritual forces of evil. Their sphere of activity is in the heavenly realms, the fifth occurrence of this phrase, which is mentioned in the New Testament only in 1:3; 20; 2:6; 3:10; 6:12. Satan, who is in the heavens (2:2) until he will be cast out in the middle of the Tribulation (Revelation 12:9-10), is trying to rob believers of the spiritual blessings God has given them (Ephesians 1:3).[5]

The apostle John tells us that a third of the angels fell with Satan in his rebellion (Revelation 12:4), and Daniel reveals a cosmic conflict where Satan's forces battle God's angels over the direction of nations (Daniel 10:13-20). There's more going on in the unseen world than we often realize.

The spirits we struggle against are described as:

- Rulers – evil supernatural beings
- Powers – demons with limited power or authority
- World forces of this darkness – cosmic rulers of the sinful world, always of the darkness of death
- Spiritual forces of wickedness in the heavenly places – a large, organized body of soldiers who wage war [6]

The enemy has a very organized army of demonic spirits. They operate in the atmosphere around the earth and are spiritual terrorists. That is why we must "be of sober spirit, be on the alert. Your adversary, the devil, prowls around like a roaring lion, seeking someone to devour" (1 Peter 5:8).

And Satan rarely comes at us with a full-frontal assault. That's not his way. He prefers the shadows. His attacks are almost always hidden, clever, and tailored for each target. He knows where we're weak. He has no moral compass, no ounce of compassion, no boundary he won't cross. He's not just evil; he is the definition of evil. And he's after us:

For still our ancient foe
Doth seek to work us woe;
His craft and power are great,
And, armed with cruel hate,
On earth is not his equal. [7]

All around us, a very real spiritual battle is being waged. The evil one is assaulting your marriage, your children, your vocation, and your self-worth. He is scheming and will not relent until he takes you out or destroys your testimony and effectiveness. He is the "thief who comes to steal, kill, and destroy" (John 10:10a).

To stand against Satan and defeat his schemes, we must know about the enemy. One of the best ways to become aware of how he works is through systematically reading through the Bible. The evil one's tactics have not changed since Genesis 3. He is constantly tempting us to doubt God's Word and then to deny God's Word to get what we want.

Friend, Satan is not a foe we can take on by ourselves. On our own, we're no match for him. The strength we need to stand firm comes from Christ. It's *In Him*, and Him alone, that we're equipped for the fight. We "suit up" to engage in the fight; then, we battle in the heavenlies through prayer. But note: This kind of spiritual warfare isn't a new concept.

4. Read 2 Kings 6:1-14. Describe what is going on between the King of Aram and Israel.

5. Read 2 Kings 6:15-19. This is probably a very familiar story. One that you may have heard, but not really studied the context. This took place during the Divided Kingdom. How was Elisha able to see in the spirit realm?

When we walk closely with the Lord, He will speak to us through His Word and His indwelling Spirit. As we pray and commune with Him, He will reveal where He is moving and working, and allow us to join Him.

As Elisha prayed, he asked the Lord to blind the army of the Arameans. And that is exactly what God did. Then Elisha led them to the king of Samaria. The king asked in 2 Kings 6:21 if he should kill his enemy. But Elisha told him to feed them and send them home. That passage closes by stating, "So he prepared a great feast for them; and when they had eaten and drunk, he sent them away, and they went to their master. And the marauding bands of Arameans did not come again into the land of Israel" (2 Kings 6:23).

Hold that thought and consider this: When Jesus was preparing for the cross and was sharing His last words with the disciples in John 14-17, He told them about the coming of the Holy Spirit. In John 16:12-13, Jesus said, "I have many more things to say to you, but you cannot bear them now. But when He, the Spirit of truth, comes, He will guide you into all the truth; for He will not speak on His own initiative, but whatever He hears, He will speak; and He will disclose to you what is to come."

Did you notice that the Holy Spirit will guide us and speak to us? He will also disclose to us what is to come. And that is what the Lord did in 2 Kings 6. He opened Elisha's eyes; therefore, he had no fear. Then, when Elisha prayed for his servant, the Lord opened his eyes as well. Maybe we need to have our spirit eyes opened. Only those who are clothed "in Christ" and in tune with His Spirit are enabled to "see."

Since "our struggle is not against flesh and blood," your issue is not with another person. This is a spiritual war, invisible, but very real. The enemy we face despises everything that belongs to Christ: His people, His Church, His mission. And yes, he's subtle. He's strategic. He's strong. But he's also defeated. Not by us, but by the One who crushed him at the cross.

At Calvary, Satan suffered his greatest defeat. What looked like a moment of victory for the enemy turned out to be his undoing. Jesus didn't just overcome sin and death, He stripped Satan and his demonic forces of their power and put them to open shame. Paul paints the picture for us in Colossians 2:15:

> When He had disarmed the rulers and authorities [those supernatural forces of evil operating against us], He made a public example of them [exhibiting them as captives in His triumphal procession], having triumphed over them through the cross (AMP).

This was a cosmic humiliation, a victory parade led by the risen Christ.

Though Satan still operates in this present world, his days are numbered. His authority is limited. He only rules where Christ is not enthroned. As John Stott says, "They were defeated at the cross and are now under Christ's feet – and ours. So the invisible world in which they attack us and we defend ourselves is the very world in which Christ reigns over them and we reign with Him." [8] But here's the catch – victory isn't automatic. If we neglect the Spirit's filling (Ephesians 5:18), if we drift from our dependence on Christ, or if we give the enemy a place in our lives, we make ourselves vulnerable. Satan cannot overpower a Spirit-filled believer, but he can certainly prey on one who is distracted or self-reliant.

So, the call is clear – Draw near to Christ. Take hold of the resources He provides. Suit up in His strength. Stand firm in triumph. Then, full of Christ, we can proclaim with Martin Luther:

And though this world with devils filled
Should threaten to undo us,
We will not fear, for God hath willed
His truth to triumph through us
The Prince of Darkness grim,
We tremble not for him;
His rage we can endure,
For lo, his doom is sure;
One little word shall fell him. [9]

Just one word from Christ, and the enemy runs. That's all it takes. The battle is not ours to win; it's already been won. Victory belongs to Jesus, and because we *are In Him*, it belongs to us too!

Day Three

Ephesians 6:13-15

So far, in Ephesians 6:10-12, we have learned that we are commanded to "be strong in the Lord" and "put on the full armor of God." Why? Because we are in a war, a struggle that is not against "flesh and blood," but is being fought on an entirely different level. We are battling against "rulers," "powers," "world forces of this darkness," and "spiritual forces of wickedness in the heavenly places." The battle we face is not one we can fight in our own strength. But the good news is: We don't have to. In Christ, God has given us everything we need to stand firm.

Read Ephesians 6:13.

As Paul prepares to teach us how to stand firm, he repeats the commands of verses 10-11 in verse 13: "Therefore, take up the full armor of God, so that you will be able to resist in the evil day, and having done everything, to stand firm." When Paul says "Therefore," he is pointing out that due to the number and power of the opposing forces (v. 12), we must put on the whole armor of God. He tells us once again that we must "suit up" to be able to "stand."

In verse 13, "take up" is drawn from military language; it speaks of a soldier preparing for combat. The armor is available, but the believer-soldier must intentionally take it up and put it on in order to be ready for the battle. Only when clothed in the armor will believers be able to "resist," a word that indicates standing against strong opposition. This is a full-force assault. And without the armor, we don't stand a chance.

1. When, specifically, does Paul say believers should be ready to resist the enemy? (v. 13)

The "evil day" is when the enemy's attack comes with extraordinary power, and the temptation to give in is intensely strong. Jim Logan explains, "The evil day is a particular day, a day of violent temptations and attacks whenever they come to us….In Luke 4, Satan left Jesus until an 'opportune time,' until another day when he could unleash his worst attacks. So the 'evil day' Paul has in mind here is the day when the great attack comes, when all hell breaks loose." [10]

2. How can you recognize when you are in an "evil day" in your own life?

When the "evil day" comes, the only way we can prevent being a casualty of the enemy's assault is to be "in Christ." We stand and are victorious *In Him.*

Now let's begin to consider the believer's armor, one vital piece at a time.

Read Ephesians 6:14-15.

As we consider each piece of the armor, it will help to connect the piece with the word that follows it. The first piece of armor is the belt of truth.

Belt of Truth

Paul lists the pieces of armor in the same order a soldier would put them on. The first piece a Roman soldier would fasten on was his belt or girdle. According to Rienecker and Rogers:

> The Romans soldiers wore one of at least three wide belts or girdles. [1] The breech like leather apron worn to protect the lower abdomen, [2] or the sword belt which was buckled on together with the sword as the decisive step in the process of preparing oneself for battle and [3] the special belt or sash designating an officer or high official. [11]

The one piece of equipment no soldier would dare forget was his belt that held his sword. Without it, he would be unarmed and vulnerable. No sane warrior would step onto the battlefield without his weapon at his side.

Francis Foulkes explains the meaning of the word "girded" in verse 14:

> Strictly the girdle is not part of the armor, but before the armor can be put on, the garments underneath must be bound together. The metaphor of girding is often used in the Bible because it describes a preparatory action necessary for a person with the flowing garments of those days before work could be done, a race run, or a battle fought (Luke 12:35; 1 Peter 1:13). [12]

The belt was a vital and functional part of the soldier's armor. It held the scabbard that carried his sword, secured his tunic to keep it from tangling around his legs during combat, and helped fasten the breastplate in place, guarding him against enemy strikes. In short, the belt held everything together.

That's exactly what truth does in the life of a believer. Truth stabilizes us. It gathers up the loose ends that trip us up. It supports righteousness by defining it, because without truth, how would we even know what is right or wrong? Truth keeps everything in its proper place so we can stand firm when the battle comes.

3. Read John 14:6 and John 17:17. What does Jesus say about what Truth is and where it comes from?

Our lives must be built upon the Truth of God. That is why it is so important for us to have a plan for reading through the Bible each year as well as doing studies like this one. We are to saturate our minds with the Truth so we can discern the schemes of the evil one and not give in to his lies.

From the beginning, the serpent has questioned and denied the Word of God. His tactics have not changed. We must build our lives upon God's Truth by making decisions and choices based on what is true, not what "feels" true. Our feelings are real, but they are not reliable, and should not govern our lives. As we choose to act based on God's Word, our emotions will eventually line up with what is true!

The second piece of armor is the Breastplate of Righteousness.

Breastplate of Righteousness

The Roman breastplate was a substantial piece of armor, made from leather, bronze, or chain mail, covering the soldier from neck to thigh – both front and back. Its purpose was critical: to shield the vital organs, the very core of a soldier's physical life. Without that protection, even a single blow could prove fatal in moments. [13]

The breastplate of righteousness is just as essential to us as the Roman soldier's breastplate was to him. Warren Wiersbe reminds us:

> It symbolizes the believer's righteousness in Christ (2 Corinthians 5:21) as well as his righteous life in Christ (Ephesians 4:24). Satan is the accuser, but he cannot accuse the believer who is living a godly life in the power of the Spirit. The life we live either fortifies us against Satan's attacks or makes it easier for him to defeat us (2 Corinthians 6:1-10). [14]

4. Read the following verses and summarize what you learn about righteousness.

   - Isaiah 61:10 –
   - Romans 5:19 –
   - Romans 8:10 –
   - 2 Corinthians 5:21 –
   - Philippians 3:9 –

Our enemy, the accuser of believers (Revelation 12:10), aims right at the heart of our faith. He works relentlessly to convince us that our sin has placed us beyond God's reach, whispering lies that question the sufficiency of His grace. He hurls accusations, shame, and condemnation, hoping we'll believe that God's love and forgiveness are conditional.

But when we stand firm, anchored in the Truth that we have been declared righteous by the blood of Christ alone, and that the Holy Spirit empowers us to live holy lives, the enemy has no choice but to retreat. His arrows fall harmless when we stand in the righteousness of Christ.

5. Are you standing firm in the truth that you are now righteous because you are "in Christ"?

6. How might our lives be different if we lived from our position of "righteous" *In Him* instead of depending on our own self-righteousness?

In verse 15, Paul turns his attention to the believer's feet, urging us to wear the third piece of armor, the sandals of the gospel of peace.

Sandals of Peace

Shoes are important. They can determine how stable and steady you can stand. A friend once told me she categorizes her shoes by how long she can comfortably wear them. She can look at a shoe and declare, "That is a one-hour shoe," "That is a three-hour shoe," or "That is an all-day shoe." The older I have gotten, the fewer shoes I have that are all-day shoes! ●

While high heels may be stylish, they're useless in combat, unstable and unreliable for battle footing. A Roman soldier, by contrast, wore specially designed sandals equipped for maximum stability and traction. These shoes gave him a firm grip, whether standing his ground or advancing against the enemy. Harold Hoehner describes these shoes, known as *caligae:* "The Roman legionaries wore heavy sandals…with soles made of several layers of leather averaging 2 centimeters (¾ inch) thick, studded with hollow-headed hobnails. They were tied by leather thongs half-way up the shin and were stuffed with wool or fur in the cold weather." [15] Similar to cleats, they were designed to function in any climate or on any terrain.

Believers also need special shoes. We can stand firm in peace, ready for battle because "the peace of God, which surpasses all comprehension, will guard [our] hearts and minds in Christ Jesus" (Philippians 4:7). We go to battle with both the inner peace that Christ has already given and the desire to see peace in the hearts of others.

There are slight variations in the translation of verse 15. The *New American Standard Bible* states it, "and having shod your feet with the preparation of the gospel of peace." This lends itself to the shoes of the gospel of peace preparing us to share the gospel. While that is true, I also believe the intent is that we would be prepared for battle with the peace of the gospel.

Stott writes that the *New English Bible* translates verse 15 this way: "'Let the shoes on your feet be the gospel of peace, to give you a firm footing.' And certainly, if we have received the good news, and are enjoying the peace with God and with one another which it brings, we have the firmest possible foothold from which to fight evil." [16]

We need to be ready to share the gospel and have the peace the gospel brings into our lives.

7. Read Ephesians 2:17. What did Jesus preach?

8. Read Isaiah 52:7. How should we incorporate the gospel and what effect will it have?

The enemy hates the gospel and fears us sharing it. That is why you will often hear thoughts like, "You won't be able to answer their questions," or "You aren't prepared." Sometimes, the enemy will use the fear of being offensive or of being rejected to stop a gospel conversation.

I have found that questions often put others at ease. Asking a person about their spiritual background is not offensive. Most people are comfortable talking about themselves. If you are feeling prompted to share the gospel with someone, you can trust that the Holy Spirit has already been working on them.

When Paul wrote to the Corinthian church, he was dealing with division. He told them that they were acting like carnal Christians. They were living in the flesh or as "mere men." Some were claiming to be "of Apollos," while others claimed to be "of Paul."

9. What does 1 Corinthians 3:5-7 say about the results of sharing the gospel?

It is the power of the word of the gospel and the work of the Holy Spirit that brings a person to Christ. It takes the conviction of the Spirit for a person to realize their lostness. We are simply instruments through which the Holy Spirit moves and works.

Who are you currently praying for to be saved? As you pray, ask the Holy Spirit to give you an opportunity to share the gospel. We must be prepared and assured as we allow the truth of Ephesians 6:15 to be manifest in our lives.

As we continue studying the armor of God, ask yourself:

Am I daily putting on what God has provided, or am I stepping into battle unprepared?

Day Four

Ephesians 6:16-17

Every piece of armor Paul describes is vital, not optional, for withstanding the enemy's attacks and standing firm in the strength that only God can provide.

Read Ephesians 6:16-17.

Next, Paul turns our attention to the shield of faith, a crucial defense in the heat of spiritual battle.

Shield of Faith

The Roman shield, known as the *scutum*, was a formidable piece of armor, roughly four feet tall and two-and-a-half feet wide, about the size of a small door. Kent Hughes offers this vivid description:

> The Roman scutum or shield was made of two layers of laminated wood, covered first with linen and then with hide, and then bound top and bottom with iron, with an iron ornament decorating the front of it. A man could put his entire body behind it as it absorbed the javelins and arrows of the enemy. In the case of flaming arrows, very often the arrow would snuff out as it buried itself in the thickness of the shield. During battles these great shields would often bristle with smoking arrows like roasted porcupines. [17]

These shields were specifically designed to extinguish flaming arrows, missiles that had been dipped in pitch, set on fire, and launched with deadly intent. When soldiers marched side-by-side, their overlapping shields formed an impenetrable wall of protection, a united defense against the fiery assault of the enemy.

Once again, we will look to Stott for insightful application:

> The devil's darts no doubt include his mischievous accusations which inflame our conscience with what (if we are sheltering in Christ) can only be called false guilt. Other darts are unsought thoughts of doubt and disobedience, rebellion, lust, malice, or fear. But there is a shield with which we can quench or extinguish all such fire-tipped darts. It is <u>the shield of faith</u>. [18]

1. What are some additional examples of flaming arrows? (v. 16)

In short, the list of fiery attacks at the devil's disposal are virtually endless. But the shield of faith offers an impenetrable defense against all of them. When raised, it extinguishes every flaming arrow the enemy hurls our way.

2. Read 1 John 5:4. What does faith help us to do?

DID YOU KNOW?

Roman soldiers had two shields at their disposal. One was small and round, about the size of a Frisbee that was carried on the forearm in battle. This is not the shield that Paul is writing about in Ephesians 6:16.

Faith overcomes. It gives us the strength to lift our eyes above the chaos and helps us see our circumstances from God's perspective. Through faith, we trust His power, His promises, and His presence, even when we can't see the way forward. In the midst of Satan's rain of fire, we take up our shield of faith and pray:

Lord, I trust You. I believe You are Who You say You are.
Though the enemy surrounds me, I will not fear, because You are with me.
Strengthen my faith, steady my heart, and help me stand firm
in the victory that is already mine in Christ.

Next comes the helmet of salvation.

Helmet of Salvation

In the first century, the helmet protected the soldier's head. Helmets were made of "bronze fitted over an iron skull cap lined with leather or cloth." [19] Charles Swindoll notes, "By Paul's day, they often had a band to protect the forehead and plates to protect the nose and cheeks. Little of the head was exposed to danger, but a soldier could still see clearly so as not to be caught off guard by swift-moving enemies or unexpected objects." [20] No sword would be able to pierce through a good helmet.

When the soldier prepared for battle, his helmet and sword were handed to him by his armor bearer. In the same way, the helmet of salvation is not something we can earn or fabricate; it's a gift handed to us by God Himself.

3. Read 1 Thessalonians 5:8. How does Paul describe the helmet?

This "hope" is a certainty – solid, sure, and unshakable. It's the confident expectation that what God has promised will indeed come to pass. Our salvation, already secured through Christ's work, will be fully realized when He returns for His people. Once you are saved, you can't be unsaved! When we wear this helmet of salvation, our minds are guarded against the enemy's attacks, the lies, doubts, and fears that try to chip away at our assurance. So, when Satan tries to flood your thoughts with doubt or condemnation, remember this: Your salvation is certain. Your hope is secure. God will complete what He has begun. The helmet of salvation is your protection. Stand firm beneath it.

As Paul wrote to the church at Rome, "hope does not disappoint" (Romans 5:5) because "our salvation is nearer to us than when we believed" (Romans 13:11).

Up to this point, every piece of God's armor has been defensive in nature. But now, Paul gives us the one offensive weapon we need to defeat the enemy, the sword of the Spirit.

Sword of the Spirit

4. What is the sword of the Spirit? (v. 17)

The sword Paul is referring to here is the short sword, called the *machaira,* that would be used up close in hand-to-hand combat. Invented by the Romans, the sword's double edge was kept razor sharp, making it a highly effective and deadly weapon.[21]

The believer's sword is the Word of God. When writing about God's Word, Paul usually uses the Greek word *logos,* referring to the written Word. But here, in Ephesians 6:17, he uses the word *rhema,* which points to the spoken word. Paul's emphasis here is not simply reading Scripture, it's on declaring it, speaking it aloud in the face of temptation and attack. It's about actively wielding God's revealed Truth as a weapon against Satan and his foul accomplices.

5. How is the Word of God described in Hebrews 4:12?

When we take up the Word of God in spiritual battle, we are wielding the most powerful weapon available. In Matthew 4, when Satan tempted Jesus in the wilderness, the Lord didn't argue or reason, He responded with Scripture. Three temptations, three strikes from the Word, all from the book of Deuteronomy (8:3; 6:16; 6:13). Jesus showed Himself to be the Master Swordsman. With one final thrust, the enemy fled, and Christ stood victorious in the silence that followed (Matthew 4:11). Let's not miss the point: If Jesus, the Son of God, met the devil with the Word, how much more should we?

6. Read Deuteronomy 32:46-47. What does Moses say about the Word of God?

DID YOU KNOW?

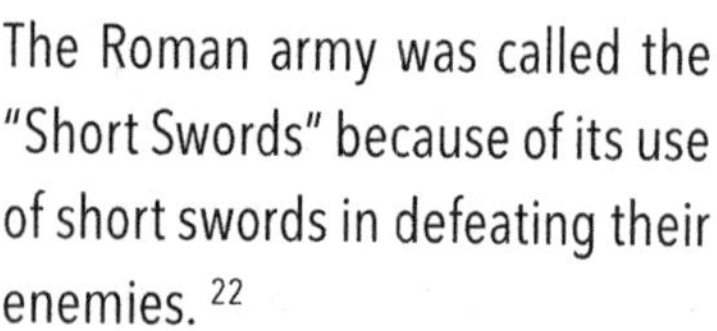

The Roman army was called the "Short Swords" because of its use of short swords in defeating their enemies.[22]

Moses reminds us that God's Word is not just helpful advice, it is our very life. It is the foundation on which we stand and the weapon we wield. That's why taking up the sword of the Spirit in spiritual warfare is so essential.

Through each piece of the armor, Paul is pointing us to Christ. The armor is not just from Christ, it is Christ. And the only way we can prevent being a casualty of war is to be "in Christ" at all times.

7. Read Romans 13:12-14. Who does Paul say we are to put on?

Paul is calling us to live in the reality of who Christ is and what He provides, every day. The armor of God is essentially a picture of putting on Christ in practical, spiritual terms. As we walk through the armor once again, let's see how Christ embodies it, and how wearing each piece is living clothed *In Him*.

The Belt of Truth – Christ is the Truth

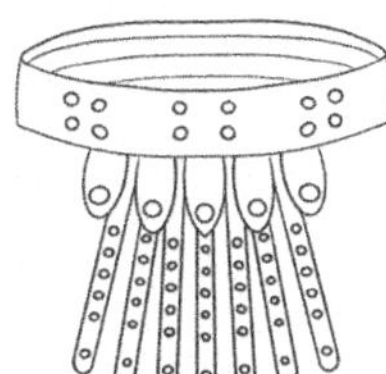

"I am the Way, and the Truth, and the Life" (John 14:6).

Jesus doesn't just speak the truth; He is the Truth. He is the fixed point that holds everything else in place, just as a belt secured the rest of a soldier's armor. To "put on Christ" is to let His truth shape your thoughts, words, and decisions.

The Breastplate of Righteousness – Christ is Our Righteousness

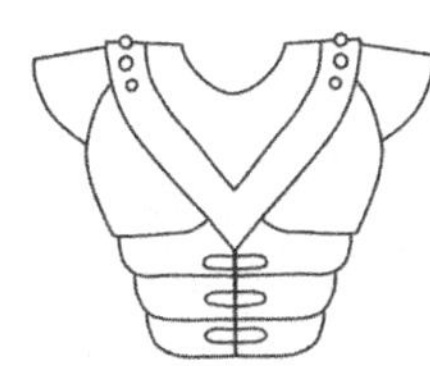

"He made Him who knew no sin to be sin on our behalf, so that we might become the righteousness of God in Him" (2 Corinthians 5:21).

Jesus is our righteousness. On our own, our best efforts fall short "like filthy rags" in God's sight (Isaiah 64:6). But in Christ, we are clothed in His perfect righteousness. The breastplate protects the heart, the seat of our identity. Putting on Christ means resting in His righteousness and living out of that right standing, not our performance.

Shoes of the Gospel of Peace – Christ is Our Peace

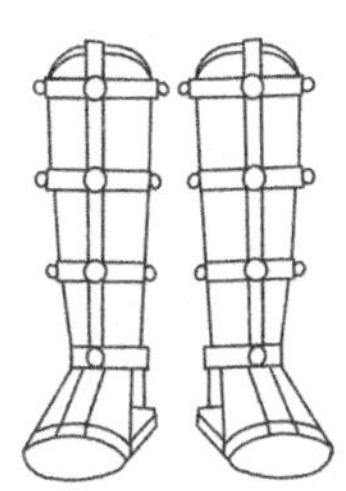

"For He Himself is our peace..." (Ephesians 2:14).

"Therefore, having been justified by faith, we have peace with God through our Lord Jesus Christ" (Romans 5:1).

Through His shed blood at Calvary, Jesus made peace between God and man. He is our peace, and He brings peace into our lives. His peace gives us stability when the ground beneath us shakes. Putting on Christ means walking in the confidence of that peace and carrying it to others.

Shield of Faith – Faith is in Christ

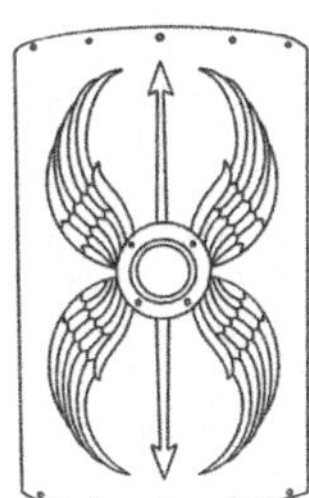

"...the life which I now live in the flesh I live by faith in the Son of God, Who loved me and gave Himself for me" (Galatians 2:20).

"Looking unto Jesus, the author and finisher of our faith..." (Hebrews 12:2, KJV).

Faith is trust in the person of Christ. He is both the object and the source of our faith. To put on Christ is to lift the shield of faith, trusting Him above every fear, temptation, or fiery dart from the enemy.

Helmet of Salvation – Christ is Our Salvation

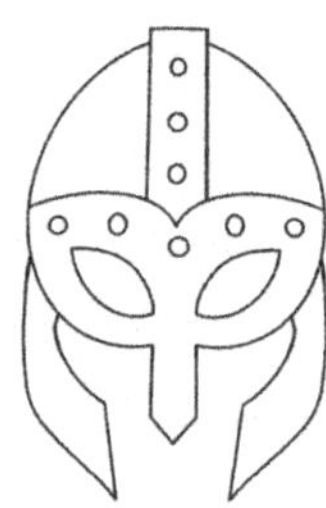

"The Lord is my light and my salvation – whom shall I fear?" (Psalm 27:1).

"You shall call His name Jesus, for He will save His people from their sins" (Matthew 1:21).

"Salvation is found in no one else" (Acts 4:12, NIV).

The helmet protects the mind; so, putting on Christ means guarding your thoughts with the assurance of your salvation *In Him*. It's rooting your security, hope, and identity in Jesus.

Sword of the Spirit – Christ is the Word of God

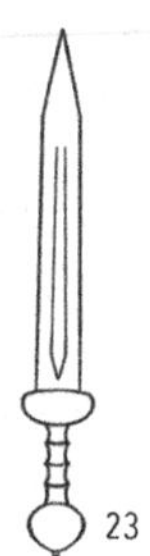
[23]

"And the Word became flesh and dwelt among us..." (John 1:14).

"His name is called The Word of God" (Revelation 19:13).

Jesus is the living Word, and Scripture is the written Word that testifies to Him. To put on Christ is to let His Word dwell "richly in you" (Colossians 3:16), equipping you to resist lies and fight spiritual battles with truth.

To "put on the armor of God" is, in very real terms, to put on the Lord Jesus Christ. And when we do, we're not just equipped, we're enveloped in the One Who has already secured the victory.

Dear believer, it's time to suit up. Your Father has provided everything you need: truth to ground you, righteousness to guard you, peace to steady you, faith to shield you, salvation to secure you, and His Word to equip you. The armor is the spiritual reality in which we live and fight. So, take it up, piece by piece, and walk forward in His strength. In Christ, the battle is already won. *In Him*, you win!

Day Five

The Believer's strategy: Dressed for War

The following passage is so familiar that we may have missed what Jesus was actually saying:

The thief comes only to steal and kill and destroy;
I came so that they would have life, and have it abundantly.
John 10:10

As He speaks, Jesus intentionally puts two statements together: There is a thief who comes to steal, kill, and destroy. But, I came to offer life abundant.

John Eldredge explains the reason Jesus married these two truths:

> I mean, He says them in one breath. And He has His reasons. By all means, God intends life for you. But right now that life is opposed. It doesn't just roll in on a tray. There is a thief. He comes to steal, kill, and destroy. In other words, yes, the offer is life, but you are going to have to fight for it because there's an enemy in your life with a different agenda. There is something set against us. We are at war. [24]

We are at war. And we have a very real enemy. If asked, "Is Satan real?", most of you reading would say, "Yes." But does that knowledge actually impact the way you live? We have a foe who is out to kill us, but too often, because the battle is being fought in the unseen realm, we tend to go through our daily lives unaware – and ineffective. And then, when the "evil day" comes, we are not prepared to do war.

But it doesn't have to be that way. If we are **dressed for war**, we will be prepared for war.

We have been given the attire we need to enable us to stand against the schemes of the enemy: the full armor of God. Our Father has provided all we need to live as more than conquerors, and that begins with God's Word. His Word is Truth. Jesus is the Truth. We read in *The Beginner's Guide to Spiritual Warfare,* "The first of the weapons is the Word of God. This is the truth that nullifies the effect of Satan's primary tactic of deception....It is the Word that is the 'sword of the Spirit' (Ephesians 6:17). It is especially the Word as appropriated by us and spoken with trust and confidence." [25]

We live in a spiritual world. The spirit realm is eternal, and we will one day be at home in it. All of us are being assaulted by demonic spirits in this cosmic war. As you have studied this week, have you become more aware of the schemes of the enemy?

1. How is the enemy attacking you or someone close to you?

2. Think about your thoughts over the past week. How has the enemy been deceiving, discouraging, or distracting you from time with the Lord and trusting Him completely?

3. Sometimes we need to examine our motives. How does the enemy seek to get you to live for yourself instead of for the Lord and His Kingdom?

Immersing ourselves in the Word of God allows us to be sensitive to the truth and more aware of the lies of the evil one, our flesh, and the world. Ingram tells us:

> The grammar in Ephesians 6 is very instructive. There is no break between verses 17 and 18. If I were to adjust the punctuation of this verse – that's okay to do, since the Greek text has no punctuation in it – it would look like this: "Take the helmet of salvation and the sword of the Spirit (which is the Word of God) with all prayer and petition. Pray at all times in the Spirit." [26]

Our next lesson, "Pray at all times in the Spirit," will take us deeper into the vital role of prayer in spiritual warfare. We've seen how God provides His armor, but prayer is what activates and empowers it in our daily lives.

During our time in Alabama, I had the privilege of being mentored by Sylvia Gunter. Her influence on my prayer life was profound and lasting. In her booklet, *For the Family*, she includes a powerful prayer designed to help believers "suit up" each day and stand firm. I've included it here for you. I encourage you to make a copy and incorporate it into your personal time with the Lord.

> Declare daily that you are obeying God's command to stand in all the armor available to intercessory soldiers in the battle for our families.
>
> *Father, our struggle is not against flesh and blood, but against the rulers, the authorities, the powers of this dark world and the spiritual forces of evil in the heavenly realms. They are merely fallen angels cast down from Heaven by the command of the true and living God. They are in subjection to Jesus Christ, the Son of God. We are in Him and stand in His already-assured victory. Therefore, we put on the full armor of God, so that when the fiery darts come, we may be able to stand our ground.*
>
> *We stand firm because we have taken up these weapons:*
>
> - *We buckle the belt of truth around our waist – Truth is the Person of our Lord Jesus. He is the Way, the Truth, and the Life.*
> - *We put on the breastplate of righteousness – The Person and sinless sacrifice of the Lord Jesus Christ is our Righteousness.*

- *We take the shield of faith which extinguishes all the flaming arrows of the evil one – The Person of the Lord Jesus Christ is the Author and Finisher of our faith. He is all the faith we need.*
- *We take the helmet of salvation – My Lord Jesus Christ Himself alone is my salvation. His mind guards our minds.*
- *We take the sword of the Spirit, which is the Word of God – The Word is the Person of Jesus who came in the flesh and defeated the works of the enemy. His Word never returns void.*
- *We clothe ourselves in all of Jesus and pray in the Spirit on all occasions with all kinds of prayers and requests.* [27]

From this day forward, choose to live from your secure position "in Christ," fully dressed and ready to stand firm *In Him.* The war has already been won at the cross, but until He returns, the skirmishes will continue. Take heart: the Prince of Peace is coming. And when He does, He will right every wrong, silence the enemy, and reign in perfect peace. *His Kingdom is forever.* [28]

166 A Mighty Fortress Is Our God

Pray at all times in the Spirit

Ephesians 6:18-24

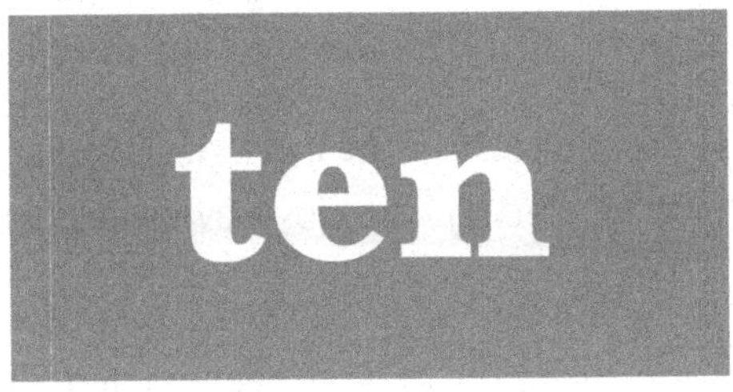

ten

"Pray at all times in the Spirit"

Ephesians 6:18-24

Years ago, as I opened the blinds on the window that faced our neighbor's house, I noticed her garage door was open. It was unlike her to leave her garage door up when she was not home, but I assumed she must have been running a quick errand and did not intend to be gone long.

I then noticed a man in work clothes inside her garage, standing near the back door. At the time, several homes were being built around us, and it was not unusual for someone from a construction crew to use an outdoor faucet with a homeowner's permission. Still, something made me pause. I then glanced back and saw the man was gone, but for a split second, I thought I caught the glint of metal flashing at her back door. Because I do have an active imagination, I immediately scolded myself for getting all worked up over what was surely nothing. But the feeling that something was off wouldn't go away.

When my neighbor returned a few minutes later with her toddler, I rushed over with my boys – who were just two and four at the time – and told her what I had seen. Alarmed, she sputtered, "I left my back door unlocked. I was only going to be gone for a few minutes!" I offered to go inside the house with her – and before you frown disapprovingly on my actions, let me go ahead and acknowledge that this was not the smartest decision I have ever made.

Cautiously, we stepped inside her house. Everything seemed normal...but then we heard heavy footsteps upstairs.

Yes, I know, we should have called the police right then. But instead, we ran toward the stairs (I honestly don't know what we were thinking). At that point the intruder flew down the stairs and tried to open the front door, which was now dead-bolted. After fumbling with it for what seemed like an eternity, he finally got it open and fled.

I hurried to her phone and called 911. Instead of reaching a person, I got a recording saying the phone company was on strike, but if it was an emergency, I could stay on the line. So, I did. Eventually, a Memphis dispatcher picked up the line, and I immediately began to blurt out the situation we were in. When I took a breath, the operator gently said, "Ma'am, you live in Shelby County, and this is the Memphis City Police station. You will need to talk to officers with Shelby County." Thankfully, she was willing to connect me with them, but first cautioned, "Stay in the house with the doors locked; help will be on the way soon."

When the county operator picked up, I began reporting the incident once again. But suddenly, my neighbor started jumping up and down, pointing frantically. The man had brazenly returned and was now trying to get in through her back door, which, thankfully, was now locked. As we peeked through her curtains, we got a close-up view and were able to give the dispatcher a vivid, detailed description. Because of that level of detail, he was quickly arrested.

In much the same way, as Paul was writing Ephesians 6:10-17, he had a close-up view of a Roman soldier in his armor. He wasn't describing it from memory or imagination; he was seeing it up close, every day, down to the last detail.

Roman guards typically guarded prisoners in 12-hour shifts. So, Paul's guards would have gotten to know him well. They would have watched as a steady line of visitors made their way to see him and, due to their proximity, couldn't help hearing the apostle as he taught and prayed.

A while later, Paul would write to the Philippians:

> Now I want you to know, brethren, that my circumstances have turned out for the greater progress of the gospel, so that my imprisonment in the cause of Christ has become well known throughout the whole praetorian guard and to everyone else, and that most of the brethren, trusting in the Lord because of my imprisonment, have far more courage to speak the Word of God without fear (Philippians 1:12-14).

The imperial guard mentioned here was the *praetorion* – an elite group of soldiers tasked with protecting high-ranking officials in Rome. Because of Paul's imprisonment, these men were regularly exposed to the gospel. Over time, many came to faith in Christ. [1]

The Romans had imprisoned Paul in an attempt to stop the spread of the gospel. But, through God's sovereign plan, Paul's imprisonment brought the very thing they were trying to stop into the inner circle of Caesar's household through his own bodyguards. Such divine irony! And what a fitting reminder: God is able to use the hard situations in our lives for good.

And we know that God causes all things to work together for good to those who love God,
to those who are called according to His purpose.
Romans 8:28

Day One
Ephesians 6:18

Whenever it is hardest to pray, it is most necessary to pray. [2]
~ Charles Spurgeon

On the heels of describing the armor of God, Paul reminds his readers of the next vital element in the Christian's battle strategy: the privilege and power of prayer. Having suited up for the battle "against the rulers, against the powers, against the world forces of this darkness, against the spiritual forces of wickedness in the heavenly places" (Ephesians 6:12), he now instructs believers to pray.

1. Read Ephesians 6:18-24. If you were to give this brief passage a title, what would it be?

2. Paul is drawing the net, bringing his letter to a close. Look back over Ephesians 6:18-24. Make a list of the key words and phrases. Use a purple pen to mark the one equivalent phrase to "In Him" in verse 21.

Key Words in Ephesians 6:18-24

As Paul writes this letter, he is not certain whether he will be released from his imprisonment or released to glory. So, we can safely assume he is measuring his words carefully, trusting the Spirit of God to frame his thoughts in a way that pleases the Lord and instructs believers in the ongoing struggle of spiritual warfare.

3. Capturing the essence of Paul's message in Ephesians 6:18-24, write a 1-2 sentence summary of this passage.

Now, let's dive into our focus verse for today's lesson: Ephesians 6:18.

Having instructed his readers to put on the whole armor of God and stand against the onslaught of the wicked one, Paul completes our battle plan with instructions to pray. Pray? That might seem like a passive position for a warrior to take. Yet, prayer is the spiritual discipline that brings God into the equation and releases the power of the Holy Spirit.

4. When does Paul say we are to pray? (v. 18)

Paul is not introducing a new concept in Ephesians 6:18. It is a continuation of thought, including prayer as a part of the believer's combat strategy. John Stott emphasizes prayer as an integral part of spiritual warfare:

> Paul adds prayer (verses 18-20), not (probably) because he thinks of prayer as another though unnamed weapon, but because it is to pervade all our spiritual warfare. Equipping ourselves with God's armour is not a mechanical operation; it is itself an expression of our dependence on God, in other words of prayer. [3]

How foolish we are if we think we can manage or manipulate any situation in our own strength. As the Old Testament prophet said, "'Not by might nor by power, but by My Spirit,' says the Lord of hosts" (Zechariah 4:6).

One of my favorite passages is Psalm 20, a prayer of David, asking God to answer the cries of His people. As a young shepherd, David had learned that his strength came from the Lord. He had already defeated a lion and a bear while protecting his father's flock (1 Samuel 17:34-37), not realizing those early victories were the training ground to prepare him to face Goliath.

5. Read David's prayer in Psalm 20:1-9. In it, there are seven prayer requests, each beginning with the word "may." Notice how specific David is in his petitions. Summarize each request in the space provided.

Scripture	Prayer Requests
v. 1a	
v. 1b	
v. 2	
v. 3	
v. 4	
v. 5	
v. 9	

6. Psalm 20:7 gives ironclad evidence that David is confident in the Lord and not in his abilities or military might. What does David say we are to do?

7. Let's do that now. Share about a time the Lord answered your prayers. Brag on Him. Then spend a few minutes glorying in His Presence and thanking Him for answered prayer.

Let's look back at Ephesians 6:18.

8. What phrases does Paul use to describe how believers should pray? (v. 18)

Stott's explanation helps us grasp Paul's meaning, "Moreover, it is prayer in the Spirit, prompted and guided by Him, just as God's Word is 'the sword of the Spirit' which He Himself employs. Thus Scripture and prayer belong together as the two chief weapons which the Spirit puts into our hands." [4]

Yet, there are times when we don't know what to pray, or we pray, but ask for something contrary to God's will.

9. Read Romans 8:26. According to this verse, Who can we confidently trust to intercede for us and present our prayers in a way that is pleasing to the Father?

Even though the Spirit helps us in our weakness, we are not called to passive prayer. Paul calls us to stay alert as we pray (Ephesians 6:18) because the enemy is prowling like a roaring lion, seeking someone to devour (1 Peter 5:8). False teachers threaten to lead many astray (Acts 20:29-30). And perhaps most urgently, the Lord is returning for His bride, the Church (Matthew 25:1-13; 1 Thessalonians 5:1-8; Revelation 16:15).

David Shepherd delves into the original language to further our understanding of Paul's prayer strategy, "The word Paul used in verse 18 for 'be alert' (better translated 'keep alert,' NRSV) means 'to stay awake, to lie sleepless, to be watchful, vigilant.'"[5]

10. Who does Paul say to pray for? (v. 18)

All believers, from the brand-new Christian to the seasoned saint, are subject to the same brutal, relentless forces of wickedness. So, beloved, pray. Pray all the time. Pray in the Spirit. Pray alertly. Pray with perseverance and supplication. Pray for all the saints. Whatever you do and in everything you do: Pray!

I pray that from His glorious, unlimited resources He will empower you with inner strength through His Spirit. Then Christ will make His home in your hearts as you trust in Him. Your roots will grow down into God's love and keep you strong. And may you have the power to understand, as all God's people should, how wide, how long how high, and how deep His love is. May you experience the love of Christ, though it is too great to understand fully. Then you will be made complete with all the fullness of life and power that comes from God (Ephesians 3:16-19, NLT).
Amen and amen!

Day Two

Ephesians 6:19-20

I was diagnosed with cancer in the fall of 2021 and completed my treatment in July 2022. Thankfully, I survived the treatment; the cancerous tumor did not. Praise God! But then, I was plunged into the unexpected process of coping with the recovery. I had wrongly believed that once the treatment was completed, I would feel like my old self again. However, I didn't realize that my old self had been replaced with a battle-scarred woman that I barely recognized in the mirror.

The medical term that encompasses the transitional phase that follows the completion of cancer treatment is known as "survivorship," and it results in a variety of issues that caught me totally by surprise. Despite my oncology team's best efforts to prepare me otherwise, I found myself pinning my hopes on the completion date of my treatment plan, assuming life would return to normal. Instead, I began to deal with brain fog, the lingering trauma of the diagnosis, an odd form of grief for what I had lost to cancer, social awkwardness after being somewhat quarantined for a year due to my weakened immune system, and multiple side effects from the medications I would be taking for the next ten years. These meds were (and still are) playing havoc with my emotions, my sleep patterns, my joints, my hair, and my skin…just to name a few of the issues. All this as I was attempting to claw my way back to my pre-cancer life and activities. Good times!

One of the first social gatherings we ventured out to was a small dinner party. I was so excited to be able to attend, but I found myself making clumsy attempts to make casual conversation. Seriously? Words are my thing! But a year of a serious health crisis had put me in a different place than I had ever been.

After our meal, we gathered in our hosts' den to share about the Lord. I was blessed to hear all that my brothers and sisters in the Lord shared. The share time was going to be followed by a time of prayer. Our dear host looked at me first and asked with great compassion, "How can we pray for you?" All the tension I had been holding in my chest began to ease at his tender concern and desire to pray for me. Beloved, one of the many gifts of being a part of the family of God is the covering of prayer that comes from one another.

Read Ephesians 6:19-20.

After asking the believers to pray for one another in the battle (v. 18), Paul asks them to pray also for him.

1. What is Paul's specific prayer for himself? (vv. 19-20)

Paul is confined in Rome, under arrest for preaching the gospel. He is separated from his brothers and sisters in Christ, and most are scattered throughout Asia Minor. This observation by Stott resonates with me and I believe will be a blessing to you:

> "Pray also for me," Paul begged (verse 19). He was wise enough to know his own need of strength if he was to stand against the enemy, and humble enough to ask his friends to pray with him and for him. The strength he needed was not just for his personal confrontation with the devil, however, but for his evangelistic ministry by which he sought to rescue people from the devil's dominion. This had been a part of his original commission when the risen Lord Jesus had told him to turn people "from darkness to light, and from the power of Satan to God" (Acts 26:18). Hence the spiritual conflict of which he was aware.
>
> Moreover he had not left the battlefield now that he was under house arrest and unable to continue his missionary expeditions. No, there were those soldiers to whom one by one, each for a shift of several hours on end, he was chained, and there were his constant visitors. He could still witness to them, and he did so. There must have been other individuals beside the fugitive slave Onesimus whom he led to faith in Christ. Luke tells of Jewish leaders who came to him at his lodging "in great numbers," and who heard him expound "from morning till evening" about the Kingdom and about Jesus. "Some were convinced," Luke added (Acts 28:17, 23-24).
>
> Thus Paul's evangelistic labours went on. For "two whole years" he "welcomed all who came to him," he proclaimed "the Kingdom of God and…the Lord Jesus Christ," and he did it "quite openly and unhindered" (Acts 28:30-31). [6]

So often our prayers are reduced to a shopping list designed to produce greater comfort for us. Had I been imprisoned like Paul, my prayer request would have been something like this, "Get me out of here!" But that was not the case with Paul. Paul's concern was that utterance may be given to him so that he might share the gospel boldly.

2. Why do you think Paul, seasoned apostle that he is, asks for prayer to speak boldly? (vv. 19-20)

DID YOU KNOW?

Paul asks that the Ephesian saints pray that God would give him a gift of utterance "in the opening of his mouth," that is, when he opens his mouth to speak. This utterance, this speech, Paul desires, should be in boldness. "Boldness" is *parresia*, literally, "all speech." The word means "fearless, confident freedom in speaking." [7]

3. Do you pray for boldness to share Christ? Why or why not?

The "mystery of the gospel" in Ephesians 6:19 refers to God's plan to bring Jews and Gentiles together as one people through Christ. This was not fully understood in the Old Testament, but has now been made clear through the life, death, and resurrection of Jesus. Paul addressed this mystery earlier in Ephesians 3:3-6. When Paul asks for prayer that he may boldly proclaim "the mystery of the gospel," he's asking for courage to preach the radical, unifying message of salvation through Christ for all people, regardless of background, status, or nationality. Preaching that message is the very reason Paul finds himself chained to a Roman soldier at this point.

4. What phrase does Paul coin to describe himself in his current situation? (v. 20)

The word "ambassador" is a political term, referring to an official representative of a government. Dispatched to a foreign land, the ambassador's role is to reflect the official position of the sovereignty that gave him authority. [8] Paul realizes that, although he is in Rome as a prisoner, he is ultimately serving as a representative of another Kingdom, the Kingdom of God.

The Apostle's description takes on a whole new slant when we consider the double meaning of the word "chains." As David Guzik explains:

> Think about Paul's wonderful self-description: an ambassador in chains. Of course, the ancient word used here for chains usually meant a prisoner's shackles. At times, Paul wore the iron bands around his wrists and carried the chain that held him to the prison. But that ancient word we translate chains could also be used for the gold adornment worn around the neck and wrists of the wealthy and powerful. On special occasions, ambassadors wore such chains to show the riches, power, and dignity of the government they represented.
>
> Which sense did Paul mean when he called himself an ambassador in chains? I think he meant it in both senses! Paul looked at his prisoner's chains and considered them to be the glorious adornment of an ambassador of Jesus Christ. [9]

5. How can you faithfully represent Christ wherever God has placed you, even in hard or limiting circumstances?

In 1887, Ernest Shurtleff wrote the stirring hymn, "Lead On, O King Eternal," for his own graduation from Andover Theological Seminary. He envisioned his graduating class singing this hymn as a prayer for God's guidance as they were moving into various ministries as ambassadors for the Lord:

> *Lead on, O King Eternal, we follow, not with fears;*
> *For gladness breaks like morning where're Thy face appears;*
> *Thy cross is lifted o'ver us; we journey in its light:*
> *The crown awaits the conquest, Lead on, O God of might.* [10]

What a beautiful prayer! It points to the reality that victory over the kingdom of darkness demands that we remain on the alert, praying with perseverance. But, the victory, the crown of conquest, belongs to the Lord.

Dear sister, Paul's words in Ephesians 6:19-20 are an urgent call for prayer. You may feel inadequate and be tempted to shrink back from this assignment, so let me encourage you with this glorious truth. Prayer is an intimate, ongoing conversation and communion with the Lord. It can be activated anytime and anywhere. It can be childlike or that of a seasoned prayer warrior. It can be made publicly or privately, whispered or made silently. Prayer takes many forms, much like the conversations between a child and her earthly father.

After the death, burial, and resurrection of Christ, He ascended triumphantly to Heaven. Steve Gaines' words make our hearts rejoice as he reminds us of Jesus' ministry in His glorified state:

> He is now in Heaven, seated on His glorious throne. And what is Jesus doing in His resurrected state? He is preparing Heaven for His followers, pardoning lost people, and preparing to come again. But Jesus is doing something else right now – praying for His people. "Therefore He is able also to save forever those who draw near to God through Him, since He always lives to make intercession for them" (Hebrews 7:25). This verse links the security of our eternal salvation with the fact that Jesus will always pray on our behalf. Thus, if you are a Christian, you are going to make it safely through this life assured of the fact that you will enter into Heaven when you die. All because Jesus is praying for you. [11]

Beloved, ponder this: Jesus is praying for you. Right now. He sees you. He knows your struggles. He loves you. And He is bending low and drawing near.

The Lord your God is in your midst, a victorious warrior.
He will exult over you with joy,
He will be quiet in His love,
He will rejoice over you with shouts of joy.
Zephaniah 3:17

Will you spend the next few minutes talking with Him? Share whatever is on your heart. Lift up those you know who need prayer today. Hear Him rejoicing over you as you do.

Day Three

Ephesians 6:21-22

As Paul is moving to the close of his letter to the believers in Ephesus, he shifts from theological instruction to personal connection.

Read Ephesians 6:21-22.

1. Who does Paul mention in verse 21?

When Paul received Christ as Lord and Savior, most of his devout Jewish family members and friends would have likely rejected him. Therefore, it was a gracious gift of the Lord to give him dear friends, like Tychicus, who became his faith family. John Phillips comments on this supernatural phenomenon, "The family of God makes brothers and sisters of all who love the Lord. Some become beloved brothers, often nearer to us than our natural siblings." [12] The words of Proverbs 18:24 confirm this, "There is a friend who sticks closer than a brother."

2. In what two ways does Paul describe Tychicus? (v. 21)

DID YOU KNOW?

The word translated "minister" in Ephesians 6:21, *diakonos*, means "an active servant." [13] Tychicus was willing to devote himself to the service of God; he was a helper to Paul and an active worker for the cause of Christ. His sole ambition was to be useful in relieving Paul's restrictions and furthering the Kingdom of God. People like Tychicus are invaluable in the Lord's work. A beloved brother and a faithful minister are titles of nobility in the Kingdom of God. We should covet them for ourselves. [14]

Paul has been arrested and is considered by Rome to be an enemy of the state. To be found in his company is risky. Tychicus could have been branded as an accomplice and placed under arrest, but he is determined to serve Paul as a faithful minister of Christ.

Tychicus was a dear friend and traveling companion of Paul. As often as I have opportunity, I encourage Christian women to build a strong support group of like-minded friends. Proverbs 27:17 says, "Iron sharpens iron, so one man sharpens another." Beloved, we need each other. Friends in the Lord divide our sorrows and multiply our joys. Girlfriends, find your people!

A wonderful example of this principle is found in Exodus when Amalek attacked Israel. As Moses sent Joshua to lead the fighting forces against them, he told the young commander, "Tomorrow I will station myself on the top of the hill with the staff of God in my hand" (Exodus 17:9).

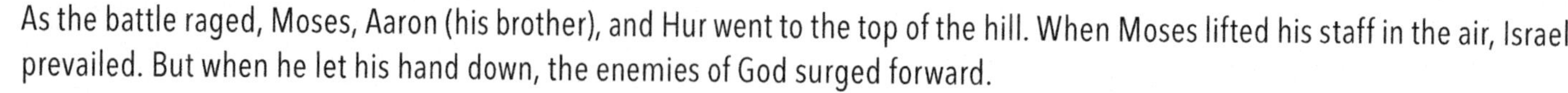

As the battle raged, Moses, Aaron (his brother), and Hur went to the top of the hill. When Moses lifted his staff in the air, Israel prevailed. But when he let his hand down, the enemies of God surged forward.

Read Exodus 17:12-13.

3. What happened to Moses' hands? (v. 12)

4. What did Aaron and Hur do to assist Moses? (v. 12)

5. What was the result? (v. 13)

God had called Moses to lead His people. The call of leadership did not extend to Aaron and Hur, but they served in a capacity of support. These men did not attempt to usurp Moses' authority or step into his role. Instead, they gave him much needed help to fulfill his calling. They were devoted companions who strengthened Moses and shared the burden. Without them, the battle would have been lost.

Friendships are vitally important. An unhealthy trend, perhaps spawned by the COVID-19 pandemic and fed by long work hours and the social changes brought on with the advent of social media, shows Americans are not cultivating friendships. According to statistics, a narrow majority of adults (53%) say they have between one and four close friends, while a significant share (38%) say they have five or more. Some 8% say they have no close friends at all. [15] The Bible emphasizes the importance of friendship, touting its value and highlighting the characteristics of true friends. It also encourages believers to choose friends wisely.

My husband and I surrendered our lives to Christ at about the same time. Because we had been living a very worldly lifestyle, our friends were not good influences (although I do not fault them for the sinful decisions we made).

Paul writes, "Do not be deceived: 'Bad company corrupts good morals'" (1 Corinthians 15:33). Amen and amen. A similar truth is expressed in Proverbs 12:26, "The righteous is a guide to his neighbor, but the way of the wicked leads them astray" (emphasis mine). So true.

After we came to Christ, we found freedom *In Him* and wanted to share what had happened in our lives with our friend group. Sadly, none of them were interested in following Jesus, and they quickly abandoned us like proverbial rats leaving a sinking ship. While we realized this was for the best, for the first time in our lives we found ourselves without a circle of close friends. During this season, God drew us close to Him and close to each other. But initially, I still felt lonely and a bit abandoned. Little did I know the wealth of dear friends that were awaiting!

Because we were so hungry to learn about Christ, we began to expand our involvement at church, where we started to cross paths with new (to us) brothers and sisters in Christ. Initially, I shrank back from approaching any of them, fearing they already had an established group of friends. In time, I learned that was the voice of the enemy in my head trying to keep me isolated and alone. When I began to attend our church's women's ministry (back then, known as the Women's Missionary Union), I began to meet other women who loved the Lord, many of whom were in my same season of life. They graciously sought me out, extending friendship. And to this day, those women remain some of my dearest friends.

6. In John 15:12-15, Jesus tells His disciples His commandment regarding interpersonal relationships. What did He say to them? (v. 12)

7. What is the greatest indicator of genuine love and what does that look like? (v. 13)

8. How does a true friend of Jesus demonstrate authentic love for Him? (v. 14)

9. Up to this point, the disciples had a rabbi/student relationship with Jesus, but all of that was changing. What is their (and our) new relationship with Him? (v. 15)

Jesus no longer called His disciples servants, but friends, known and loved by Him. What a gift, to be called His friend! And what a reminder: Friendship is a holy thread in the fabric of life. Paul understood this, too. He had beloved companions who encouraged him and served alongside him. And as he makes clear in closing words to the Ephesians, one of those trusted friends is Tychicus. He joined the ranks of other faithful friends of Paul like Timothy, Luke, Mark, Aquila, Priscilla, and Phoebe.

10. For what purpose (in addition to delivering the letter) does Paul send Tychicus to Ephesus? (Ephesians 6:21)

We don't know a lot about Tychicus, other than he was a native of Asia Minor (Acts 20:4) and possibly of Ephesus (Acts 21:29). Paul also mentions Tychicus in Colossians 4:7-8 as the one who he commissioned to carry his letter to the church at Colossae.

It seems that Paul entrusts his younger colleague to serve as the courier for both letters as well as acting as Paul's personal representative to update the churches on his wellbeing. Phillips adds,

> There would be stories about soldiers won to Christ, news of Paul's latest Epistles, a description of the house where Paul lived, the remarkable account of a vital Christian ministry being carried on despite chains, tales of visitors coming to Rome from all over the world. Tychicus would have to relay all this information. It would be grist for the mill of prayer. [16]

The news concerning Paul from his dear companion, Tychicus, will comfort their hearts.

Paul doesn't just send a letter to Ephesus, he sends a person. Someone who can look the Ephesian believers in the eye, respond to their questions, allay their fears, share how God was using the apostle to reach people for Christ, and report back to Paul on the state of the church in Ephesus. Although Paul prefers personal, physical presence to written correspondence, his incarceration in Rome prevents that. So, sending Tychicus with the letter is the next best thing. The Apostle understands the value of physical presence. Charles Swindoll chimes in:

> In our techno-crazed world, in which we can carry on virtual "face-to-face" conversations over the Internet, take university courses and earn degrees without setting foot in a real classroom, and get powerful Bible teaching and preaching 24/7 at the touch of a button, we too quickly forget the need for flesh-and-blood presence. Nothing can ever take the place of a real person spending real time and sharing real space with other real people (see 1 Thessalonians 2:7-9). Paul did not just send Tychicus to Ephesians to share information; that could have been accomplished through a letter. Rather, Tychicus was to share his very self, something that would comfort the hearts of the Ephesian believers (Ephesians 6:22). [17]

While Tychicus may not be a well-known figure, his role in the life and ministry of Paul – and in the encouragement of the early church – was anything but small. He was a trusted messenger, a faithful servant, and a friend. And through his ministry, we're reminded that God often works through quiet faithfulness and behind-the-scenes obedience to strengthen the Body of Christ. God is calling all of us to that same kind of faithfulness. Like Tychicus, we may not always be in the spotlight. But our obedience, our presence, and our friendships can have a lasting impact on the Kingdom of God.

11. Who in your life needs encouragement right now?

12. How can you be a "Tychicus" this week?

Father, give us eyes to see those around us who need encouragement. May we carry Christ well in every conversation, every act of kindness, and every relationship. Strengthen our friendships and let them be holy ground where Your love is made visible.
In Jesus' name, Amen.

Day Four

Ephesians 6:23-24

Paul doesn't end his letter with casual words. His benediction is as intentional and doctrinally packed as the rest of the epistle. Every word here matters. Paul's concern for all who are *In Him* is evident and endearing as he speaks a blessing over his readers, centering around four key words: peace, love, faith, and grace.

Read Ephesians 6:23-24.

With his parting words, it is almost as if Paul is recapping the touchstones of his entire letter to the Ephesians.

Peace. Love. Faith. Grace. Paul's prayer is that these blessings will be the shared experience of all who are *In Him*.

1. From Whom do these blessing come? (v. 23)

DID YOU KNOW?

It was the custom in the ancient world for correspondents to end their letters with a wish – usually a secular wish, even if the gods were invoked – for the reader's health or happiness. Paul sees no reason to abandon the convention in principle. But as he has Christianized the opening greeting, so now he Christianizes his final wishes. Indeed, what he writes is half wish, half prayer. [18]

Now, let's consider these attributes one at a time.

Peace

2. Peace has been a recurring theme throughout Paul's letter. Look back at Ephesians 2:14-18. What did we learn about peace from this passage?

Since Christ has established peace with God and between believers, those who bear His name are called to live accordingly, "being diligent to persevere the unity of the Spirit in the bond of peace" (Ephesians 4:3).

But this peace is not just external. Internally, it will protect our hearts and minds.

3. Look up Philippians 4:6-9. Paul reminds us to refuse anxious thoughts and turn to the Lord in prayer. What will be the result? (v. 7)

4. Paul exhorts us to dwell on these characteristics of Jesus. If we practice these spiritual disciplines, what will be the result? (v. 9)

Beloved, did you notice Paul's turn of phrase? When anxious thoughts attack, turn to God in prayer and the peace of God (v. 7) will guard your hearts and minds. Fill your mind with the things of the Lord and the God of peace (v. 9) will be with you. Peace is one of the love gifts that accompany our salvation.

A peaceful way of life is first on Paul's mind, and close behind it comes the second element of Paul's benediction: love.

Love

Love is what makes peace possible. It's a key theme woven throughout Paul's letter to the Ephesians. And it's one in which the Ephesian believers stand out; they are known for their love for all the saints. Paul affirms this early in his letter: "For this reason I too, having heard of the faith in the Lord Jesus which exists among you and your love for all the saints, do not cease giving thanks for you, while making mention of you in my prayers" (Ephesians 1:15-16).

It is easy to love some of the saints, isn't it? But all? That is a different matter!

Theologically, everything we need to love our fellow believers is already in place. Peace has been made through Christ. As Romans 5:5 tells us, "the love of God has been poured out within our hearts through the Holy Spirit Who was given to us." And 1 John 4:19 reminds us, "We love, because He first loved us." The capacity to love is ours. What remains is our choice to act on it. As with so many truths grounded in deep spiritual reality, the practical outworking often comes down to our human will. In his companion letter to the Colossians, Paul writes, "Put on love" (Colossians 3:14). Is it hypocritical to act lovingly toward someone we don't naturally "like"? Not at all. It is never hypocrisy to bend our wills to obey the Word of God. And as we put on love, over and over again, we will begin to wear it without even thinking about it.

The third blessing Paul invokes is connected to love: "love with faith."

Faith

What Paul has in mind is both saving faith and practical daily faith. Kent Hughes explores the reality of faith in the life of believers:

> Real faith has two elements: belief and trust. To have true faith we must believe what is revealed about God in the Scriptures and what is said about us. Faith begins with belief, but belief alone is not faith. There must, along with belief, be trust – trusting God on the basis of what we believe. Paul wants the Ephesians to "button up intellectually" in relation to the deep truths he has given them, and then he wants them to trust those truths in the living out of life. [19]

Trust is resting on what you believe. Does your trust match your belief?

5. Is there an area in your life where you say you trust God, but are living like you don't? If so, what is it?

6. What are some ways you can realign the way you live with what you believe?

Lastly, Paul blesses the Ephesians with grace.

Grace

Paul's final prayer is for the grace of God, His unmerited divine favor, to be with all who love Jesus with "incorruptible love" that is permanent and genuine. "Grace" is the first word in Paul's formal greeting to the Ephesians (1:2), and it is the final thought as he closes.

Grace is God's free gift. As Paul has already explained, "For by grace you have been saved through faith; and that not of yourselves, it is the gift of God; not as a result of works, so that no one may boast" (Ephesians 2:8-9).

But after receiving saving faith by grace, there is a condition to maintaining its undisturbed flow, and that is to "love our Lord Jesus Christ with incorruptible love" (6:24). Loving Him is foremost.

> But when the Pharisees heard that Jesus had silenced the Sadducees, they gathered themselves together. One of them, a lawyer, asked Him a question, testing Him, "Teacher, which is the great commandment in the Law?" And He said to him, "'You shall love the Lord your God with all your heart and with all your soul, and with all your mind.' This is the great and foremost commandment." (Matthew 22:34-38)

Sadly, years later, the church in Ephesus would receive a stern rebuke from the Lord.

7. Read Revelation 2:1-5. What has befallen the Ephesians?

8. Jesus says, "Remember." "Repent." "Or else." What fate awaits the church of Ephesus if they fail to heed the Lord's warning?

DID YOU KNOW?

The Greek word used for "incorruptible" is *aphtharsia*, meaning sincere. [20] The NIV translates this verse as "undying love," a picture of eternal love for Christ. The same word is used in Romans 1:23, describing the glory of our "incorruptible God."

We are prone to wander from the Lord. The world, the flesh, and the devil are all conspiring together to disrupt our relationship with Jesus. If we fail to remain vigilant, a chink in our armor will appear, and we will find ourselves drifting away from the Lord.

The central question for each of us is this: Do we love Christ? Do we delight *In Him*? Is our love for Him growing, deepening, and maturing? Do we love Him more now than when we first believed? More than we did a year ago?

What a great way for Paul to end his letter! Love Jesus! Soon and very soon, we will see Him.

Until that day, may grace be with all who love our Lord Jesus Christ with an incorruptible love. May we be found faithful - watching, worshiping, and walking in step with the Spirit - eyes fixed on the One we love.

Day Five

The Believer's strategy: Armed for War

Ephesians 6 outlines the believer's strategy for standing firm in the midst of spiritual battle – not through human strength, but by putting on the full armor of God. Paul is clear: The fight is not against flesh and blood, but against spiritual forces of evil. Therefore, the strategy isn't offensive power but spiritual preparedness – truth like a belt, righteousness like a breastplate, peace as our footing, faith as a shield, salvation as a helmet, and the Word of God as our sword. Each piece is essential, not optional, and all are activated through constant, Spirit-led prayer. In other words, victory doesn't come by charging ahead in our own power, but by standing our ground in prayer, fully armed, fully dependent, fully alert, **armed for war**.

Prayer is not something we do in preparation for the battle; prayer is the battle. The battle "against the rulers, against the powers, against the world forces of this darkness, against the spiritual forces of wickedness in the heavenly places" (Ephesians 6:12) is prayer. Samuel Chadwick wrote, "The one concern of the devil is to keep saints from prayer. He fears nothing from prayerless studies, prayerless work, and prayerless religion. He laughs at our toil, mocks at our wisdom, but trembles when we pray." [21]

The cosmic battle is taking place in heavenly places, in the spiritual realm. The opposition is real, but not visible to the naked eye. But be assured, beneath the surface, an invisible spiritual battle is raging. We win this war not with tangible weapons like guns and ammunition, or roundhouse kicks and punches. We win by daily putting on the whole armor of God, standing firm, and staying alert in prayer. When we pray, we unleash angelic beings to draw swords and rout Satan's minions. Is it any wonder the enemy attempts to keep us from prayer? Phillips writes:

> Satan does not fear eloquence in prayer...He does not fear perseverance. (Quite often prayer is the most spasmodic and disjointed of our activities.) He does not fear our understanding of the way prayer works. No, he fears the simple fact that a needy child of God is at the mighty throne of God. Satan harnesses all his minions to bar the way to the throne of God. But no demon, no angel-prince, no fallen angel can face the Spirit's flaming Sword. The Word of God clears the way to the throne of God for the child of God. [22]

Because Satan cannot block our access to God, he often turns to more subtle tactics. One of Satan's devices designed to get the upper hand in spiritual warfare is the construction of strongholds in our minds. Strongholds are spiritual fortresses built with Satan's lies. They can be negative thought patterns, deeply ingrained habit patterns held over from our life prior to Christ, or false belief systems that contradict God's Word. They hinder our relationship with God and negatively affect our spiritual growth.

1. Read 2 Corinthians 10:3-5, one of the key passages on tearing down destructive thought patterns.

   - In verses 3-4, Paul speaks of weapons that are "not of the flesh." What are these weapons, and what makes them powerful for tearing down strongholds?

- Verse 5 speaks of "destroying speculations and every lofty thing raised up against the knowledge of God."

- What do you think Paul means by "speculations and every lofty thing"?

- What are some modern examples of these?

- How do we tear down strongholds? (v. 5b)

The Bible speaks of using spiritual weapons like the Word of God and prayer to dismantle these strongholds, replacing them with God's Truth.

Ralph Waldo Emerson is often credited with having said: "Sow a thought and you reap an action; sow an act and you reap a habit; sow a habit and you reap a character; sow a character and you reap a destiny." [23] Every action begins as a seed thought. That is why Satan targets our minds, seductively wedging his lies in among the truth. His nefarious practice dates all the way back to Eve in the Garden when he said to the woman, "Indeed, has God said?" (Genesis 3:1).

2. If God's truth is the key to successfully demolishing existing strongholds and keeping our minds from becoming fertile ground for the establishment of future ones, how can we combat the enemy's tactic?

3. Spend a few minutes with the Lord in prayer. Ask Him to reveal any strongholds that you have wittingly or unwittingly allowed the enemy to build in your mind. Write them down. Then write out a prayer of contrition and commitment, seeking His divine power for the destruction of those fortresses.

Now for some good news! Conversely, in Scripture, God is also presented as a stronghold, a place of refuge and protection for believers.

4. Read Psalm 59:16-17. David penned this psalm while Saul was seeking to put him to death. How does David describe our God?

Beloved, we are locked in a fierce battle with a relentless enemy. Satan is cunning and deceitful. He entices us with our desires, tempts us to take what we think we deserve, and encourages us to follow a path of destruction, often dragging others down along with us.

So how do we, in our human weakness, stand against the enemy? Willpower won't win this battle. From a human standpoint, victory is impossible. But Paul gives us the answer: "Be strong in the Lord and in His mighty power" (Ephesians 6:10, NLT). Our strength lies not in ourselves, but *In Him*. God is our stronghold, "our refuge and strength, a very present help in trouble" (Psalm 46:1). "He will cover [us] with His pinions, and under His wings [we] may seek refuge" (Psalm 91:4). The Lord is our Shepherd (Psalm 23) and we can come to Him in prayer with confidence, knowing that every cry is heard, every burden is welcomed, and every battle met with His strength. *In Him,* we win!

Beloved, your writing team thanks you for joining us on this journey through Ephesians. We pray God's blessings on you as you lay hold of "the riches of His grace which He lavished on us" (Ephesians 1:7-8) and experience all the riches of Christ *In Him.* Grace to you and peace from God our Father and the Lord Jesus Christ!

Heavenly Father, thank you for blessing us with unfathomable riches in Christ. We have been blessed with every spiritual blessing in the heavenly places in Him. We were chosen before the foundation of the world to be holy and blameless. We have been adopted as daughters and accepted in the Beloved. We have redemption through the blood of Christ who loved us and gave Himself up for us, an offering and a sacrifice to God as a fragrant aroma. In Him we have the forgiveness of our trespasses. We are sealed by the Holy Spirit of God for the day of redemption.

We were dead in our trespasses and sins, but You saved us and seated us in heavenly places in Christ Jesus. We have been set on display so that the manifold wisdom of God might be made known to rulers and authorities in the heavenly places.

In the strength of Your might, we put on the whole armor of God and stand firm against the schemes of the devil. May we learn to pray more fervently, serve more faithfully, and walk more fully in line with Your perfect will. May we love you with an incorruptible love and desire to be found faithful to the finish.

Now to Him Who is able to do far more abundantly beyond all that we ask or think, according to the power that works within us, to Him be the glory in the church and in Christ Jesus to all generations forever and ever.

Amen and Amen.

165 Lead On, O King Eternal

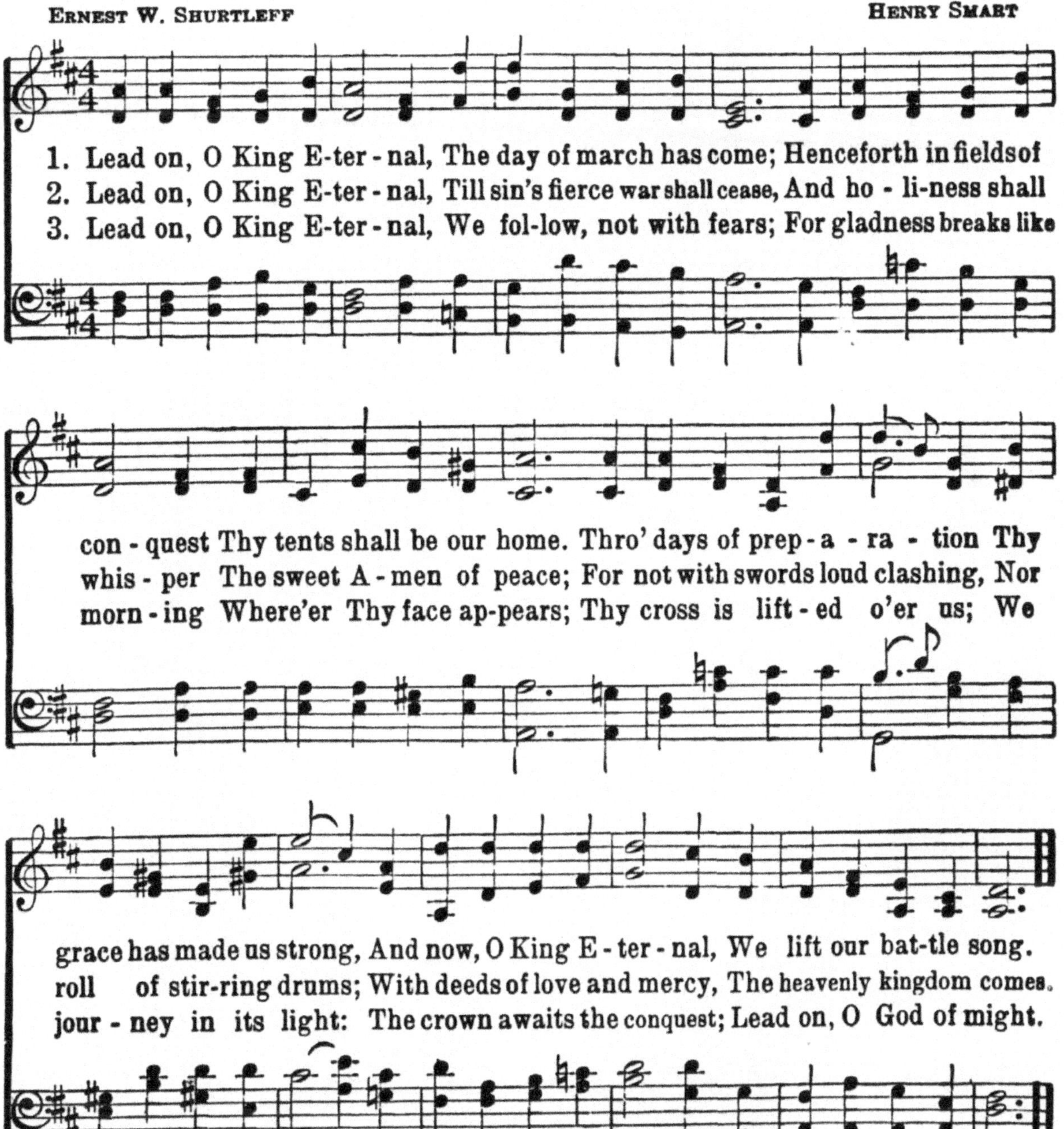

HOW TO BECOME A CHRISTIAN

Have you ever come to the place where you've put your full trust in Jesus Christ? Do you know with confidence that if you were to die today, you would be with Him forever? Ephesians tells us that every spiritual blessing is found in Christ, but that kind of life begins with a response of faith. If you are unsure where you stand with God, this is the most important moment in this study. Let's walk through how you can know that you belong to Jesus and how to step into the new life He offers.

Admit Your Sin

Ephesians 2 tells us that, before being made alive in Christ, we were "dead in our trespasses and sins" (Ephesians 2:1). Sin isn't just something we do, it's the condition of our hearts apart from God – the condition we were born into (Psalm 51:5, NLT). Romans 3:23 reminds us, "All have sinned and fall short of the glory of God." And the consequence is clear: "The wages of sin is death" (Romans 6:23). Sin separates us from God, and apart from His mercy, we are without hope, cut off from the life only He can give (Ephesians 2:12).

Abandon Self-Effort

We cannot rescue ourselves. No amount of good works, religious activity, or personal improvement can make us right with God. "For by grace you have been saved through faith; and this is not of yourselves, it is the gift of God; not a result of works, so that no one may boast" (Ephesians 2:8-9). Salvation is not something we earn. It is something we receive.

Acknowledge Christ's Work

At the center of Paul's message in Ephesians is the person and work of Jesus: Christ "loved us and gave Himself up for us" (Ephesians 5:2, NIV). Romans 5:8 says, "God demonstrates His own love toward us, in that while we were yet sinners, Christ died for us." His blood, shed on the cross, paid the penalty for your sin. *In Him*, you are redeemed and forgiven (Ephesians 1:7).

Accept Him as Savior

But friend, the blood of Christ does you no good until you receive Him by faith into your life. The Bible says, "Believe in the Lord Jesus, and you will be saved" (Acts 16:31). This is not about religion. It's about relationship, being united with Christ through faith. You must place your faith in Jesus Christ and Him alone for your salvation. Are you ready to take that step? If so, pray something like this:

> *Lord Jesus, I confess that I am a sinner and cannot save myself. I believe You died for my sins and rose again. I receive You now as my Savior and Lord. Forgive me, cleanse me, and make me Your own. I want to walk with You from this day forward. Thank You for saving me. Amen.*

If you prayed that prayer and meant it, you are now in Christ! Welcome into life forever, *In Him*!

End Notes

Introduction: In Him

1. Murray, A. *Abide in Christ*, p. 31. Kindle edition.
2. Stott, John. *Life in Christ*, p. 41.
3. Murray, A. *Abide in Christ*, p. 1. Kindle edition.
4. Vines, W.E. (1970). *Vines's Complete Expository Dictionary of the Old and New Testament Words*, p. 1. Nashville, TN: Thomas Nelson.
5. Wilbourne, R. (2016). *Union with Christ*, p. 60. Colorado Springs, CO: David Cook.
6. Voskamp, A. (2025). *Loved to Life*, p. 271. Carol Stream, IL: Tyndale House.

Introduction to Ephesians

1. Hughes, K. (1990). *Ephesians*, LOC. 136. Wheaton, IL: Crossway.
2. Vaughan, Curtis. (2002). Ephesians, p. 15. Cape Coral, FL: Founders Press.
3. Brisco, T.V. (1998). *The Holman Bible Atlas*, pp. 254-55. Brentwood, TN: B&H Publishing.
4. Brisco, T.V. (1998). *The Holman Bible Atlas*, pp. 255. Brentwood, TN: B&H Publishing.
5. Powell, M. A. (2011). *Harper Collins Bible Dictionary*, pp. 247-248.
6. Hoehner, H. (2002). *Ephesians: An Exegetical Commentary*, p. 83. Grand Rapids, MI: Zondervan.
7. Vos, H. (1999). *Bible Manners and Customs*, pp. 519-520. Nashville, TN: Thomas Nelson.
8. Brisco, T.V. (1998). *The Holman Bible Atlas*, pp. 254. Brentwood, TN: B&H Publishing.
9. Thielman, F. (2010). *Ephesians,* LOC. 1394. Grand Rapids, MI: Baker Academic.
10. Thielman, F. (2010). *Ephesians,* LOC. 1357. Grand Rapids, MI: Baker Academic.
11. Thielman, F. (2010). *Ephesians,* LOC. 1349. Grand Rapids, MI: Baker Academic.
12. Swindoll, p. 165 Swindoll, C. (2015). *Swindoll's Living Insights, New Testament Commentary Galatians, Ephesians,* p. 165. Carol Stream, IL: Tyndale House Publishers.

Lesson One

1. Reymond, R. (2010). *A New Systematic Theology of the Christian Faith*, dccclix. Nashville, TN: Thomas Nelson.
2. *Clarin.com*. (2017, February 24). "Buscan a un hombre ques heredo US $6.000.000 y no lo sabe." (Translated)
3. Swindoll, C. (2015). *Swindoll's Living Insights, New Testament Commentary Galatians, Ephesians,* p. 157. Carol Stream, IL: Tyndale House Publishers.
4. Vines, W.E. (1970). *Vines's Complete Expository Dictionary of the Old and New Testament Words*, p. 30. Nashville, TN: Thomas Nelson.
5. Wiersbe, W. (1979). *Be Rich*, p. 20. Colorado Springs, CO: Chariot Victor Publishing.
6. Ephesians 1:1, 15, 18; 2:19; 3:8, 18; 4:12; 5:3; 6:18. (NASB95)
7. Vines, W.E. (1970). *Vines's Complete Expository Dictionary of the Old and New Testament Words*, p. 544. Nashville, TN: Thomas Nelson.
8. Boice, J. M. (2006). *Ephesians*, p. 6. Ada, MI: Baker Books.
9. Stott, J. (1979). *The Message of Ephesians*, p. 6. Downers Grove, IL: Inter-Varsity Press.
10. Stott, J. (1979). *The Message of Ephesians*, pp. 22-23. Downers Grove, IL: Inter-Varsity Press.
11. *Hymnal.net*. (n.d.). "It is Well." Retrieved from https://www.hymnal.net/en/hymn/h/341
12. *Hymnary.org*. (n.d.). "What a Friend We have in Jesus." Retrieved from https://hymnary.org/text/what_a_friend_we_have_in_jesus_all_our_s
13. Elliot, E. (2021, March 4). *Elisabeth Elliot*. "Waiting." Retrieved from https://elisabethelliot.org/resource-library/devotionals/waiting-3/#:~:text=Restlessness%20and%20impatience%20change%20nothing,and%20hatred%20of%20the%20people
14. Barton, B. (1996). *The Life Application Bible Commentary*, p. 7. Wheaton, IL: Tyndale.
15. Vines, W.E. (1970). *Vines's Complete Expository Dictionary of the Old and New Testament Words*, p. 70. Nashville, TN: Thomas Nelson.
16. Swindoll, C. (2015). *Swindoll's Living Insights, New Testament Commentary Galatians*, Ephesians, p. 167. Carol Stream, IL: Tyndale House Publishers.

17. Coekin, R. (2015). *Ephesians for You*, p. 11. UK: The Good Book Company.
18. Wiersbe, W. (1979). *Be Rich*, p. 13. Colorado Springs, CO: Chariot Victor Publishing.
19. Wiersbe, W. (1979). *Be Rich*, p. 13. Colorado Springs, CO: Chariot Victor Publishing.
20. Swindoll, C. (2015). *Swindoll's Living Insights, New Testament Commentary Galatians*, Ephesians, p. 167. Carol Stream, IL: Tyndale House Publishers.
21. Osborne, G. (2017). *Ephesians*, p 23. Bellingham, WA: Lexham Press.
22. Vines, W.E. (1970). *Vines's Complete Expository Dictionary of the Old and New Testament Words*, p. 544. Nashville, TN: Thomas Nelson.
23. Vines, W.E. (1970). *Vines's Complete Expository Dictionary of the Old and New Testament Words*, p. 68. Nashville, TN: Thomas Nelson.
24. Willard, D. (1998). *The Divine Conspiracy: Rediscovering Our Hidden Life in God,* p. 310. San Francisco, CA: William Collins.
25. Vines, W.E. (1970). *Vines's Complete Expository Dictionary of the Old and New Testament Words*, p. 482. Nashville, TN: Thomas Nelson.
26. Barton, Bruce. (1996). *Life Application Bible Commentary*, p. 15. Wheaton, IL: Tyndale House.
27. Phillips, J. (1993). *Exploring Ephesians and Philippians*, p. 3. Grand Rapids, MI: Kregel Publications.
28. *Hymnary.org.* (n.d.). "Doxology." Retrieved from https://hymnary.org/text/praise_god_from_whom_all_blessings_ken
29. *Museum of the Bible.* (n.d.). "A Wretch Like Me: The Story of John Newton. Retrieved from https://www.museumofthebible.org/a-wretch-like-me#:~:text=But%20by%20age%20eleven%2C%20Newton's,and%20embraced%20life%20at%20sea
30. Vines, W.E. (1970). *Vines's Complete Expository Dictionary of the Old and New Testament Words*, p. 516. Nashville, TN: Thomas Nelson.
31. Swindoll, C. (2015). *Swindoll's Living Insights, New Testament Commentary Galatians, Ephesians*, p. 169. Carol Stream, IL: Tyndale House Publishers.
32. Voskamp, A. (2025). *Loved to Life*, p. 33. Carol Stream, IL: Tyndale Momentum.
33. Vines, W.E. (1970). *Vines's Complete Expository Dictionary of the Old and New Testament Words*, p. 704. Nashville, TN: Thomas Nelson.
34. Coekin, R. (2015). *Ephesians for You*, p. 20. UK: The Good Book Company.
35. "Lavish." (n.d.). *Merriam-Webster Dictionary.* Retrieved from https://www.merriam-webster.com/dictionary/lavish
36. *Hymnary.org.* (n.d.). Retrieved from https://hymnary.org/text/marvelous_grace_of_our_loving_lord
37. Osborne, G. (2017). *Ephesians*, p. 33. Bellingham, WA: Lexham Press.
38. Shepherd, D. (1998). *Shepherd's Notes: Ephesians*, p. 28. Nashville, TN: Broadman & Holman Publishers.
39. *Got Questions.* (n.d.). Retrieved from https://www.gotquestions.org/co-heirs-with-Christ.html
40. Acts 19:1-7.
41. Vines, W.E. (1970). *Vines's Complete Expository Dictionary of the Old and New Testament Words*, p. 553. Nashville, TN: Thomas Nelson.
42. "Pledge." (n.d.). *Merriam-Webster Dictionary.* Retrieved from https://www.merriam-webster.com/dictionary/pledge?src=search-dict-box
43. Wiersbe, W. (1979). *Be Rich*, p. 24. Colorado Springs, CO: Chariot Victor Publishing.
44. Hughes, K. (1990). *Ephesians*, LOC. 241. Wheaton, IL: Crossway.
45. Vines, W.E. (1970). *Vines's Complete Expository Dictionary of the Old and New Testament Words*, p. 676. Nashville, TN: Thomas Nelson.
46. Sullivan, A. (2016, September 19). *The New York Magazine.* "I Used to Be a Human Being." Retrieved from https://nymag.com/intelligencer/2016/09/andrew-sullivan-my-distraction-sickness-and-yours.html
47. Lewis, C.S. (1942). *The Screwtape Letters*, p. 120. New York, NY: HarperOne.
48. *World Health Organization.* (2024). Retrieved from: https://www.who.int/europe/news/item/25-09-2024-teens--screens-and-mental-health
49. DeAngelis, Tori. (2024, April1). *Monitor on Psychology, 55* (3). "Teens are spending nearly 5 hours daily on social media. Here are the mental health outcomes." Retrieved from https://www.apa.org/monitor/2024/04/teen-social-use-mental-health
50. *APA.* (2024). "Stress in America." Retrieved from https://www.apa.org/pubs/reports/stress-in-america/2024
51. Staton, Tyler. (2025). *The Familiar Stranger,* p. 119. Nashville, TN: Thomas Nelson.
52. Staton, Tyler. (2025). *The Familiar Stranger,* p. 121. Nashville, TN: Thomas Nelson.
53. Foster, R. (1978). *Celebration of Discipline*, p. 15. New York, NY: HarperCollins Publishers.
54. Pokluda, J. (2025). *Your Story Has a Villain*, p. 71. Nashville, TN: W Publishing Group.

Lesson Two

1. Thomas, I. *The Indwelling Life of Christ: All of Him in All of Me*, p. 8. PRH Christian Publishing. Kindle Edition.
2. Wilbourne, R. (2016). *Union with Christ*, p. 30. Colorado Springs, CO: David Cook.
3. Swindoll, C. (2015). *Swindoll's Living Insights, New Testament Commentary Galatians, Ephesians,* p. 176. Carol Stream, IL: Tyndale House Publishers.
4. Worley, K. (2025). *Home with God: Our Union with Christ,* p. 103. Nashville, TN: B&H Publishing Group.
5. Worley, K. (2025). *Home with God: Our Union with Christ,* p. 49. Nashville, TN: B&H Publishing Group.
6. *Study Light.* (n.d.). Retrieved from https://www.studylight.org/lexicons/eng/greek/4678.html
7. *Biblehub.com.* (n.d.). Retrieved from https://biblehub.com/greek/602.htm
8. Hoehner, H. (2002). *Ephesians: An Expositional Commentary,* p. 259. Grand Rapids, MI: Baker.
9. Quoted in Barton, B. (1996). *Life Application Bible Commentary: Ephesians*, p. 30. Wheaton, IL: Tyndale House Publishers.
10. Lemmel, H. H. (1951). "Turn Your Eyes Upon Jesus." *Inspiring Hymns*, p. 379. Grand Rapids, MI: Singspiration Sacred Music Publishers.
11. Barton, B. (1996). *Life Application Bible Commentary*, p. 30. Wheaton, IL: Tyndale House.
12. Wilbourne, R. *Union with Christ: The Way to Know and Enjoy God*, p. 17. David C. Cook. Kindle Edition.
13. Stott, J. (1979). *The Message of Ephesians*, p. 56. Downers Grove, IL: Inter-Varsity Press.
14. Swindoll, C. (2015). *Swindoll's Living Insights, New Testament Commentary Galatians, Ephesians,* p. 179. Carol Stream, IL: Tyndale House Publishers.
15. Stott, J. (n.d.). *The Message of Ephesians*. Logos.
16. Barton, B. (1996). *Life Application Bible Commentary: Ephesians*, p. 30. Wheaton, IL: Tyndale House Publishers.
17. Osborne, G. (2017). *Ephesians*, p. 47. Bellingham, WA: Lexham Press.
18. Camp, J. (2015). *Genius.* "Same Power." Retrieved from https://genius.com/Jeremy-camp-same-power-lyrics
19. Osborne, G. (2017). *Ephesians*, p. 47-48. Bellingham, WA: Lexham Press.
20. Eldredge, J. (2016). *Waking the Dead*, p. 185-86. Nashville, TN: Nelson Books.
21. Foulkes, F. (n.d.) *Ephesians: An Introduction and Commentary*, Logos.
22. Wilbourne, R. (2016). *Union with Christ*, pp. 13-14. Colorado Springs, CO: David Cook.
23. Nee, Watchman. (2024). *The Normal Christian Life,* 13. Kindle Edition.

Lesson Three

1. Wiersbe, W. (1979). *Be Rich,* p. 51. Colorado Springs, CO: Chariot Victor Publishing.
2. "Dead." (n.d.). *Merriam-Webster Dictionary.* Retrieved from https://www.merriam-webster.com/dictionary/dead
3. Wiersbe, W. (1979). *Be Rich,* p. 52. Colorado Springs, CO: Chariot Victor Publishing.
4. Wright, N.T. (2023). *Ephesians, Philippians, Colossians and Philemon for Everyone,* p. 15. Louisville, KY: Westminster John Knox Press.
5. Piper, J. (2024, June 3). *Desiring God.* "Satan, the 'Prince of the Air' – What Does That Mean?". Retrieved from https://www.desiringgod.org/interviews/satan-the-prince-of-the-air-what-does-that-mean.
6. Swindoll, C. (2015). *Swindoll's Living Insights, New Testament Commentary Galatians, Ephesians,* p. 185. Carol Stream, IL: Tyndale House Publishers.
7. Wright, N.T. (2023). *Ephesians, Philippians, Colossians and Philemon for Everyone,* p. 15. Louisville, KY: Westminster John Knox Press.
8. Wilbourne, R. (2016). *Union with Christ*, p. 30. Colorado Springs, CO: David Cook.
9. Wilbourne, R. (2016). *Union with Christ*, p. 30. Colorado Springs, CO: David Cook.
10. Wright, N.T. (2023). *Ephesians, Philippians, Colossians and Philemon for Everyone,* p. 16. Louisville, KY: Westminster John Knox Press.
11. Lucado, M. (2018). *Life Lessons from Ephesians*, p. 27. Nashville, TN: HarperChristian Resources.
12. Cole, S. (2013, September 5). *Bible.org.* "What Does it Mean to be Saved?". Retrieved from https://bible.org/seriespage/lesson-2-what-does-it-mean-be-saved-ephesians-28-10.
13. Wiersbe, W. (1979). *Be Rich,* p. 56. Colorado Springs, CO: Chariot Victor Publishing.
14. Sproul, R.C. (2020, September 28). *Ligonier Ministries.* "What Does 'Soli Deo Gloria' Mean?". Retrieved from https://learn.ligonier.org/articles/soli-deo-gloria-god-alone-be-glory.

15. McGee, J. (1983). *Thru the Bible with J. Vernon McGee Vol. V*, p. 237. Nashville, TN: Thomas Nelson.
16. Wilbourne, R. (2016). *Union with Christ*, p. 111. Colorado Springs, CO: David Cook.
17. Vines, W.E. (1970). *Vines's Complete Expository Dictionary of the Old and New Testament Words*, p. 385. Nashville, TN: Thomas Nelson.
18. Swindoll, C. (2015). *Swindoll's Living Insights, New Testament Commentary Galatians, Ephesians*, p. 192. Carol Stream, IL: Tyndale House Publishers.
19. Wiersbe, W. (1979). *Be Rich*, p. 57. Colorado Springs, CO: Chariot Victor Publishing.
20. Reid, J. (2016, November 24). *Ligonier Ministries*. "Why Remember?". Retrieved from https://learn.ligonier.org/articles/why-remember
21. Barclay, W. (1976). *The Letters to the Galatians and Ephesians (Revised Edition)*, p. 107. Philadelphia, PA: The Westminster Press.
22. *Life Application Study Bible, New Living Translation*, p. 2,617. (2007). Carol Stream, IL: Tyndale House Publishers.
23. Wiersbe, W. (1979). *Be Rich*, p. 66. Colorado Springs, CO: Chariot Victor Publishing.
24. Wright, N.T. (2023). *Ephesians, Philippians, Colossians and Philemon for Everyone*, p. 21. Louisville, KY: Westminster John Knox Press.
25. *Life Application Study Bible, New Living Translation*, p. 2,617. (2007). Carol Stream, IL: Tyndale House Publishers.
26. Wiersbe, W. (1979). *Be Rich*, p. 71. Colorado Springs, CO: Chariot Victor Publishing.
27. McGee, J. (1983). *Thru the Bible with J. Vernon McGee Vol. V*, pp. 239-240. Nashville, TN: Thomas Nelson.
28. *Genius.com*. (n.d.). "We Are Family." Retrieved from https://genius.com/sister-sledge-we-are-family-lyrics
29. *Got Questions*. (n.d.). Retrieved from https://www.gotquestions.org/what-is-a-Gentile.html
30. Wiersbe, W. (1979). *Be Rich*, p. 73. Colorado Springs, CO: Chariot Victor Publishing.
31. *Life Application Study Bible, New Living Translation*, p. 2618. (2007). Carol Stream, IL: Tyndale House Publishers.
32. *Got Questions*. (n.d.). Retrieved from https://www.gotquestions.org/Jesus-Christ-cornerstone.html
33. Wiersbe, W. (1979). *Be Rich*, p. 74. Colorado Springs, CO: Chariot Victor Publishing.
34. Anders, M. (1999). *Holman New Testament Commentary – Galatians, Ephesians, Philippians, Colossians*, p. 177. Nashville, TN: Broadman & Holman Publishing.
35. Lucado, M. (2018). *Life Lessons from Ephesians*, p. 35. Nashville, TN: HarperChristian Resources.
36. Eldredge, J. (2003). *Waking the Dead*, p. 68. Nashville, TN: Nelson Books.
37. Eldredge, J. (2003). *Waking the Dead*, pp. 70-71. Nashville, TN: Nelson Books.
38. Rushford, J. (2020, May 14). *Pepperdine Libraries*. "Hymns of the Season: Come, Thou Fount of Every Blessing." Retrieved from https://library.pepperdine.edu/news/posts/hymns-of-the-season-come-thou-fount-of-every-blessing.htm
39. Eldredge, J. (2003). *Waking the Dead*, p. 228. Nashville, TN: Nelson Books.

Lesson Four

1. Lawrence, B. & Laubach, F. (2020). *Practicing His Presence*, Kindle Edition, p. 54. Jacksonville, FL: SeedSowers Christian Publishing.
2. Osborne, G. (1996). *Life Application Bible Commentary: Ephesians*, p. 59. Carol Stream, IL: Tyndale House Publishers.
3. Osborne, G. (1996). *Life Application Bible Commentary: Ephesians*, p. 60. Carol Stream, IL: Tyndale House Publishers.
4. Stott, J. (1979). *The Message of Ephesians*, p. 116. Downer's Grove, IL: Inter-Varsity Press.
5. Swindoll, C. (2015). *Swindoll's Living Insights, New Testament Commentary Galatians, Ephesians*, p. 214. Carol Stream, IL: Tyndale House Publishers.
6. Wiersbe, W. (1979). *Be Rich*, p. 70. Colorado Springs, CO: Chariot Victor Publishing.
7. Osborne, G. (1996). *Life Application Bible Commentary: Ephesians*, p. 62. Carol Stream, IL: Tyndale House Publishers.
8. Spurgeon, C.H. (1990). *The New Park Street Pulpit, Volumes 1-6 and The Metropolitan Tabernacle Pulpit, Volumes 7-63*. Pasadena, TX: Pilgrim Publications. Retrieved from https://enduringword.com/bible-commentary/ephesians-3/
9. Spurgeon, C.H. (1990). *The New Park Street Pulpit, Volumes 1-6 and The Metropolitan Tabernacle Pulpit, Volumes 7-63*. Pasadena, TX: Pilgrim Publications. Retrieved from https://enduringword.com/bible-commentary/ephesians-3/
10. Wiersbe, W. (1979). *Be Rich*, p. 73. Colorado Springs, CO: Chariot Victor Publishing.
11. Vines, W.E. (1970). Vines's Complete Expository Dictionary of the Old and New Testament Words, p. 80. Nashville, TN: Thomas Nelson.
12. Wiersbe, W. (1979). *Be Rich*, p. 74. Colorado Springs, CO: Chariot Victor Publishing.
13. Osborne, G. (1996). *Life Application Bible Commentary: Ephesians*, p. 65. Carol Stream, IL: Tyndale House Publishers.

14. Swindoll, C. (2015). *Swindoll's Living Insights, New Testament Commentary Galatians, Ephesians,* p. 216. Carol Stream, IL: Tyndale House Publishers.
15. Swindoll, C. (2015). *Swindoll's Living Insights, New Testament Commentary Galatians, Ephesians,* p. 216. Carol Stream, IL: Tyndale House Publishers.
16. Merida, T. (2014). *Exalting Jesus in Ephesians*, Kindle Edition, p. 82. Brentwood, TN: B&H Publishing.
17. Merida, T. (2014). *Exalting Jesus in Ephesians*, Kindle Edition, p. 86. Brentwood, TN: B&H Publishing.
18. Munger, R. (1986). *My Heart - Christ's Home.* Downer's Grove, IL: Inter-Varsity Press.
19. Wiersbe, W. (1979). *Be Rich,* p. 86. Colorado Springs, CO: Chariot Victor Publishing.
20. Sproul, R.C. (2023). *Ephesians: An Expositional Commentary,* p. 49. Sanford, FL: Ligonier Ministries.
21. Sproul, R.C. (2023). *Ephesians: An Expositional Commentary,* p. 50. Sanford, FL: Ligonier Ministries.
22. *Got Questions.* (n.d.). Retrieved from https://www.gotquestions.org/doxology.html
23. Sproul, R.C. (2023). *Ephesians: An Expositional Commentary,* p. 50. Sanford, FL: Ligonier Ministries.
24. This concept of "or something better" was an idea one of our leaders had read in another study. The original author of that study is unknown.
25. Hymnary.org. (n.d.). "To God Be The Glory." Retrieved from https://hymnary.org/text/to_god_be_the_glory_great_things_he_hath

Lesson Five

1. Phillips, J. (2009). *Exploring Ephesians & Philippians: An Expository Commentary.* p. 107. Grand Rapids, MI: Kregel Publications; WORDsearch Corp.
2. Swindoll, C. (2015). *Insights on Galatians, Ephesians*, p. 230. Carol Stream, IL: Tyndale House.
3. *Life Application Study Bible* (1996). p. 74. Wheaton, IL: Tyndale House Publishers, Inc.
4. Swindoll, C. (2015), *Insights on Galatians, Ephesians*, p. 229. Carol Stream, IL: Tyndale House.
5. Merida, T. (2014). *Exalting Jesus in Ephesians*, pp. 96-97. Brentwood, TN: B&H Publishing.
6. Swindoll, C. (2015), *Insights on Galatians, Ephesians*, p. 232. Carol Stream, IL: Tyndale House.
7. *Hymnal.net* (n.d.). "Be Thou My Vision." Retrieved from: https://www.hymnal.net/en/hymn/ns/345
8. *Life Application Study Bible* (1996). p. 79. Wheaton, IL: Tyndale House Publishers, Inc.
9. Merida, T. (2014). *Exalting Jesus in Ephesians*, p. 97. Brentwood, TN: B&H Publishing.
10. Phillips, J. (2009). *Exploring Ephesians & Philippians: An Expository Commentary,* p. 115. Grand Rapids, MI: Kregel Publications; WORDsearch Corp.
11. *Crossway.org*. (n.d.). Retrieved from: https://www.crossway.org/articles/why-are-there-so-many-versions-of-the-bible/#:~:text=That's the main reasonwe, to an English-language ear.
12. Swindoll, C. (2015), *Insights on Galatians, Ephesians*, p. 239. Carol Stream, IL: Tyndale House.
13. *Life Application Study Bible* (1996). p. 80. Wheaton, IL: Tyndale House Publishers, Inc.
14. Swindoll, C. (2015), *Insights on Galatians, Ephesians*, p. 239. Carol Stream, IL: Tyndale House.
15. Wiersbe, W. (1979). *Be Rich*, p. 101. Colorado Springs, CO: Chariot Victor Publishing.
16. *Lwf.org*. (n.d.). Retrieved from: https://www.lwf.org/daily-devotionals/you-are-set-apart-for-Page of 24 34a-holy-purpose.
17. Tripp, P. (2002). *Instruments in the Redeemer's Hands*, p. 20. Phillipsburg, NJ: P & R Publishing.
18. Vines, W.E. (1970). *Vines's Complete Expository Dictionary of the Old and New Testament Words*, p. 752. Nashville, TN: Thomas Nelson.
19. Phillips, J. (2009). *Exploring Ephesians & Philippians: An Expository Commentary.* p. 120. Grand Rapids, MI: Kregel Publications; WORDsearch Corp.
20. Pokluda, J. (2025). *Your Story has a Villian*, pp. 96-97. Nashville, TN: W Publishing.
21. Peterson, E. (2007). *The Jesus Way*, p. 230. Grand Rapids, MI: William B. Eerdmans Publishing Company.

Lesson Six

1. Tozer, A.W. (1972). *I Talk Back To The Devil*, p. 19. Chicago, IL: Moody Publishers.
2. Dauphinee, D. (2019). *When You Find My Body: The Tragic Story of Gerry Largay.* Camden, ME: Down East Books.
3. *Study Light.* (n.d.) Barclay, W. "Acts 19." Retrieved from https://www.studylight.org/commentaries/eng/dsb/acts-19.html
4. *Bible Hub.* (n.d.). "Strong's Lexicon." Retrieved from https://biblehub.com/greek/3153.htm
5. Osborne, G. (2017). *Ephesians*, p. 137-138. Bellingham, WA: Lexham Press.
6. Eldredge, J. (2008). *Walking with God*, p. 179. Nashville, TN: Nelson Books.
7. Vines, W.E. (1970). *Vines's Complete Expository Dictionary of the Old and New Testament Words*, p. 290. Nashville, TN: Thomas Nelson.
8. *Bible Hub.* (n.d.) "Strong's Lexicon." Retrieved from https://biblehub.com/greek/524.htm
9. Osborne, G. (2017). *Ephesians*, p. 139. Bellingham, WA: Lexham Press.
10. Swindoll, C. (2015). *Swindoll's Living Insights, New Testament Commentary Galatians*, Ephesians, p. 253. Carol Stream, IL: Tyndale House Publishers.
11. Swindoll, C. (2015). *Swindoll's Living Insights, New Testament Commentary Galatians*, Ephesians, p. 253. Carol Stream, IL: Tyndale House Publishers.
12. Wiersbe, W. (1979). *Be Rich*, p. 121. Colorado Springs, CO: Chariot Victor Publishing.
13. Thielman, F. (2010). *Ephesians*, p. 300. Grand Rapid, MI: Baker Academic.
14. Merida, T. (2014). *Exalting Jesus in Ephesians*, p. 108. Brentwood, TN: B&H Publishing.
15. Osborne, G. (2017). *Ephesians*, p. 143. Bellingham, WA: Lexham Press.
16. Swindoll, C. (2015). *Swindoll's Living Insights, New Testament Commentary Galatians*, Ephesians, p. 254. Carol Stream, IL: Tyndale House Publishers.
17. Swindoll, C. (2015). *Swindoll's Living Insights, New Testament Commentary Galatians*, Ephesians, p. 254. Carol Stream, IL: Tyndale House Publishers.
18. Anders, M. (1999). *Holman New Testament Commentary – Galatians, Ephesians, Philippians, Colossians*, p. 235. Nashville, TN: Broadman & Holman Publishing.
19. Swindoll, C. (2015). *Swindoll's Living Insights, New Testament Commentary Galatians, Ephesians*, p. 154. Carol Stream, IL: Tyndale House Publishers.
20. Wilbourne, R. (2016). *Union with Christ*, p. 18. Colorado Springs, CO: David Cook.
21. *Three Steps Forward, Two Steps Back* is the title of a book written by Charles Swindoll.
22. "Process." (n.d.). *Merriam-Webster.* Retrieved from https://www.merriam-webster.com/dictionary/process
23. *Hymnary.org.* (n.d.). "Love Divine All Love Excelling." Retrieved from https://hymnary.org/text/love_divine_all_love_excelling_joy_of_he
24. Swindoll, C. (2015). *Swindoll's Living Insights, New Testament Commentary Galatians*, Ephesians, p. 255. Carol Stream, IL: Tyndale House Publishers.
25. Swindoll, C. (2015). *Swindoll's Living Insights, New Testament Commentary Galatians*, Ephesians, p. 257. Carol Stream, IL: Tyndale House Publishers.
26. Vines, W.E. (1970). *Vines's Complete Expository Dictionary of the Old and New Testament Words*, p. 576. Nashville, TN: Thomas Nelson.
27. Vines, W.E. (1970). *Vines's Complete Expository Dictionary of the Old and New Testament Words*, p. 472. Nashville, TN: Thomas Nelson.
28. Phillips, J. (1993). *Exploring Ephesians and Philippians*, p. 135. Grand Rapids, MI: Kregel Publications.
29. Vines, W.E. (1970). *Vines's Complete Expository Dictionary of the Old and New Testament Words*, p. 747. Nashville, TN: Thomas Nelson.
30. Vines, W.E. (1970). *Vines's Complete Expository Dictionary of the Old and New Testament Words*, p. 732. Nashville, TN: Thomas Nelson.
31. Ironside, H.A. (2000). *Ephesians*, pp. 134-135. Neptune, NJ: Loizeaux.
32. Osborne, G. (2017). *Ephesians*, p. 156. Bellingham, WA: Lexham Press.
33. Swindoll, C. (2015). *Swindoll's Living Insights, New Testament Commentary Galatians*, Ephesians, p. 259. Carol Stream, IL: Tyndale House Publishers.
34. Eldredge, J. (2008). *Walking with God*, p. 37. Nashville, TN: Nelson Books.

Lesson Seven

1. Keller, T. (2011). *The Meaning of Marriage*, p. 40. London: Penguin Books.
2. Merida, T. (2014). *Exalting Jesus in Ephesians*, Kindle Edition, p. 118. Brentwood, TN: B&H Publishing.
3. Sproul, R.C. (2023). *Ephesians: An Expositional Commentary*, p. 49. Sanford, FL: Ligonier Ministries.
4. Merida, T. (2014). *Exalting Jesus in Ephesians*, Kindle Edition, p. 121. Brentwood, TN: B&H Publishing.
5. Merida, T. (2014). *Exalting Jesus in Ephesians*, Kindle Edition, p. 120. Brentwood, TN: B&H Publishing.
6. Osborne, G. (1996). *Life Application Bible Commentary: Ephesians*, p. 61. Carol Stream, IL: Tyndale House Publishers.
7. Osborne, G. (1996). *Life Application Bible Commentary: Ephesians*, p. 62. Carol Stream, IL: Tyndale House Publishers.
8. Vines, W.E. (1970). *Vines's Complete Expository Dictionary of the Old and New Testament Words*, p. 743. Nashville, TN: Thomas Nelson.
9. Swindoll, C. (2015). *Swindoll's Living Insights, New Testament Commentary Galatians, Ephesians*, p. 266. Carol Stream, IL: Tyndale House Publishers.
10. Merida, T. (2014). *Exalting Jesus in Ephesians*, Kindle Edition, p. 122. Brentwood, TN: B&H Publishing.
11. Vines, W.E. (1970). *Vines's Complete Expository Dictionary of the Old and New Testament Words*, p. 136. Nashville, TN: Thomas Nelson.
12. Wood, A.S. (1978). "Ephesians" in *The Expositor's Bible Commentary, 11*, p. 30. Grand Rapids, MI: Zondervan.
13. Swindoll, C. (2015). *Swindoll's Living Insights, New Testament Commentary Galatians, Ephesians*, p. 267. Carol Stream, IL: Tyndale House Publishers.
14. Swindoll, C. (2015). *Swindoll's Living Insights, New Testament Commentary Galatians, Ephesians*, p. 267. Carol Stream, IL: Tyndale House Publishers.
15. Wiersbe, W. (2009). *Be Rich*, p. 136, Colorado Springs, CO: David C. Cook.
16. Snodgrass, K. (2022). *You Need a Better Gospel: Reclaiming the Good News of Participation with Christ*, p. 276. Grand Rapids, MI: Baker Academic.
17. Hughes, K. (1990). *Ephesians*, LOC. 2534. Wheaton, IL: Crossway.
18. Osborne, G. (1996). *Life Application Bible Commentary: Ephesians*, p. 105. Carol Stream, IL: Tyndale House Publishers.
19. Wiersbe, W. (2009). *Be Rich*, pp. 137-138, Colorado Springs, CO: David C. Cook.
20. Osborne, G. (1996). *Life Application Bible Commentary: Ephesians*, p. 105. Carol Stream, IL: Tyndale House Publishers.
21. Osborne, G. (1996). *Life Application Bible Commentary: Ephesians*, p. 106. Carol Stream, IL: Tyndale House Publishers.
22. Osborne, G. (1996). *Life Application Bible Commentary: Ephesians*, p. 107. Carol Stream, IL: Tyndale House Publishers.
23. Wiersbe, W. (2009). *Be Rich*, p. 140, Colorado Springs, CO: David C. Cook.
24. Merida, T. (2014). *Exalting Jesus in Ephesians*, Kindle Edition, p. 128. Brentwood, TN: B&H Publishing.
25. Wiersbe, W. (2009). *Be Rich*, p. 142, Colorado Springs, CO: David C. Cook.
26. *Hymnary.org*. (n.d.). "Take My Life and Let it Be." Retrieved from https://hymnary.org/text/take_my_life_and_let_it_be
27. *Blue Letter Bible*. (n.d.). "Strong's Lexicon." Retrieved from https://www.blueletterbible.org/lexicon/g810/esv/mgnt/0-1/
28. Ortlund, D. (2021). *Deeper: Real Change for Real Sinners*, p. 67. Wheaton, IL: Crossway.

Lesson Eight

1. Wiersbe, W. (1979). *Be Rich*, p. 152. Colorado Springs, CO: Chariot Victor Publishing.
2. Allen, J. [@jennieallen]. (2025, June 2). "These two questions will change your life" [Instagram photo]. Retrieved from https://www.instagram.com/jennieallen/p/DKZkpuVOaUr/.
3. Wiersbe, W. (1979). *Be Rich*, p. 153. Colorado Springs, CO: Chariot Victor Publishing.
4. Nee, W. (1957). *Sit, Walk, Stand*, pp. 22-23. Carol Stream, IL: Tyndale House Publishers.
5. Wright, N.T. (2023). *Ephesians, Philippians, Colossians and Philemon for Everyone*, p. 50. Louisville, KY: Westminster John Knox Press.
6. McGee, J. (1983). *Thru the Bible with J. Vernon McGee Vol. V*, p. 268. Nashville, TN: Thomas Nelson.
7. Wiersbe, W. (1979). *Be Rich*, p. 153. Colorado Springs, CO: Chariot Victor Publishing.
8. Wright, N.T. (2023). *Ephesians, Philippians, Colossians and Philemon for Everyone*, p. 50. Louisville, KY: Westminster John Knox Press.
9. *Life Application Study Bible, New Living Translation*, p. 2,625. (2007). Carol Stream, IL: Tyndale House Publishers.
10. Lucado, M. (2018). *Life Lessons from Ephesians*, p. 89. Nashville, TN: Thomas Nelson.

11. Wiersbe, W. (1979). *Be Rich,* p. 156. Colorado Springs, CO: Chariot Victor Publishing.
12. Piper, J. (2013, October 29). *Desiring God.* "Parents, Require Obedience of Your Children." Retrieved from https://www.desiringgod.org/articles/parents-require-obedience-of-your-children.
13. *Life Application Study Bible, New Living Translation,* p. 2,626. (2007). Carol Stream, IL: Tyndale House Publishers.
14. Wiersbe, W. (1979). *Be Rich,* p. 163. Colorado Springs, CO: Chariot Victor Publishing.
15. McGee, J. (1983). *Thru the Bible with J. Vernon McGee Vol. V,* p. 273. Nashville, TN: Thomas Nelson.
16. Wiersbe, W. (1979). *Be Rich,* p. 165. Colorado Springs, CO: Chariot Victor Publishing.
17. Keathley, J. (2004, June 29). *Bible.org. "The Principle of Nurture (Training Your Child)."* Retrieved from https://bible.org/seriespage/principle-nurture-training-your-child.
18. Cole, S. (2013, May 14). *Bible.org.* "The Spirit-filled Home, Part 1 (Ephesians 6:1-3)." Retrieved from https://bible.org/seriespage/lesson-51-spirit-filled-home-part-1-ephesians-61-3.
19. McGee, J. (1983). *Thru the Bible with J. Vernon McGee Vol. V,* p. 276. Nashville, TN: Thomas Nelson.
20. Vines, W.E. (1970). *Vines's Complete Expository Dictionary of the Old and New Testament Words,* p. 562. Nashville, TN: Thomas Nelson.
21. McGee, J. (1983). *Thru the Bible with J. Vernon McGee Vol. V,* p. 275. Nashville, TN: Thomas Nelson.
22. Armstrong, S. (2017, April 24). *Verse By Verse Ministry International.* "Ephesians – Lesson 6A." Retrieved from https://versebyverseministry.org/lessons/ephesians-lesson-6a.
23. Cole, S. (2013, May 15). *Bible.org.* "Working for God (Ephesians 6:5-9)." Retrieved from https://bible.org/seriespage/lesson-54-working-god-ephesians-65-9.
24. Wiersbe, W. (1979). *Be Rich,* p. 168. Colorado Springs, CO: Chariot Victor Publishing.
25. *Life Application Study Bible, New Living Translation,* p. 2,627. (2007). Carol Stream, IL: Tyndale House Publishers.
26. McGee, J. (1983). *Thru the Bible with J. Vernon McGee Vol. V,* p. 276. Nashville, TN: Thomas Nelson.
27. "Delectation." (n.d.). *Merriam-Webster Dictionary.* Retrieved from https://www.merriam-webster.com/dictionary/delectation
28. "Dysfunction." (n.d.). *Merriam-Webster Dictionary.* Retrieved from https://www.merriam-webster.com/dictionary/dysfunction
29. Lewis, C.S. (1967). *Christian Reflections,* p. 33. Grand Rapids, MI: William B. Eerdmans Publishing Company.
30. Eldredge, J. (2025). *Experience Jesus. Really.,* p. 56. Nashville, TN: Nelson Books.
31. Eldredge, J. (2025). *Experience Jesus. Really.,* p. 56. Nashville, TN: Nelson Books.
32. Nee, W. (1957). *Sit, Walk, Stand,* p. ix. Carol Stream, IL: Tyndale House Publishers.
33. Nee, W. (1957). *Sit, Walk, Stand,* p. 58. Carol Stream, IL: Tyndale House Publishers.
34. *Godtube.com.* (n.d.). "Blessed Assurance." Retrieved from https://www.godtube.com/popular-hymns/blessed-assurance/.

Lesson Nine

1. Ingram, C. (2006). *The Invisible War,* p. 106. Grand Rapids, MI: Baker House Books.
2. Barton, B. (1996). *Life Application Bible Commentary,* p. 128. Wheaton, IL: Tyndale House.
3. Brooks, T. (2023). *Precious Remedies Against Satan's Devices,* pp. 36-43. Carlisle, PA: Banner of Truth.
4. Ingram, C. (2006). *The Invisible War,* p. 51. Grand Rapids, MI: Baker House Books.
5. Walvoord, J. and Zuck, R. (1983). *The Bible Knowledge Commentary ,p. 643.* Wheaton, IL: Victor.
6. Descriptions and definitions from Baker's Encyclopedia of the Bible, and Factbook, Logos.
7. Luther, M. (1951). "A Mighty Fortress Is Our God." *Inspiring Hymns,* p. 166. Grand Rapids, MI: Singspiration Sacred Music Publishers.
8. Stott, J. (1980). *God's New Society,* p. 266. Downers Grove, IL Intervarsity Press.
9. Luther, M. (1951). "A Mighty Fortress Is Our God." *Inspiring Hymns,* p. 166. Grand Rapids, MI: Singspiration Sacred Music Publishers.
10. Logan, J. (1995). *Reclaiming Surrendered Ground,* p. 179. Chicago, IL: Moody Press.
11. Rienecker, F., & Rogers, C. L. (1976). *A Linguistic Key to the Greek New Testament,* p. 541. Grand Rapids, MI: Zondervan.
12. Foulkes, F. (n.d.). *Ephesians: An Introduction and Commentary,* Logos.
13. Swindoll, C. (2015). *Swindoll's Living Insights, New Testament Commentary Galatians, Ephesians,* p. 309. Carol Stream, IL: Tyndale House Publishers.
14. Wiersbe, W. (1979). *Be Rich,* p. 178. Colorado Springs, CO: Chariot Victor Publishing.

15. Hoehner, H. (2002). *Ephesians: An Expositional Commentary*, p. 842. Grand Rapids, MI: Baker.
16. Stott, J. (n.d.). *The Message of Ephesians*, Logos.
17. Hughes, K. (1990). *Ephesians*, LOC. 3689. Wheaton, IL: Crossway.
18. Stott, J. (n.d.). *The Message of Ephesians*, Logos.
19. Hoehner, H. (2002). *Ephesians: An Expositional Commentary*, p. 842. Grand Rapids, MI: Baker.
20. Swindoll, C. (2015). *Swindoll's Living Insights, New Testament Commentary Galatians, Ephesians*, pp. 311-12. Carol Stream, IL: Tyndale House Publishers
21. Vines, W.E. (1970). Vines's Complete Expository Dictionary of the Old and New Testament Words, p. 732. Nashville, TN: Thomas Nelson.
22. Barton, B. (1996). *Life Application Bible Commentary*, p. 134. Wheaton, IL: Tyndale House.
23. Armor of God art inspired by Lifeway's study on the same topic.
24. Eldredge, J. (2016). *Waking the Dead*, p. 13. Nashville, TN: Nelson Books.
25. Anderson, N. and Warner, T. (2000). *The Beginner's Guide to Spiritual Warfare*, p. 140. Ventura, CA: Regal 2000.
26. Ingram, C. (2006). *The Invisible War*, p. 156. Grand Rapids, MI: Baker House Books.
27. Gunter, S. (1994). *For the Family*, p. 15. Birmingham, AL: The Father's Business.
28. Luther, M. (1951). "A Mighty Fortress Is Our God." *Inspiring Hymns*, p. 166. Grand Rapids, MI: Singspiration Sacred Music Publishers.

Lesson Ten

1. BibleRef. (n.d.). Retrieved from: https://www.bibleref.com/Philippians/1/Philippians-1-13.html
2. Spurgeon, C. (n.d.). "When Should We Pray?" *Christian Classics Ethereal Library*. Retrieved from https://ccel.org/ccel/spurgeon/sermons43/sermons43.xxii.html
3. Stott, J. (1979). *God's New Society: The Message of Ephesians*, p. 283. Lisle, IL: InterVarsity Press.
4. Stott, J. (1979). *God's New Society: The Message of Ephesians*, p. 283. Lisle, IL: InterVarsity Press.
5. Shepherd, D. (1998). *Shepherd's Notes*, p. 333, Nashville, TN: B & H Publishing Group.
6. Stott, J. (1979). *God's New Society: The Message of Ephesians*, p. 285. Lisle, IL: InterVarsity Press.
7. Vines, W.E. (1970). *Vines's Complete Expository Dictionary of the Old and New Testament Words*, p. 72. Nashville, TN: Thomas Nelson.
8. Got Questions. (n.d.). *What does it mean to be an ambassador for Christ (2 Corinthians 5:20)?* Retrieved from https://www.gotquestions.org/ambassador-for-Christ.html
9. Guzik, D. (2024, January 7). *Enduring Word*. "The Ambassador in Chains." Retrieved from https://enduringword.com/ambssador-in-chains/
10. Shurtlea, E. (1951). "Lead On, O King Eternal." *Inspiring Hymns*, p. 165. Grand Rapids, MI: Singspiration Sacred Music Publishers.
11. Gaines, S. (2013). *Pray Like it Matters*, p. 19. Tigerville, SC: Auzano Press.
12. Phillips, J. (2009). *Exploring Ephesians & Philippians: An Expository Commentary*, p. 209. Grand Rapids, MI: Kregel Publications.
13. Vines, W.E. (1970). *Vines's Complete Expository Dictionary of the Old and New Testament Words*, p. 562. Nashville, TN: Thomas Nelson.
14. Phillips, J. (2009). *Exploring Ephesians & Philippians: An Expository Commentary, p. 209.* Grand Rapids, MI: Kregel Publications.
15. Goddard, I. (2023, October 12). *Pewresearch.org*. "What does friendship look like in America?" Retrieved from https://www.pewresearch.org/short-reads/2023/10/12/what-does-friendship-look-like-in-america/
16. Phillips, J. (2009). *Exploring Ephesians & Philippians: An Expository Commentary*, p.210. Grand Rapids, MI: Kregel Publications.
17. Swindoll, C. (2015), *Insights on Galatians-Ephesians*, p. 318-319. Carol Stream, IL: Tyndale House Publishing.
18. Stott, J. (1979). *God's New Society: The Message of Ephesians*, p. 289–290. Lisle, IL: InterVarsity Press.
19. Hughes, K. (1990). *Ephesians*, LOC. 4207. Wheaton, IL: Crossway.
20. Vines, W.E. (1970). *Vines's Complete Expository Dictionary of the Old and New Testament Words*, p. 577. Nashville, TN: Thomas Nelson.
21. Samuel Chadwick as quoted by J.D. Greear. (2017, April 26). *J.D. Greear Ministries*. "Seven Ways to Overcome Satan." Retrieved from https://jdgreear.com/seven-ways-overcome-satan/#:~:text=7
22. Phillips, J. (2009). *Exploring Ephesians & Philippians: An Expository Commentary*, p. 202. Grand Rapids, MI: Kregel Publications.
23. This quote is commonly attributed to Ralph Waldo Emerson but the original author is unknown.

Hymns

1. And Can It Be
Wesley, C. (1967). "And Can It Be that I Should Gain?" *Favorite Hymns of Praise*, p. 95. Wheaton, IL: Hope Publishing Company. https://hymnary.org/hymn/FHOP/page/95
2. Amazing Grace
Newton, J. (2023). "Amazing Grace." *Psalms and Hymns to the Living God*, p. 314. Douglasville, GA: G3 Ministries. https://hymnary.org/hymn/PHLG2023/314
3. Turn Your Eyes Upon Jesus
Lemmel, H. H. (1951). "Turn Your Eyes Upon Jesus." *Inspiring Hymns*, p. 379. Grand Rapids, MI: Singspiration Sacred Music Publishers. https://hymnary.org/hymn/IH1951/379
4. Come Thou Fount of Every Blessing
Robinson, R. (1951). "Come, Thou Fount." *Inspiring Hymns*, p. 405. Grand Rapids, MI: Singspiration Sacred Music Publishers. https://hymnary.org/hymn/IH1951/405
5. To God Be the Glory
Crosby, F. (1951). "To God Be the Glory." *Inspiring Hymns*, p. 227. Grand Rapids, MI: Singspiration Sacred Music Publishers. https://hymnary.org/hymn/IH1951/227
6. Be Thou My Vision
Byrne, M. (2023). "Be Thou My Vision." *Psalms and Hymns to the Living God*, p. 413. Douglasville, GA: G3 Ministries. https://hymnary.org/hymn/PHLG2023/page/413
7. Love Divine, All Loves Excelling
Wesley, C. (1951). "Love Divine." *Inspiring Hymns*, p. 83. Grand Rapids, MI: Singspiration Sacred Music Publishers. https://hymnary.org/hymn/IH1951/83
8. Take My Life and Let It Be
Havergal, F. (1951). "Take My Life and Let It Be." *Inspiring Hymns*, p. 375. Grand Rapids, MI: Singspiration Sacred Music Publishers. https://hymnary.org/hymn/IH1951/375
9. Blessed Assurance
Crosby, F. (1951). "Blessed Assurance." *Inspiring Hymns*, p. 311. Grand Rapids, MI: Singspiration Sacred Music Publishers. https://hymnary.org/hymn/IH1951/311
10. A Mighty Fortress Is Our God
Luther, M. (1951). "A Mighty Fortress Is Our God." *Inspiring Hymns*, p. 166. Grand Rapids, MI: Singspiration Sacred Music Publishers. https://hymnary.org/hymn/IH1951/166
11. Lead On, O King Eternal
Shurtlea, E. (1951). "Lead On, O King Eternal." *Inspiring Hymns*, p. 165. Grand Rapids, MI: Singspiration Sacred Music Publishers. https://hymnary.org/hymn/IH1951/165

Made in the USA
Columbia, SC
08 July 2025